D1253032

MONEY, CAPITAL, AND FLUCTUATIONS:
EARLY ESSAYS

By the same author

Law, Legislation and Liberty
  Volume 1   Rules and Order*†
  Volume 2   The Mirage of Social Justice*†
  Volume 3   The Political Order of a Free People*†
  (Also available in a one-volume edition*)

*Prices and Production**
Monetary Theory and the Trade Cycle
(ed.) *Collectivist Economic Planning**
Monetary Nationalism and International Stability
*Profits, Interest and Investment**
*The Pure Theory of Capital**†
*The Road to Serfdom**†
*Individualism and Economic Order**†
*John Stuart Mill and Harriet Taylor**†
*The Sensory Order**†
The Counter-Revolution of Science
(ed.) *Capitalism and the Historians*†
*The Constitution of Liberty**†
*Studies in Philosophy, Politics and Economics**†
A Tiger by the Tail‡
The Denationalization of Money‡
New Studies in Philosophy, Politics, Economics
  *and the History of Ideas**†

* Published by Routledge & Kegan Paul, London
† University of Chicago Press
‡ Institute of Economic Affairs, London

MONEY, CAPITAL, AND FLUCTUATIONS: EARLY ESSAYS

F. A. Hayek
Edited by Roy McCloughry

The University of Chicago Press

The University of Chicago Press, Chicago 60637
Routledge & Kegan Paul, London WC1E 7DD
© 1984 by Routledge & Kegan Paul
All rights reserved. Published 1984
Set in Baskerville 10/12pt by Input Typesetting Ltd., London SW19 8DR
Printed in Great Britain by Redwood Burn Ltd., Trowbridge, Wiltshire

93   92   91   90   89   88   87   86   85   84   5   4   3   2   1

Library of Congress Cataloging in Publication Data

Hayek, Friedrich A. von (Friedrich August), 1899–

Money, Capital, and Fluctuations.
Includes index.
1. Money—addresses, essays, lectures.   2. Capital—
addresses, essays, lectures.   3. Business cycles—
addresses, essays, lectures.   I. McCloughry, Roy.
II. Title.
HG221.H346   1984   332.4   84–227

ISBN 0–226–32092–8

Shr. 20.00/12.00/10/2/84

CONTENTS

PREFACE AND ACKNOWLEDGMENTS

The impetus for these translations arose from work which I was doing at the time of the fiftieth anniversary of the delivery of 'Prices and Production' as lectures at the London School of Economics. The critical appraisal of Professor Hayek's early monetary theory on which, as a 'non-Austrian', I was then engaged, led me to have these seminal essays translated, which were previously available only in German. It is my hope that the appearance of these essays will enable the economics profession to make an assessment of Hayek's extensive contribution to the 'great debate' of the interwar years.

This project has taken a number of years to complete and in that time many people have given time and help. I would like to thank Meghnad Desai in particular for many conversations on Hayek and on monetary theory and also Morris Perlman for helpful advice. Translating from the German is never easy at the best of times and the translators were faced with an extremely difficult task. I am especially grateful to Dr Michael Hudson of Leeds University who has brought clarity and style to the whole manuscript and who acted as senior translator. My thanks go also to Mr Max Alter of the London School of Economics for his hard work on several of the translations. Mrs Christine Blackmore assisted with the translation, especially the fifth essay. Thanks are due to the Wincott Foundation for a grant to cover editorial costs and to Elizabeth Fidlon of Routledge & Kegan Paul who has been the epitome of a patient and supportive editor. I am grateful to Sue Kirkbride and Susan Doidge who typed the manuscript with great speed and accuracy. Lastly my thanks to Professor Hayek who was willing to meet on several occasions to discuss the contents of this volume.

Roy McCloughry

EDITOR'S INTRODUCTION

Friedrich von Hayek made his debut in England in February 1931 at the London School of Economics when he gave four lectures at the invitation of Lionel Robbins, published in September of that year as *Prices and Production*. At that time Hayek was Director of the Austrian Institute for Trade Cycle Research and a member of the 'Mises Group' in Vienna. The lectures were to prove the fulcrum of his early work in that much of his early work in the 1920s was fulfilled in them and much of his later effort was devoted to exposition and elaboration of the position they represented. Although intensely analytical they created a controversy in the economics profession which must have caused envy amongst many who heard them. The journals became preoccupied with Hayek's method and message and the debate attracted names such as Hicks, Lerner, Durbin, Robbins, Shackle and Sraffa, not to mention Keynes.

Many reasons have been given for this explosion of interest. 'Austrian' economics was foreign in more than one sense. It provided British economists with a new paradigm within which to think. It was also highly technical in content at a time when economics was beginning to ally itself with higher analytical and mathematical techniques. Undoubtedly another reason for the extended discussion was that Hayek's model contained an essential ambiguity characteristic of many great models but fatal to all but the greatest. Such ambiguity was heightened by the fact that few English-speaking economists had read Böhm-Bawerk or were familiar with Hayek's earlier writings, published in the German literature. *Prices and Production* thus seemed to protrude like an iceberg out of the water, nine-tenths below the surface. Hayek's contribution to the history of economic analysis in the 1930s has always been difficult to assess because of these missing paragraphs of the 'Hayek story'. These essays are offered in translation to enable the profession to make that assessment.

vii

Although Hayek's position has changed over the years, sometimes with great subtlety, one of the most enduring qualities of his statements has been their consistency. There can be few economists alive today who in writing to *The Times* in the 1980s can say '. . . as I said in 1931. . . .' Hayek has persisted in his crusade against inflationary policies whether regarded as *à la mode* or not. Yet those who are familiar only with Professor Hayek's most recent writings on economics will be surprised at many of the emphases they will find in these essays. If one looks at his work on the nature of equilibrium through the eyes of the modern Austrian school one is reminded of the market process as an existential discovery procedure to which equilibrium is irrelevant; the price mechanism as an information-signalling device and the essential ignorance of market participants. Hayek would be sharply critical of those economists working within the Arrow-Debreu tradition of General Equilibrium theory in that it assumes the very thing to be explained, *viz.*, the givenness of the information. This 'givenness' of market information was questioned by Hayek in his famous paper on 'Economics and knowledge' published in 1937, a year which marks a watershed in Hayek's thought. Previous to that date Hayek's own thought was dominated by General Equilibrium theory. This comes out repeatedly in *Monetary Theory and the Trade Cycle* (1929, English edition 1933), where he talks of 'the unquestionable methods of equilibrium theory' (p. 57), and also in *Prices and Production*. He says, 'It is my conviction that if one wants to explain economic phenomena at all, we have no means available but to build on the foundations given by the concept of a tendency toward equilibrium' (*PP*, p. 31, 1st edition). Hayek points out in a footnote that by equilibrium he means the Lausanne formulation of General Equilibrium (*MTTC*, pp. 42–3). Nor is he committed only to the framework but also to fast speeds of convergence within the model, leading him to ignore periods of transition between equilibria and to describe only the new equilibrium. This absence of wage rigidities and other contractual frictions was at the heart of Hayek's debate with Pierro Sraffa in the pages of the *Economic Journal*, and led to his attempt to include them in his description of the downswing in his essay in 'Capital consumption'.

Although Hayek was aware of the fictitious nature of barter equilibrium he also believed that a tendency to equilibrium was ascertainable in the empirical world. In fact, the only way in which economics could claim to be an empirical science and cease to be an exercise in pure logic was to demonstrate that a tendency to equilibrium existed in the 'real world'.

Market forces, in other words, potentially terminate in a state of equilibrium. This is very different to modern Austrian analysis, as Professor Ludwig Lachmann has pointed out.

> Professors Hayek and Mises both espouse the market process, but do not ignore equilibrium as its final stage. The former whose early work was clearly under the influence of the general equilibrium model, at one time, appeared to regard a strong tendency towards general equilibrium as a real phenomenon of the market economy. (Ludwig Lachmann, 'From Mises to Shackle', *Journal of Economic Literature*, 1975, vol. 14, p. 60)

Alongside this paradox between logical and empirical analyses of equilibrium which Hayek finally separated in 1937, there is a distinction between statics and 'dynamics' which is central to this period. In the 1920s economists such as W. C. Mitchell and Simon Kuznets were devoting their energies to statistical research, believing that only accurate statistical techniques could capture the business cycle in all its complexity. Kuznets, especially, believed that the concept of equilibrium was responsible for monocausal explanations of the cycle, which were totally inadequate as explanations of complex cycles. W. C. Mitchell in particular held views almost diametrically opposed to those of Hayek, stating that 'to determine how the fact of cyclical oscillation in economic activity can be reconciled with the general theory of equilibrium or how that theory can be reconciled with the facts' was not part of his objective. How different it might have been if the early Hayek had been exposed to Frisch's econometric approach with its emphasis on the role of theory and systems determination rather than Mitchell's 'congeries of economics statistics'. Although Hayek was impressed by the advance in statistical technique during his visit to the United States in 1923–4, he maintained his belief in the primacy of theoretical reasoning.

Yet Hayek became aware that the monetary economy required a different definition of equilibrium to the barter economy in that although simultaneous exchange could be assumed for barter transactions, indirect exchange must require a causal analysis in time.

> For the moment at which the analysis is no longer concerned exclusively with prices which are (presumed to be) simultaneously set, as in the elementary presentation of pure

theory, but go on to consideration of the monetary economy
with prices which necessarily are set at successive points in time,
a problem arises for whose solution it is vain to seek in the
existing corpus of economic theory. ('Intertemporal
equilibrium', this volume p. 72).

Hayek's paper on *Intertemporal Price Equilibrium and Movements in the
Value of Money* (1928) is undoubtedly one of the most important
pieces of theoretical work which Hayek ever wrote. It undergirds
the entire argument of *Prices and Production*. Although the first signs
of his distinctive theory of the cycle appeared as early as 1925 (this
volume, pp. 27–8, n. 4), it is in 1928 that he works out the relationship between the changes in relative prices over time and the intertemporal allocation of resources, which was to prove so seminal in
1931.

Hayek's paper preceded Lindahl's work on the subject and was
part of a larger work on monetary theory which was never published. Yet it did not completely suit the task which Hayek had set.
Instead of setting prices at 'successive points in time' prices were
set in the first period. It was a perfect foresight equilibrium and in
such a model there is no motive to hold money *qua* money.

Others were working from different assumptions. J. R. Hicks in
his paper 'Gleichgewicht und Konjunktur' (1933) expounded a
model in which agents were myopic and in which monetary disturbances were imposed on more fundamental problems. Two strands
began to emerge in the literature on monetary theory in the 1930s.
On the one hand there was Hayek's seminal insight into intertemporal equilibrium and the misdirection of investment due to
credit inflation. This strand led to the definition of monetary
neutrality. On the other hand there was a school growing which
based its thought on Gunnar Myrdal's concepts of *ex ante* and *ex
post* which incorporated 'genuine' uncertainty from period to period.
Alongside this went Hicks's insight into the theory of money as
represented by his paper, 'A suggestion for simplifying the theory
of money' (1935) in which Hicks described money as having a
positive marginal utility due to its demand as an asset under conditions of uncertainty. Although frequently confused with one another
in the early 1930s, monetary equilibrium (the latter approach) and
monetary neutrality were conceptually distinct in the definitions of
equilibrium and the demand for money implicit in them. For if
Hayek had no concept of monetary equilibrium, neither as we have

mentioned above did he have any theory of barter disequilibrium. What Hayek had discovered was an essentially theoretical tool, which enabled real analysis to be conducted in monetary terms. Although there was much discussion of neutrality as an operational goal of monetary policy it was never intended to fulfil that function, as his note on 'Neutral money' points out.

Many of the difficulties encountered by Hayek in this early work have had to be rediscovered for what Hayek was really up against was the problem of the incorporation of money into a general equilibrium framework. The extensive contribution which he made in these essays and in the wider debate, for which he was awarded the Nobel Prize, will take some time to assess and certainly cannot be attempted in the space available here. I hope to make a contribution towards that assessment elsewhere.

Roy McCloughry

INTRODUCTION

These essays which friends have judged worthy of republication in English date from a period more than fifty years ago when I was slowly developing my own distinct interests in economic theory but had not yet clearly perceived which of them were to become my chief concerns in the field. The essays clearly show the decisive impact of an early visit to the United States that had shifted my interest a little from the pure theory of value and price to the problems of the steering process in the market economy. I was then becoming increasingly aware that the guide function of the process determining the effectiveness of our efforts, on which we had become irrevocably dependent, could operate satisfactorily only if monetary demand corresponded to real demand, not so much in the aggregate as in the relative proportions of the different goods which were demanded and supplied. Looking back on my endeavours in this particular field, more than half a century later, I find it difficult to say how much of what I am now inclined to read into these early attempts I was clearly aware of at the time.

My initial university training at Vienna had been short but intense: thanks to the special privileges granted to soldiers returning from the war I was allowed three years from 1918 to 1921 to obtain a law degree, which was, in fact, chiefly directed to economics and psychology. Ultimately, external circumstances forced me to choose between the two. In economics it was my teacher Friedrich von Wieser who directed my interest to the intricacies of the subjective theory of value, on one particular problem of which, the theory of 'imputation', I wrote during the following year and a half a doctoral dissertation while employed in a temporary government office. Good fortune brought it that I found myself there under the direction of another economist whom I had scarcely known at the university but who, for the next ten years, became the chief guide in the development of my ideas: Ludwig von Mises. His then more than ten years old *Theory of Money* and his work on socialism that

1

appeared during the first year I served under him determined the chief direction of my work during these years until, after my return from the United States in 1924, I became for seven years a regular member of the discussion group known as the 'Mises Seminar'.

Aware that as an economist some knowledge of the English-speaking world and particularly the United States was essential, I managed in 1923 and 1924, on leave from my government job but before Austrians were eligible for Rockefeller fellowships, to spend, at my own expense and risk, fifteen months at New York, being officially connected with New York University but also gate-crashing at Columbia and the New School of Social Research. I must confess that in spite of a dozen letters of introduction from Josef Schumpeter, which I presented to the leading economists of the east coast all of whom received me very kindly, I found the situation of pure theory in the States somewhat disappointing. Interests had shifted to more concrete factual questions. What I found most interesting and instructive was the work done on monetary policy and the control of industrial fluctuations connected on the one hand with the Harvard Economic Service and on the other with the new experiments in central banking policy of the Federal Reserve System. I even commenced work there on a further PhD thesis on problems of monetary stabilization under the direction of Professor J. D. Magee, but which I never completed.

Returning to Vienna and my government job I began working up my American experiences in preparation for a major work on monetary theory with which I hoped to qualify for a university position. The essays here reproduced date from this period of the later part of the 1920s. But various unforeseen interruptions slowed down my progress. My interest was mainly directed to the theoretical aspects, but what was then mainly appreciated were the concrete knowledge of particular facts and the acquaintance with statistical techniques I had acquired in the United States and which were then still largely unfamiliar on the European continent. So it was in the studies of my descriptive work on American monetary policy that I was led to develop my theories of monetary fluctuations.

One episode in the growth of my expositions may perhaps be worth recording here. In the draft of my account of American monetary policy after 1920 I had made use of what I thought was a theory of Ludwig von Mises that was familiar to us in the Vienna circle. But another member of our group with whom I was in daily contact, Gottfried Haberler, persuaded me after reading my first draft that no sufficient exposition of the theory I had used was to be found in Mises's published work, and that if I was to expect to be understood, I must give a fuller account of the theory underlying my report of the events described. Thus arose the long footnote now recorded on page 27 of this volume containing the first statement of my version of Mises's theory.

Another interruption of my efforts caused by my limited acquaintance with the newly developed American statistical methods was my selection as the director of the new institute for trade cycle studies that, as in several other countries about the same time, was opened at Vienna at the beginning of 1927. This appointment helped me greatly in many ways but inevitably much delayed my theoretical work. An invitation to fill the one remaining gap in the great series of Max Weber's monthly *Grundrisse der Sozialökonomik*, the volume on money, proved another distraction but caused me to alter the plans of my efforts. I had become convinced that a satisfactory textbook on monetary theory and policy required a long introduction describing the historical development of these subjects. My free time during the last two or three years at Vienna that was not taken up by my institute and eventually also by lecturing at the University of Vienna, was devoted to an extensive study of the literature on money. The first four chapters of this, from the seventeenth to the nineteenth centuries, had just been written when an invitation arrived to give some lectures at the University of London. Into these I compressed within a few weeks an outline of what I thought was going to be the most original part of my planned systematic exposition. In the end the work I had done before remained a fragment because of my assumption of the London professorship and, two years later, the rise of the Hitler regime which finally forced the German publisher to abandon his plans for the big textbook on money.

What I had actually published during the years preceding this in the form of articles in professional journals, and now partly published here in English translation, are the by-products of these endeavours and are inevitably not systematic. Yet they contain the beginning of those ideas which I was later able to work out at greater leisure in London. There I had the opportunity to approach the subject, as I thought it required, more systematically via its necessary formation in the theory of capital. I had intended, in a second volume of this work, to return in much greater detail to the

3

monetary applications and had even postponed that refutation of
the revived fallacy of the determination of employment by aggregate
demand which I became increasingly aware was the more urgent
task. But after a highly specialized effort of seven years with only
half the task completed I must confess I had become so tired of it
that I used the outbreak of war as an excuse to publish the first
part and then to turn to what had come to appear to me more
pressing problems. It would have been difficult for me to decide
what parts of these early efforts towards an unachieved goal would
be worth preserving and I was glad to leave the choice wholly to
the sympathetic judgment of Mr Roy K. McCloughry who, after
all the efforts and care he has devoted to these early endeavours of
mine, certainly knows now more than I do about what I thought
fifty years ago. I have not altogether given up hope to have the
chance to explain 'what I really meant'. But for the present I
can only be profoundly grateful to Mr McCloughry's conscientious
endeavours to find out what indications of this hope my early efforts
may perhaps provide.

Freiburg, November 1982   F. A. Hayek

THE MONETARY POLICY OF THE UNITED STATES AFTER THE RECOVERY FROM THE 1920 CRISIS*

Before looking in detail at the policies of the Federal Reserve Banks in the period under consideration it is important first to look at a new aspect of policy, of which they had to take particular note in the period concerned. This is the exercise of a systematic control of credit with the aim of smoothing out cyclical fluctuations and preventing economic crises. At earlier points in this essay,† the relationship between credit policy and cyclical movements has been repeatedly emphasized so as to indicate the way in which attempts to obviate the damaging effects of gold imports necessitated deviations from the policy traditionally followed by the banks in this respect. In what follows, we shall be concerned with the efforts to replace the policy previously pursued by the banks which was an almost exclusively repressive policy directed solely towards the alleviation of a crisis that had already made its appearance, by one which sought to prevent cyclical and crisis phenomena from evidencing themselves at all.

This new tendency originated in a change in the way in which the scientific examination of cyclical movements is undertaken. During the course of the last decade, at least in the Anglo-Saxon countries, the investigation of the alternation of periods of prosperity and stagnation[1] that had been correctly observed by the representatives of the 'currency school' almost a hundred years ago completely displaced the analysis of the crisis viewed as an isolated pheno-

---

* The following article constitutes an extract from a much longer work first published as 'Die Wahrungspolitik der Vereinigten Staaten seit der Überwindung der Krise von 1920' in *Zeitschrift für Volkswirtschaft und Sozialpolitik*, n.s. 5 (1925), in two parts: vols 1–3, pp. 25–63 and vols 4–6, pp. 254–317. Section 6 (pp. 255–82), published here, represents the theoretical core of the paper. This section is subtitled, 'The theoretical foundations of attempts to influence the level of economic activity by banking policy'.

† A reference to sections not printed in this volume (ed.).

menon. Related to this change, the problem which had until then stood in the forefront of the discussion, i.e. the overcoming of crises regarded simply as an unavoidable phase of every wave-like movement in the economy, was replaced by that of exerting a systematic influence upon the course of the cycle in all its phases. In the United States above all, an extraordinary amount of attention has been paid to the investigation of cyclical phenomena in recent years, not least because they appear to offer a reliable predictor of future economic developments, with the hope that economic science can thus be of service for immediately practical purposes. Since the crisis of 1920, this area of research has perhaps had an excessive amount of effort devoted to it, and the results achieved have drawn the attention of the lay public to this research to an extent that has not been conferred upon any other branch of economic investigation for a long time. This is the reason why the more recent scientific views in this field became effective relatively rapidly and even the official institutions could not completely close their eyes to them.

Thanks to the intensified attention devoted to this field, our understanding of the course followed by the ebb and flow of the economy and its causes have actually made such significant progress that we can hope that it will be possible quite soon to prevent a large part of the damage done by the cycle. Certainly, these advances cannot as yet be integrated into a recognized, unified theory similar to those theories of the cycle that already exist. To do so is made more difficult by the very methods of investigation themselves which most American researchers employ in this field. They do not begin from a definite, basic theoretical conception of the economic process, but content themselves with gaining as detailed as possible a picture of the typical course of a cycle with the aid of detailed statistical investigation of the behaviour of the individual factors in each phase of the cycle. It is their hope that, from the insights they thereby gain into the relative behaviour of the individual branches of production, etc., they will then be able to derive theories as to the nature of the interrelationships between them.[2] The result is a type of *symptomatology* of the course of the cycle. By tracing out the far-reaching similarities that exist between the different economic cycles, it establishes the characteristic feature of each phase of the cycle. On this basis, and hence not merely by relation to current statistical data, it makes possible the appropriate diagnosis of the current economic situation. Furthermore, as already noted, to a certain extent it enables us to forecast the behaviour of economic activity that can be expected in the coming period. It may be that such a procedure will ultimately arrive at a complete description embracing all the essential characteristics of the cycle, which is the task of theory, but it must be said that being still in its early stages of development, it does not offer the comprehensive understanding attainable with a theory derived from general economic principles. It is of little help when what is at issue is not detailed interconnections but the cause of cyclical fluctuations in general. If the aim is to combat cyclical fluctuations at their root, then most researchers into the cycle also have recourse consciously or unconsciously to the explanations offered by 'abstract' theories.

Nevertheless, the main results of that inductive research have effected a not inconsiderable strengthening of certain generally theoretical concepts as to the cause of economic fluctuations. The statistical investigations of the relative behaviour of the individual factors in the course of economic activity, very expressively termed 'cyclic chartology' because of their predominantly graphical methods of presentation, have brought to our attention especially the chief bases of the most important group of business cycle theories. They have shown, firstly, that in the upswing it is the rise in prices which becomes the strongest force driving up the level of activity. They have also shown, secondly, that it is the excessive expansion of the producer-goods industries, in general terms the relatively greater expansion of the output of goods of higher order as compared to those of lower order, and the increase in the demand for consumption goods, that are the most important causes of the regularly recurring economic crises. There is not the space here for a more extensive consideration of the other linkages and interrelationships upon which these investigations have thrown new light. Similarly, only brief mention can be made of the most striking features of the depiction of what is regarded as a typical cyclical fluctuation. The greater attention paid to this can be ascribed to the fact that, in the theory of business cycles, decisive significance has for some time been attributed once again to explanations drawn from the field of the monetary and credit system.

The data which are available to American researchers in especial abundance consist mainly of comprehensive figures as to quantities of output, stocks, turnover and the level of employment in individual industries and branches of production, in addition to the particular and general price statistics which have always been available. Also there are the particularly copious banking statistics, available in monthly series but often also even on a weekly basis. After the detection and elimination of certain tendencies of movement within each of these series which are independent of the particular stage of the cycle, such as the regular fluctuations that occur within any one year, and the developments which proceed uniformly over decades with the growth of population and technical progress, their comparison then shows the relative behaviour of each of them in the individual phases of the cycle and thus permits conclusions to be drawn as to the connection which exists between them. What emerges is a quite definite, regularly recurring succession of undulating movements of production, prices, trade and credit, so that one is accustomed to speak of particular cycles in each of the factors. To explain the causal relationships existing between them must be the next task of the theory of cyclical phenomena. The most important of these empirically established regularities in the course of the individual phases of the cycle are as follows: the depression comes to an end when the existing commodity stocks have fallen to a minimum in all sectors, and the beginnings of the upswing evidence themselves first in an increase in the output of the industries producing raw materials and capital goods, while prices often still continue to fall. The further increase in productive activity and later the rise in prices is larger and happens earlier, the further removed from the stage of consumption are the goods concerned. Correspondingly, this increase comes to an end soonest in industries producing raw materials and industrial equipment which exhibit the greatest fluctuations. Then at a later stage the production of intermediate goods and semi-finished products is affected, and last of all activity in the industries producing consumption goods and goods which satisfy the needs of consumers directly. The same relationship is shown by turnover and prices in wholesale and retail trade. In general terms, the rise in prices continues beyond the rise in output in the sector concerned, but within the individual commodity groups its movement corresponds to that of output. So far as the financial aspects of the movement are concerned, it is the prices of stock market securities that are as a rule among the earliest to be affected by the general upswing, while rates of interest are among the last. The extremely rapid growth of bank credit in the later part of the upswing continues after the general peak has been reached, and its volume is extended right up to the capacity of the banks to lend. In the downturn and the downswing, the individual factors maintain much the same sequence, with what were the leading elements likewise showing the strongest declines.

This sequence in the movements of the individual sectors of the economy is to be attributed to the well-known circumstance that any change in the demand for finished products has a magnified effect upon the next highest stage of production, calling forth changes in that stage which are a multiple of it. It is not necessary at this point to enter into details about the intermediate steps through which this cumulative effect is mediated. The more recent American literature on the 'business cycle' is rich in excellent studies in this field, and the reader is referred to them.[3] All that needs to be emphasized in this context is that they are all based upon the proposition that, during the upswing, the production of goods of higher order is orientated towards not merely an increased but a rising level of demand, and therefore has also to make possible the enlargement of commodity stocks, the extension of the production apparatus, etc., and so by its very nature is orientated towards a temporary demand. But the latter must come to an end as soon as the demand for final products ceases to *increase*. In addition, in the later stages of the upswing especially the expectation of a further rise in prices stimulates ever greater purchases in anticipation of expected future demand, which gives rise to a particularly large increase in areas of production more distant from the consumer as compared to the actual growth in demand for consumer goods. However, it is the excessive growth in the production of goods of higher order, necessary only to satisfy a rapidly growing need for finished products, which is the main reason why productive activity in general can no longer be maintained at the level it has already attained if for any reason the *increase* in demand comes to an end. If the tempo of the upswing flattens out, or if it even merely slows down, there must be a decline in employment in those industries and as a result a consequential diminution in the demand for finished products. The outcome must then be a general reaction, in which as in the upswing the effects of any partial retrogression are multiplied in their further repercussions ultimately leading to a general depression. Among the causes which bring the upward movement to an end, and thus make a downswing inevitable, a main role is played – in addition to the necessity to restrict credit with which the banks find themselves faced – by the differences which emerge between the situations in which the various sectors of the economy find themselves. Such differences must inevitably arise when there

9

is a rapid rise in general prices, for such a rise is never felt equally in each of the various sectors.

The excessive development of the industries producing raw materials and capital goods, whose regular recurrence is thus to be regarded as the main cause of the periodic economic crises, necessarily arises from and is chiefly due to the much praised elasticity of our modern credit system. The cumulative effect which any increase in the demand for finished products exerts upon the output of goods of higher order finds its expression in the accumulation of excessive stocks of commodities, a disproportionate expansion of the apparatus with which they are produced, and especially a greater rise in the prices of raw materials and capital goods and thereby the elimination of profits. This can take place only because the extension of credit by the banking system is not strictly linked to the growth of savings. The banks can make purchasing power available to the entrepreneur even if no one else has refrained from exercising to a corresponding extent the purchasing power which they possess. The banks are especially prone to behave in this way if a favourable economic situation appears to reduce the risks involved in doing so. Since the increased demand thereby making its appearance in the market is confronted by an unchanged supply, it must bring about a rise in prices which is particularly great in the case of goods of higher order. The reason is that the possibility of expanding the supply of money capital to a level in excess of that of real capital also puts the banks in a position to offer the former at a rate which is *cheaper* then that which corresponds to the proportion which the increased demand bears to the supply of real capital. It thereby makes capital investments continue to appear to be profitable though in fact they exceed the economically permissible level[4] and hence must[5] sooner or later be partly lost. The most significant phenomena of the upswing, over-investment and a general rise in prices, and at the same time the causes of the crises which always follow upon the upswing, are therefore largely a result of an extension of credit which is from time to time excessive (or, to utilize Wicksell's terminology to put the same thing in another way, of an occasional fall of the money rate of interest below the real rate). This extension of credit gives rise to a short-lived inflation and leads to the emergence of the disproportions between the individual sectors of the economy to which the accompanying stimulation of business always gives rise. The crisis then becomes the only way of eliminating these disproportions. This recurrent inflation

10

therefore works like a drug giving rise not merely to a short-lived increase in well-being but also to an extended nightmare later.

Certainly, if a gold currency exists, the banks can never create more credit *in the long run* than the volume which corresponds to the accumulation of real capital. But the mechanism which prevents their doing so is clumsy and delayed in its operation and does not go fully into effect before the inflation of credit has already inflicted heavy damage. If the rise in prices takes on too great a dimension, the gold currency or a currency system of the same type forces the banks to check or even to restrict any further extension of credit in order to maintain their liquidity. If the expansion of credit and thus the rise in prices is confined to one country, the outflow of gold after a time forces the banks to impose credit restrictions. If, on the other hand, the rise in prices is either international or extending to all countries with the same monetary basis, the point at which it is checked will be still later. That point will be reached when the increase in the demand for cash resulting from the rise in prices exposes the banks to the danger of being unable to maintain the ratio between their cash and their liabilities which is either legally imposed upon them or to which they traditionally adhere. Experience shows that this mechanism is not sufficient to preserve the economy from the pronounced fluctuations of prices over a few years which is characteristic of cyclical movements. It is necessary for the rise in prices to have already become rather strong, or to have persisted for some time, before those counteracting influences become operative. In the period before the latter occurs, all those characteristics develop which unavoidably produce a severe reaction when the rise in prices eventually comes to an end. In the downswing, in turn, too long a time elapses before the inflow of gold from abroad or the reflux of cash from circulation into the banks induces them to abandon their reluctance to grant credit. But it is the latter which until then has contributed to intensifying the fall in prices and hence the depression.

If the gold currency exists in connection with a developed system of bank credit, its automatic operation therefore does not suffice to obviate the possibility of a dangerous inflation caused by bank credit. In an economic system which makes extensive use of bank credit, the alien element of bank credit seems to make necessary certain elaborate precautions if even that degree of stability in economic activity is to be achieved which is automatically secured if gold is the only medium of circulation. Once such interconnections

11

are grasped, it seems but a short step to suggest that the elimination of any disproportion which emerges between the various sectors of the economy because of an excessive creation of credit should not be left to the mechanical forces of the economy, which only works slowly, especially since this process always operates through crisis-ridden convulsions of the whole of economic life. Instead, it is concluded, a purposive intervention should be made to regulate the volume of credit as soon as it becomes evident that it has been granted excessively and therefore threatens to lead to dangerous developments. Steps to restrict the volume of credit at the right moment in the ascending phase of the cycle, before it actually becomes necessary to do so with respect to the liquidity of the banks and the maintenance of the gold standard, then appears to become the tool with which economic activity can be stabilized and crises prevented. 'Control of credit' has in this way become the slogan of and the sovereign remedy advanced by those who seek to combat crises. Almost all the discussion of how to prevent crises revolves around the possibilities of credit control and the forms it should take, in comparison with which only subordinate significance is attributed to all other measures which enter into consideration. It is scarcely possible to deny that, among US economists, expectations of this type have been set too high and in this respect they have probably often asked too much of a good thing. But we should certainly not underestimate the significance of this whole area of enquiry, which has scarcely ever been treated in an appropriate way on the European continent.[6] And this may also serve as our excuse for devoting somewhat more space to this matter here than is absolutely necessary within the framework of this essay.

It must be emphasized that what has come to light in the preceding brief presentation of the evolution of thought which leads to the above conclusions (in so far as they are concerned with the connection between bank credit and crises), was in many cases theoretical views which did not originate from American research but are due to the work of European economists, especially K. Wicksell, L. v. Mises and G. Cassel. As has already been pointed out, however, what shifted the policy of influencing the course of the cycle by means of banking policy into the foreground in the United States was not so much the widening dissemination of *crisis theories*, which see the main cause of crises in the over-capitalization due to the excessive extension of credit by banks. Rather, the shift was due in the first instance to the results derived from statistical investigations, which led to the recognition that the movement of prices was the strongest driving-force of cyclical fluctuations. When this recognition was linked with what were often very simple quantity theory conceptions, the stimulus to devote one's chief attention to the policies of the banks was created.[7] To these circumstances is also certainly to be attributed, at least in part, the fact that no unanimity of opinion exists as to the type of measures which should be employed to prevent severe cyclical fluctuations and the efficacy which can be expected of them. Without such unanimity, however, it is impossible to produce any theoretical concepts which can be linked up with each other. Hence the proposals put forward differ totally from one another and are mostly rather like rules of thumb which were discovered and developed in the course of practical attempts to control the cycle.

The main aim of the great banking reform of 1913–14 was to create an authority which would help to avoid, by expanding the credit it made available at times of crisis ('panic financing'), the financial panics of the type that had occurred until then with especial frequency and violence in the US. But in addition to that, it also aimed at offering a means of lessening cyclical fluctuations by the creation of an authority capable of conducting a systematic credit policy. The particular frequency with which financial panics occurred in the United States was generally attributed – rightly or wrongly – to the decentralization of its banking system.[8] The expectations of a system with a central bank were so high that the Federal Reserve Bank bill brought before the House of Representatives sought to establish explicitly the maintenance of as high as possible a degree of stability in the price level as the guiding principle of the new bank's discount policy.[9] Though this wide-reaching provision did not survive the committee hearings, there can be no doubt that especially the (as yet to be discussed) 'open market operations' of the Federal Reserve Banks were justified largely with respect to their possible use to influence the course of economic activity.[10]

In this context, however, there is another aspect from which the significance of the reform of 1913–14 must be viewed, though it is scarcely mentioned in the entire discussion relating to this matter. What this reform did was not merely to make a systematic credit policy by a central authority possible but it also made it *indispensable* if a counterweight was to be provided to the greater possibilities of inflation which its creation made possible.[11] The reform guaranteed a greater elasticity of the credit system as a whole and of the note circulation in particular. But in doing so, it suppressed a series of factors which the most recent views see as operating beneficially precisely by imposing a check upon the expansion of credit during the upswing. The elimination of these factors therefore necessarily intensified the danger of an excessive expansion of credit and increased the need for special precautions to be taken against it. One of the features of the former system which was most censured was that a scarcity of money automatically arose precisely during upswings. The first reason was that, at a high level of the interest rate, the issue of new National Bank notes was less profitable. The second was that the more abundant receipts from customs duties and indirect taxes, which comprised the most important revenues of the state, accumulated in the treasuries as large money balances and thus were withdrawn from circulation. But the automatic braking effects upon the expansion of credit formerly exercised by these two features was eliminated by the introduction of the 'elastic' Federal Reserve Bank notes and the abolition of the 'independent treasury system', the latter also implying that state funds could not be withdrawn from circulation. Certainly, these automatic brakes had not always gone into operation at the most appropriate time and in the most appropriate way. That for the most part they did so at a very late stage of the upswing then also rendered more difficult the satisfaction of the increased demand for money in the crisis and, as an unintended by-product, gave rise to the impression that they were responsible for an undesirable disturbance of the overall system. Yet it is odd to observe that the same authors who stigmatize the tendency towards a scarcity of money during the boom as a severe deficiency of the old system will also and often within the same work recommend precisely the creation of such a scarcity as a systematic policy for the prevention of economic crises. The justice of the attacks made on the old system under *this* heading must appear to be quite questionable. No error is involved in assimilating this as many other parts of the reform to those policies whose unintentional effect is inflationary, a danger which is all the greater in view of the great influence exerted upon the American currency experts by ideas originating from the 'banking school'.

So far as the conduct of a systematic policy for the prevention of cycles is concerned, the Americans do not have much to learn from the great European central banks which have in so many respects provided a model for the American banking reform. Certainly, in his repeated attacks upon the Bank of England which attained their lasting form in his classic work *Lombard Street*, Walter Bagehot gained general acceptance for the doctrine that, at times of crisis, the central banks should not follow a policy of an essentially private nature. Rather than concentrating upon the maintenance of their liquidity, they should be led by wider general economic considerations, and intervene to ameliorate the distress by an abundant extension of credit albeit at a high interest rate. There have been scarcely any attempts to go beyond a policy of this type, which aims simply to facilitate the process of recovery after a crisis has already broken out, to the adoption of a purposive, preventative counter-cyclical policy.[12] The credit policy of the central banks restricted itself to keeping the movements in the value of money within certain limits set by the gold currency, and only to checking the expansion of credit when their reserves or the maintenance of the gold parity of the national currency appeared to be under threat. Within the limits set by the gold currency, they saw no occasion to work against a general price rise even if it must inevitably lead to an economic crisis with all its evil consequences. 'So long as credit is regulated with reference to reserve proportions, the trade cycle is bound to recur.'[13] In this proposition, which rapidly became famous, the English monetary theorist R. G. Hawtrey summed up the judgment of more recent writers as to the worth of the guidelines hitherto followed in central banking policy. At the same time he pointed out that the way to reform was to neglect the reserve proportion in favour of other criteria as the guidelines for discount policy.[14] The concrete problem around which the greatest part of the relevant discussion turns is what *other* data will now have to replace the reserve proportion as the guide for discount policy.

It has been shown above that, in addition to these general considerations, America has had to abandon the traditional guiding principles of discount policy because it is now isolated as the only country still on the gold standard. It is probably due more to this circumstance than to theoretical considerations that the problem under discussion here has been so generally raised in recent years. There remains a third fact that has contributed to making the question as to the lines of credit policy most appropriate for central banks to follow especially topical in America. The traditional views on the guiding principles of discount policy are almost exclusively derived from the experience of the Bank of England and hence from the particular conditions under which it operates. Such principles were scarcely relevant or were not adequate even for the continental European banks, who were thus obliged to supplement them with other approaches. In doing so, however, they did not develop an independent theory of discount policy. In the United States, on the other hand, it soon became evident that some of the presuppositions for the applicability of the guiding principles of discount policy as developed in England were either altogether absent or present to only an insufficient extent. This was true above all of that factor which played so large a role in the theory of discount policy: the issue of any excessive extensions of credit into a severe 'internal drain', a withdrawal of ready money from the central institution to cover the increased demand for currency (*Geldzeichen*) to cover the increased demand arising from internal trade.

Due to the provision for simply proportional coverage of the note issue and the extended use of cheques in place of ready money (a factor absent on the continent of Europe), the Federal Reserve Banks lose almost no gold at all to the circulation, especially in the early stages of a credit expansion. For this reason, the reserve proportion is not the sensitive indicator of credit conditions in America that it is in England.[15] It is solely due to this that the change in demand operates to a greater extent upon currency than upon deposit money, with an effect upon the reserve proportion that remains small. Hence, the credit banks need to secure reserves with the Federal Reserve Banks which are merely a proportion of the amount by which they expand their deposits. To acquire Federal Reserve notes, on the other hand, they must rediscount assets with the Federal Reserve Banks to the full amount of the expansion of their deposits. Now the evidence is that the ratio between deposit money and notes changes in favour of the latter during an upswing. Hence in the later part of the upswing the credit banks utilize the Federal Reserve Banks to an extent which far exceeds that of the increase in bank credit, to satisfy the demand for currency. It is this which is somewhat analogous to the 'internal drain' to which the Bank of England is subject.[16] The so-called 'external drain' as well is far less operative than in London because of the smaller significance of foreign credits on the American money market, and hence it does not possess the same importance for discount policy in America as it does in London.

The new conception of the aims and guidelines of discount policy which differs most from that previously held demands that it must be exclusively or predominantly directed towards the stabilization of the general price level. Accordingly, movements in the price index are to be employed as a signal for action to be taken. Any rise in the index by a definite percentage is immediately to be met with a rise in the discount rate or other restrictions on credit, and every fall in the general price level by a reduction of the discount rate.[17] The passage in the draft version of the Federal Reserve Act to which attention has already been drawn, but which was deleted in the final version of the act, sought to prescribe this policy to the Federal Reserve Banks. The authorities actually charged with the conduct of credit policy were most decisive in their rejection of this demand, and also referred to the refusal of Congress to accept it.[18] But it met with heavy opposition from most theoreticians as well. A proposal of this type has been advanced by Irving Fisher in the United States and J. M. Keynes in England, and most sharply argued against by B. M. Anderson. The main objection raised against it is that the average movement of all prices does not at all proceed parallel with that of other important factors in cyclical fluctuations, especially levels of output. The general price level in particular normally continues to decline for some time while the level of economic activity is rising once again.[19] In addition, it is argued, the effect of a rise in prices is initially completely beneficial, because of the stimulus it gives to a further expansion of output. A credit policy orientated solely towards price movements would therefore, through the granting of the larger volume of credit it would facilitate, act in a quite inappropriate way in that it would impart an excessive stimulus to a level of economic activity which was already beginning to rise again. And it would check its further rise, by leading to the imposition of credit restrictions at a time when that rise in output was still far from having achieved its possible maximum. But those price rises which can no longer call forth an expansion in productive activity, because this existing productive apparatus is already fully employed, are in the view of most economists dangerous and thus should be prevented. The objection that appears to us to be much more serious is that the cyclical movement finds its initial expression not in the behaviour of the general price level but in that of the relative prices of the individual groups of commodities. Hence an index of the general price level cannot yield any relevant information as to the course of the cycle nor more importantly can it do so at the right time. Our discussion of this controversial issue cannot go into any further detail at this point, and similarly with respect to two other issues: whether – as is often asserted – fluctuations in the general price level may not arise from causes other than those of a monetary nature and hence cannot or must not in all cases be rectified by monetary means; and to what extent index numbers in general afford an appropriate picture of movements in the value of money.

In place of this method, which seeks to solve the problem under discussion in what is certainly too simple a fashion, various people have sketched out other, more refined procedures. Their aim is to enable the prevention of unduly severe cyclical fluctuations or even the elimination of cycles in general, by means of discount policy. The development already noted in the statistical observation of cyclical phenomena in the United States offers an abundance of clues for the assessment of the current position, in the form of the various 'cycle barometers'. The correct interpretation of them should therefore facilitate a far more systematic conduct of stabilization policy than is permitted by looking solely at price statistics. The need is mainly to develop, from the complicated methods used to observe economic activity, a method which is simple, operable in practice and as clear as possible, and from which one will be able to derive in a virtually automatic fashion the measures of credit policy called for at any moment. In the United States, there is a wide level of agreement that the most important task of a credit policy which seeks to eliminate crises is the reduction of the volume of credit at the right time, i.e. when any further expansion of credit apparently gives rise to a disproportion between the output of capital goods and the demand for consumer goods. Given this level of agreement, then, what is necessary above all is to ascertain the signals by which it can be recognized that the time has arrived for credit to be restricted.

While this problem has often attracted passing attention from various authors and been discussed in articles,[20] it has not hitherto been subjected to any systematic treatment. The appearance of a larger-scale work by Professor O. W. M. Sprague,[21] anticipated with impatience, was originally announced for 1923, but has not yet happened. It was Sprague who with some emphasis first directed general attention to this problem, and whose exploratory proposals formed the starting point for its discussion. Mitchell, like Adams, has taken up the suggestion made by Sprague in his published works, and outlines it thus:[22]

Professor Sprague proposes to use index numbers of physical product such as have been made recently by Day, King, Snyder, and Stewart as a basis for discount policy. This series shows that the increase in the volume of business after a depression is for some time produced mainly by a rapid increase in the output of serviceable goods. During that phase of the cycle expansion is economically desirable. But whenever the existing industrial equipment is booked to capacity and the industrial army is fully employed then future growth in the supply of serviceable goods slows down to the rate at which new equipment and new hands can be provided and improved technical methods devised. After that point has been reached in the cycle a further rise of prices does not increase the current supply of serviceable goods, but creates confusion in the markets, stimulates harmful speculation, and produces the credit entanglements which cause so much anxiety during the crises and prolongs the period of liquidation. *Our aim accordingly should be to check the rise of prices when the index numbers of physical output indicate that the limit of existing capacity is being approached.* At that point it would be desirable to raise discount rates – even though the reserve ratios might still be high.

The italicized passage in the quotation embodies the basic concept; that credit should be restricted so as to check the rise in prices, as soon as this rise no longer can call forth a corresponding increase in output. In addition to the statistics of physical production emphasized in the first line of the passage quoted, it is above all the level of employment or unemployment which is taken to be the most important indication that a further expansion of output can no longer be effected by an expansion of credit. Why is the level of employment chosen as the indicator? Because, according to recent American investigations, especially those by W. A. Burridge,[23] and in agreement with the conclusions reached by German researchers (such as Jastrow), it is regarded as that which provides the most accurate picture of the general economic situation. J. R. Bellerby[24] would go further and make the index of general employment the criterion by which in the first instance the volume of credit would be regulated: the aim would be to prevent any further rise in prices once employment had reached the level which could be regarded as normal for any country. A related proposal by F. W. Pethick Lawrence[25] regards the statistics as to stocks of finished products

19

as the most important indicator of the business situation. When such stocks are rising, the discount rate should be raised, and vice versa. Bellerby[26] is correct when he comments that the value of this index as a criterion would be considerably increased if it could be broken down into separate indexes for retail trade, wholesale trade and output.

The discussion has as yet made little progress beyond the acceptance of the basic principles common to these proposals. What is still missing is the extension and the refinement of the methods necessary if their utilization is to be attended with an adequate degree of certainty. Only after years of practical testing will it be possible to decide which of the methods proposed can actually be used. In precisely the same way as the proposal for a pure stabilization of the price level, all the improved suggestions still continue to run up against one fact: that the economic situation is not revealed by the movement of any one of the factors that they take as their indicator, such as the level of output, employment, or commodity stocks, or their relationship to one another or to the movement of prices. Rather, it is in the first instance the relationship between the behaviour of these factors in the individual sectors of the economy that reveals the situation. Yet these relationships are neither so regular in their recurrence nor have been subjected to sufficient basic research to enable easily recognizable criteria for credit policy to be derived from them. The comprehension of these statistics is faced with the problem that the usual dividing lines drawn between the sectors of the economy, and even the combination of different activities within a single enterprise, do not always coincide with those demarcations which correspond to the theoretical categories that must be employed in the explanation of cyclical movements. Hence even the most precise production statistic cannot yield any reliable conclusion as to the way in which the emphasis is shifting between the production of goods of higher order and that of lower, and whether this relationship is in accordance with the capital accumulation actually taking place.

Yet it is not simply in the derivation of the statistics for the most important variables which might serve as criteria that difficulties arise. On the contrary, it is precisely the dominantly statistical basis and the lack of interest in theory characteristic of American researchers that prevents them from taking up the most difficult problems. And it causes them, too, to overlook basic difficulties pertaining to their procedure.

A special treatise would be needed to provide a more detailed critique of the various proposals from the aspect of the theory of crises. All that can be emphasized here is that, from the theoretical viewpoint, it must appear highly doubtful whether a complete prevention of crises is possible while our present credit system is maintained, at least in its basic features. Mere alterations in the credit policy pursued by banks can have only a minor effect upon the underlying causes of crises. The naive confidence in this respect which is shared by many of the most eminent American scholars[27] can be explained only by the derogatory attitude displayed by most of them towards the insight into the necessary interrelationships between economic phenomena provided by theory. Although theory seems to offer the possibility of eliminating the cause of crises by thorough-going changes in the present organization of economic life, it must be asked whether too high a price would have to be paid to achieve such stability. Thus, it is not improbable that any 'additional' credit newly created by the banks in excess of the current accumulation of savings must sooner or later lead to a reaction against the more rapid progress of the economy which it has made possible. The reason is that the development of the productive apparatus of society to the same extent would have swallowed up a part of its income greater than that which it wanted to or is able to permanently withdraw from consumption. The losses which arise from the revelation that the capital outlay made is not yet economically justified are the price of an undesirably rapid progress, a rate of progress which exceeds that which people are ready to purchase for themselves by a corresponding voluntary sacrifice of current enjoyments.

There can be no doubt at all that the development of the capitalistic economy over the last 100 years would not have been possible without the 'forced saving' effected by the extension of additional bank credit. Hence economic fluctuations must probably be regarded as a necessary accompaniment of the accelerated development experienced by countries of the Western world in the last 150 years. Such fluctuations, in turn, could be entirely eliminated only if the tempo of this development was substantially lessened, i.e. to the rate made possible by voluntary saving. The extent of the reduction necessary would then have to be much greater than appears at first sight, because certainly the overwhelming part of the private accumulation of wealth taking place today is made from entrepreneurial profits. This would necessarily show a large decline

21

if growth were substantially reduced, with the result that the volume of private savings would also thereby necessarily decline. But if one is not ready to take this step, one will have to adopt a more modest goal. After a careful weighing-up of the advantages and disadvantages to be expected, an attempt could be made to maintain a more rapid growth rate within such limits as will lessen the all too severe damage wrought by crises. Growth will thus not be permitted to exceed the rate which appears justified by the more rapid progress whose causes are the same as those of crises. But if this is accepted, all the new proposals lose that revolutionary character claimed for them by their advocates; all they do then is to provide a clearer elaboration of an old problem and new angles for its solution. But on the other hand, it will thereby become evident that the practical questions arising in this context cannot be answered in any clear-cut way by science alone. For they are also partly questions of one's outlook on life, and hence are in the widest sense matters of judgment upon which sharply divergent views may be held. However, through such discussion, awareness will also be gained of the dangers that could appear if, because of all too bold an experimentation in this field, the traditional established rules of credit policy become neglected before the new rules have obtained an equal measure of authority. This would leave the door wide open to abuse. Certainly, it is a very significant gain that new approaches are being worked out for central banking policy in addition to the incomplete principles that have existed for some time. Their incorporation into the discussion should also make possible the provision of positive guidance for policy in situations in which the previous criteria have failed to operate, proved inadequate, or have transmitted their signals at too late a stage. Central banking policy has been for too long the step-child of science and it is only just that it should now have somewhat more attention paid to it. An appropriate credit policy will probably turn out to be able to restrain cyclical fluctuations within narrower limits than has hitherto been the case. But there is nothing that would so put paid to the possibilities opening up in this field as to impose too strenuous demands upon central banking policy at this early stage of the discussion, and thereby lead it to undertake premature and unwise experimentation. To do so would not merely be to cause immeasurable damage directly, but would probably also call forth political intervention. If this were to occur, not only would the central banks be stripped of the possibility of exercising that beneficial regulatory influence which they possess today, but our entire money and credit system would become, to an even greater extent than previously, an object of contention between the political parties. Then it would constitute a source of continuous disturbances of economic life, instead of exerting a stabilizing influence upon it.

One further comment may be made upon the particular concrete proposals for an active[28] stabilization policy on the part of the banks. Many of them hope to achieve a complete elimination of cyclical fluctuations. But, even leaving aside the fact that such fluctuations are undoubtedly caused by factors other than an excessive expansion of credit, it is safe to say that they will never be able to do so. The reason is that the prevention of a reversal in the level of economic activity would probably require a rise in interest rates to be effected before they could be *recognized* as actually being too low. Presumably it would be necessary to keep the interest rate at a level significantly higher than would appear usual throughout the depression, or at least from the moment at which the decline in production came to an end. Yet it is precisely at the beginning of an upswing that the central banks can exert only minor influence. Hence it seems quite doubtful whether such a policy could ever be operated in practice. Suppose the stabilization policy of the banks was orientated toward the movement of prices, whether prices in general or their relationship to each other for the particular commodity groups. It must always become operative at too late a stage to prevent a reversal in economic activity, because the misfortune has already occurred and capital has been locked up to too great an extent when once the expansion of credit begins to work itself out in a rise in prices.

Up till now, however, scarcely sufficient attention seems to have been paid to another element of cyclical movements which can be given statistical expression and changes in which could usefully be considered by a banking policy aiming at economic stabilization. What we have in mind is the total volume of bank credit in use at any time. If it is changes in the volume of credit in use which are to be considered as the chief cause of the unequal development of supply and demand, and hence of cyclical movements, a policy which maintained the volume of bank credit approximately stable would have most to contribute to the prevention of cyclical fluctuations. We shall content ourselves with advancing this proposition here, without going into the practical and theoretical difficulties relating to it.[29]

Our discussion of contemporary opinion as to the aims of credit policy has arrived at its conclusion. It remains for us to briefly describe the simultaneous development of thought regarding the tools to be employed by credit policy. In this context, the first question to be answered is: which authorities should work together in conducting such a policy, and are in a position to do so successfully? It has long been believed that only the central banks should be required to conduct a credit policy guided by overall economic considerations, as only they could be expected to be successful. But in recent times, the conviction has grown that the tools available to the central bank for this purpose are inadequate. It is now felt that, if credit control measures are to be penetrating and swift in action, this will involve the voluntary and independent co-operation of at least all the large commercial banks.[30] By pointing out their private economic interests to them, it is hoped to induce these banks to conduct a policy which runs parallel to the stabilization policy being pursued by the central bank.

Bearing in mind the necessarily limited duration of every upswing, they should at least go so far as to base their lending on a more cautious evaluation of the assets of borrowers than is necessary during a stagnation, which brings less surprises with it than the boom. It is not completely utopian to expect the individual commercial banks to behave in a way thus orientated towards general economic considerations.

The fact that in recent years a large number of the leading American banks have set up their own economic bureaux is evidence of this. The findings of such bureaux whose main task is to accurately observe and investigate cyclical movements receive full consideration by the managements of these banks. The expectation that a turn-around is imminent when the level of activity appears to near its peak will doubtless cause the banks to exercise greater restraint in the later part of the upswing. As a result, the necessary braking effect which should be the aim of the central banks at this point in time will be exerted from the side of the commercial banks as well.

Of course, it is natural to expect the great central banks to exercise the credit control demanded with the tool of discount policy. But it has been a subject much discussed whether and to what extent they can exert the necessary influence upon the total volume of bank credit simply by changing their discount rate, and what additional measures may be needed. The sceptical view holds that a rise or a reduction in the discount rate of the central banks cannot exert any significant influence upon the total volume of bank credit outstanding. Two reasons are advanced to support this view. Firstly, it is argued, the change in the interest burden borne by industry in general which follows upon a change in the rate plays far too small a role as a cost element to lead to significant changes in the level of output, and especially to outweigh the prospects of profits opened up by rising prices. Secondly, it is said, the credits directly affected by the change, those granted to the customers of the central banks themselves, form only a increasingly small fraction of all bank credits outstanding at any time. To these arguments, however, Hawtrey in particular has provided an excellent counter. He argues that the interest rate plays a large role in the calculations of two particular groups: the wholesale dealer above all, working with capital which to an overwhelming extent he has borrowed from others, and the demand exercised by whom determines the volume of output in the first instance; and in the securities markets. It is via its influence upon these two groups that a change in the interest rate exerts its effect. Again, the credit extended by the central banks themselves is the only portion of the overall structure of credit whose volume can easily be varied. Hence as a rule it constitutes the marginal supply of credit and as such its price determines that of all bank credit. Yet the view seems to be becoming ever more widespread that a rise in discount rate takes too long to exert its influence upon the volume of bank credit outstanding for it to be successful by itself in influencing the economy in the desired direction – above all, because all orders already placed must be met despite any rise that may occur in the interest rate. Hence, changes in the discount rate must be supplemented, it is felt, by the sale of securities by the central banks, so-called 'open market operations', which will bring about a direct reduction of the loans they have made. In recent times, many authors have even apparently come to regard these open market operations as the most important tool of discount policy (in the wider sense of the term), and recommend its employment not merely alongside and in support of changes in the discount rate but in many cases instead of such discount rate changes.

The Federal Reserve Banks were empowered by law to buy and sell bank acceptances, treasurers' notes (*Schatzscheine*) and certain other securities on the open market and hence to enter into dealings with non-members of the Reserve System, though they were restricted in all their other business to dealings with member banks alone. But the reasons for empowering them to undertake such operations were various. The first aim was to enable them both to invest their funds profitably at times when there was little demand upon them for rediscounting, and to promote the introduction of certain types of commercial paper (bills of exchange, bank acceptances) by forming a regular source of demand for them. But the main reason for enabling the Federal Reserve Banks to undertake 'open market operations', was to make available a weapon with which they could make their discount rate effective. Examples of this were provided by the practice of the Bank of England and the German Reichsbank. To make their discount rate effective, they sold or raised money on Treasury bills (consols) and first-class bills bought for this purpose at the private rate, and by the withdrawal of funds thereby created they forced the banks to make use of their rediscounting facilities.[31] Conversely, by purchasing such securities, the central bank is able to ease the money market if the rate of interest demanded by the banks appears to it to be inappropriately high. Since the rate of interest at which such purchases are undertaken is as a rule higher than that at which sales to absorb excessive funds are made, the central bank can in this way make a quite respectable profit on its dealings in discountable or fixed-interest paper.

In discount policy in the strict sense, the central bank must basically remain passive and wait to see the extent of the demands made upon it for rediscounting. It can then determine the price at which it will meet this demand. But by being able to intervene in the open market, it can influence the supply of credit directly and thus regulate that demand which it must satisfy by rediscounting and for which the official discount rate is therefore effective. In this way it gains the initiative, and can influence the policy of the commercial banks far more directly than often is possible through changes in its official discount rate.

The practices followed by the Federal Reserve System in its activity up till now have stimulated discussion of some of the other basic questions of discount policy in the wider sense of the term. Only the most important can be briefly mentioned here. In addition to distinguishing between the effects of rediscounting according to the point of origin and the time for which they are operative, recent discussion has primarily been concerned with the question: what should be the relationship between discount rate of the central bank and the rate on the open market? The policy followed by the system in recent years has almost invariably been to keep its discount rate below that on the open market for the same classes of securities. The demand has been voiced, however, that the central bank's discount rate should basically be kept above that prevailing in the open market.[32] Any rediscount rate that enables a profitable use to be made of funds borrowed from the Federal Reserve Banks, it is argued, must stimulate inflation. The excellent book on the discount policy of the Federal Reserve System by B. H. Beckhart, which has already been cited in this essay, must be referred to for further discussion of these and other questions.

Notes

1 One of the most eminent representatives of this school, Lord Overstone, had already in 1837 pointed out with the utmost rigour the basic tenets of the modern theory of 'business cycles'. In his *Reflections Suggested by a Perusal of Mr J. Horsley Palmer's Pamphlet on the Causes and Consequences of the Pressure on the Money Market*, he says: 'The state of trade revolves apparently in an established cycle. First we find it in a state of quiescence – next improvement – growing confidence – prosperity – excitement – overtrading – convulsion – pressure – stagnation – distress – ending again in quiescence.' (Cited from A. Marshall, *Money, Credit and Commerce*, London, 1923, p. 246.)

2 This approach is an outflow from a general trend in more recent American economics. Under the influence of the objective (behaviouristic) psychology which has come to the forefront there in recent years, American economics has turned to an ever increasing extent away from purely theoretical research aimed at an understanding (*Verstehen*) of economic activity. Drawing extensively upon statistical series, it now seeks primarily to construct a picture of the path typically followed by all economic processes. This school is customarily described as 'the institutional school' because of the particular attention it pays to the concrete forms assumed by economic life. Its main achievements lie precisely in the field of research into the business cycle, and the leading American scholar in this field, W. C. Mitchell (main work: *Business Cycles*, Berkeley, 1913), is also the acknowledged leader of the new trend.

3 See particularly the classical presentation of W. C. Mitchell, *op. cit.*

4 A rate of interest which is inappropriately low offers to the individual sectors of the economy an advantage which is greater the more remote is their product from the consumption stage. This is so because the time over which interest is saved with respect to the ultimate final product is correspondingly longer, and the price which the purchaser at the next stage can offer is higher by the entire amount of the interest saved on the path to the consumer. It is not so much the effect of

interest as a cost element in one's own production – this could be the same in all branches of production – which is decisive in this context. Rather, it is the summation of the increased demand exerted by all those participating at later stages of production (inclusive of commerce), because of the greater possibilities of profit offered to each of them by the lower interest rate. In addition, the value of fixed capital depends not upon a price achieved at any point in time but on the yield expected over a longer time period. Hence it is influenced to a much greater degree by the current interest rate at which the yield is capitalized than is the price of circulating capital (materials, labour), which is consumed during a period of production and obtains a single price which must be discounted. A relatively lower interest rate therefore raises the price of fixed capital, and hence the prospects of profit in its production, far more than is the case with circulating capital. In the production of producer goods, a higher percentage of fixed capital is normally employed than in that of consumer goods and especially than that in the last stage of production in the wider sense, commerce. Consequently, this factor makes an essential contribution to explaining why an interest rate which is too low calls forth an expansion of the individual sectors of the economy which is greater the more remote is their product from the consumption stage.

To prevent a disproportionate development of the production of goods of higher order, the interest rate must always be sufficiently high to restrict it to that level at which the capital necessary for the maintenance of output in the later stages under unchanged conditions can also be procured. Since the interest on capital – as all modern (catallactic) theories agree – represents the necessary limit to a disproportionate expansion of the capitalistic mode of production, an interest rate which is temporarily too low must give rise to an excessive accumulation of capital. This would be equivalent to an ever-intensifying widening of the basis of the pyramid of the capitalistic structure of the economy while the savings necessary to raise its height are not available. The initial strengthening of the demand for raw materials, due to the prospects of increased profits in the sectors converting them into manufactures, must decline as soon as the savings used up in the production of goods of higher order are no longer sufficient to permit a corresponding expansion of the output of goods of lower order (i.e. under equally profitable conditions, hence at an interest rate which has not risen).

5 Cf. in this context, L. v. Mises, *Theorie des Geldes und der Umlaufsmittel*, 2nd edn, Munich, 1924, pp. 373ff.

6 Among German authors, to our knowledge it has only been K. Wicksell, A. Spiethoff, G. v. Schulze-Gävernitz, L. v. Mises, J. Schumpeter and A. Hahn who have occasionally concerned themselves with this problem.

7 The situation has been different in England. There, under the influence of A. Marshall, theoretical interest has been more lively, and R. G. Hawtrey especially has made an essential contribution to our understanding of the relationships between credit and cyclical phenomena. The role played by economic theory in the American and English schools has in fact been like that in the German and Austrian schools:

the former has placed the greater weight on historical-statistical research, the latter on theoretical.

8 See, e.g., B. H. Beckhart, *The Discount Policy of the Federal Reserve System*, New York, 1924, pp. 100ff.:

> The diffused character of the National banking system, the lack of any but local cooperation amongst the members, and the scattered nature of the reserves *prevented any pretence at credit control. Cyclic fluctuations were consequently greatly sharpened and intensified.* On the upward swing of the cycle, always a time when business men over-capitalise future earnings, credit was freely extended. No check was placed on the expansion. The boom periods regularly terminated in severe crises, which as regularly degenerated into panics, followed by severe and prolonged depressions. *The asperities of cyclic fluctuations were much more severe in America than in England, France or Germany, where some degree of control* was exercised by the central banks over credit extensions.

(The emphasis in the above and all succeeding quotations from this work have been added by the present author.) Similarly H. G. Moulton, *The Financial Organisation of Society*, Chicago, 1921, pp. 522ff.; V. Morawetz, *The Banking and Currency Problem in the United States*, New York, 1909, pp. 4–50; and H. Bilgram and E. Levy, *The Causes of Business Depressions*, Philadelphia, 1914, pp. 762ff.

9 Section 11d of the first draft, and section 15 of the text: '[the rate of discount] shall be made with a view to accommodating the commerce of the country and promoting a stable price level.' Cf. H. P. Willis, *The Federal Reserve System*, New York, 1923, pp. 1585 and 1605.

10 See H. P. Willis, *op. cit.*, pp. 332, 1626.

11 Only W. F. Gephart in *Inflation in Relation to the Bank Reserves and the Business Cycle*, Federal Reserve Bank of St. Louis, June 1928, p. 13, seems to have stated this with the necessary degree of clarity.

12 As we have already emphasized, the older English theoreticians of the currency school had a firmer grasp of this than the majority of economists who came after them. The currency school hoped also to prevent cyclical fluctuations by the regulation of the note issue they proposed. But since they took only the effects of the note issue into account and neglected those of deposit money, and the restrictions imposed upon bank credit could always be got round by an expansion of transfers through bank deposits, Peel's Bank Act and the central bank statute modelled upon it could not achieve this aim. The problem of the prevention of crises would have received a radical solution if the basic concept of Peel's act had been consistently developed into the prescription of 100 per cent gold cover for bank deposits as well as notes.

13 *Monetary Reconstruction*, London, 1923, p. 144.

14 Obviously, what is at issue here is not the replacement of a credit policy orientated strictly towards the maintenance of a sufficient degree of liquidity by a laxer policy. On the contrary, it is whether, taking the maintenance of liquidity fully into account, still further and stricter regulations should be drafted. In particular, further extensions of credit

which seem permissible with respect to the liquidity of the banks, and demanded because of the striving for profitability, are nevertheless to be abstained from for general economic reasons. The more abundant granting of credit after the crisis, which is demanded, would likewise not have to take place at the cost of greater liquidity, since the restriction of credit at the right time during the upswing would mean for the banks a higher degree of liquidity after the reversal than was the case with the previous policy.

15 O. W. M. Sprague in particular has emphasized this: 'Bank of England practice however loses significance and is positively misleading when it is applied to a banking system which loses no gold for purposes of domestic circulation as credit expands.' *The Discount Policy of the Federal Reserve System*, p. 26.

16 See in this connection the interesting remarks on pp. 23ff. in the *Tenth Annual Report of the Federal Reserve Board, covering the operations for the year 1923*, Washington, 1924, especially p. 25:

> This is the usual sequence – an increase of deposits followed by an increase of the currency. Ordinarily the first effect of an increase in business activity on the banking position is a growth in loans and deposits. . . . There comes a time when the increase of business activity and the fuller employment of labor and increased payrolls call for an increase of actual pocket money to support the increased wage disbursements and the increased volume of purchases at retail. At this stage the rough parallelism between growth of loans and deposits of the banks gives way to a divergent movement between these items. Loans may continue to increase while deposits will remain stationary or show a decline. . . . What in the first instance was the creation of bank credit in the convenient form of a checking account has now become a demand for cash. . . . The ratio of loans to deposits rises with an increased demand for currency.

Again, p. 27:

> Under the Federal Reserve System, as before, fluctuations in the ratio of loans to deposits are occasioned by changes in the country's demand for currency. This increased demand however, under present conditions leads to increased borrowing at the reserve banks. In the absence of gold imports in sufficient volume to meet the currency demand, it will be reflected in larger rediscounting at the Federal Reserve Banks for the purpose of obtaining currency. . . . It is then that the resources of the reserve bank are brought more fully into play and its loans mount rapidly. So long as the member bank's customers required only book money, the amount of member bank credit which a dollar of reserve bank credit would sustain was on the average in the ratio of about 10 to 1. But as the demand for currency increases, this ratio declines and eventually reaches a point where a dollar of reserve bank credit must be obtained for each dollar of currency taken from the bank by its customer.

17 Thus, e.g., I. Fisher, Beckhart, Foster and Catchings, and many others.
18 See Annual Report of the Federal Reserve 1923, p. 31: 'No credit system could undertake to perform the function of regulating credit by reference to price without failing in the endeavor'; also the views as to the various functions of the Federal Reserve System quoted in Beckhart, *op. cit.*, pp. 524ff.
19 Cf. W. C. Mitchell, *op. cit.*, p. 457.
20 See particularly the works by Gephart, Mitchell and Sprague, *op. cit.*, as well as Foster and Catchings, *Money* (Boston and New York, 1923) and the article by Thomas Adams, 'Financial devices for controlling or mitigating the severity of business cycles', in *Business Cycles and Unemployment* Report of the Committee of the President's Conference on Unemployment, (New York, 1923).
21 *Bank Credit and Business Cycles*, announced as No. 5 of the Publications of the Pollak Foundation for Economic Research.
22 W. C. Mitchell, 'The crisis of 1920 and the problem of controlling business cycles', *Am. Ec. Review* (supplement) XII, 1922, pp. 20–32, p. 25; also in L. Edie (ed.), *The Stabilisation of Business*, New York, 1923, pp. 42ff.
23 *Cycles of Unemployment in the United States*, Boston, 1923.
24 J. R. Bellerby, *Control of Credit as a Remedy for Unemployment*, London, 1923, p. 90.

In the meantime, the employment index, rough as it may be, if taken in conjunction with the movement of the price level itself, would form an admirable criterion for the guidance of discount policy. A tendency on the part of the employment index to turn down toward the horizontal (after a comparatively high level of employment, varying according to the country, had been reached) coupled with an upward turn of the price index number, would be the strongest possible evidence that the time had come to regulate credit strictly in accordance with the needs of industry as expressed in the volume of goods coming to the market. In other words, after this point had been reached, the movement of the price level would be the principal guide, the object of credit policy being to prevent the rate of movement from attaining any degree of rapidity.

25 *Unemployment*, Oxford, 1922, p. 53:

What would really help to regulate trade would be to begin to contract credit as soon as stocks of finished articles unmarketed showed signs of increasing (instead of waiting as now until they have become considerable), and to begin to expand it as soon as they show signs of diminishing. In this way both the extreme height of the boom and the extreme depths of the slump would be avoided.

26 *Op. cit.*, p. 75.
27 See, for example, Mitchell, 'The crisis of 1920 and the problem of controlling business cycles', p. 31:

For since the money economy is a complex human institution, it is subject to amendment. What we have to do is to find out just how the rules of our own making thwart our wishes and to change them in detail or change them drastically as the case may require.

28 Active, in the sense of a policy directed towards modifying the course of economic activity, as compared to a passive policy, whose aim is merely an adjustment to the given course of activity.

29 In this context, see R. G. Hawtrey, *Monetary Reconstruction*, London, 1923, pp. 123ff.:

Traders and Bankers often deprecate changes in the discount rate as being unsettling to business. *But what is unsettling is the alternation between expanding and contracting credit.* If credit, and therefore the flow of purchasing power, are kept approximately steady, the short period changes in the rate of discount cause no trouble except in the highly specialised calculations of the discount market itself.

30 Cf. especially O. W. M. Sprague, *Bank Management and the Business Cycle*, n.p., n.d., pp. 20ff.; Gephart, *op. cit.*, p. 7; and Kemmerer (cited by Adams, *op. cit.*, p. 268).

31 Cf. Beckhart, *op. cit.*, pp. 61ff.

32 Especially by Anderson and Hepburn, *op. cit.*, pp. 4ff.

TWO

SOME REMARKS ON THE PROBLEM OF IMPUTATION*

1 The concept of economic imputation and its origin

The doctrine of marginal utility makes it possible to equate the subjective value of economic goods with a certain level of utility yielded by them if the good yields this utility directly and in isolation. In this case, as is generally known, the level of utility which determines the value of a certain quantity of a good is the lowest level of utility attainable by using this quantity of the good without neglecting any of the higher levels of utility obtainable from it. However, this principle is not immediately applicable to those goods which cannot by themselves satisfy certain needs and wants but which are able to do so only in combination with other economic goods. Following Menger's practice, these goods are called complementary goods. For these goods, the utility obtained in each individual case is brought about by and is dependent on several goods. Hence, the values of several goods are to be derived from it if one wants to retain the explanation of value by utility. The problem thereby posed is of the greatest importance since the relationship between value and utility, on which it is based, does not exist merely in cases in which the satisfaction of a need or want requires the uses of several consumer goods. It also arises with all those needs and wants which are satisfied by a *product* and which indirectly require a multitude of (producer) goods for their satisfaction. While the first case is usually neglected as being of no importance, the problem of the derivation of the value of the individual producer goods from the jointly produced level of utility has entered into the economic literature under the name of *Zurechnung* (English: imputation; French: *imputation*; Italian: *imputazione*), a term introduced by Wieser in analogy with the use of the word in jurispru-

---

* First published as 'Bemerkungen zum Zurechnungsproblem', in *Jahrbücher für Nationalökonomie und Statistik*, 69 (1926), pp. 1–18.

dence. In the course of the elaboration of the subjective theory of value, this problem has been extensively dealt with by the so-called Austrian school.

2 The position of the doctrine of imputation in modern economic theory

In the modern subjective theory of value individual valuation has been made the basis of the explanation of the determination of prices. From Ricardo onwards, however, there was little dispute that it was knowledge of the determinants of income which constituted the objective of theoretical economics. Such knowledge is at the same time generally sought by way of an investigation of the elements determining the prices of the factors of production. Consequently, the whole of economic theory rests on the explanation of the value of producer goods and thus on the theory of imputation. A satisfactory solution of the problem of imputation is therefore the precondition which must be satisfied if the theory of distribution is to be definitively established on the basis of the subjective theory of value. Now, subjective value itself is the cause of exchange and the determining cause of prices, but subjective value is itself to be explained by exchange. Hence, the solution of the problem of imputation has to be attempted without recourse to exchange. Any solution, therefore, has to be based on the assumption of an economy guided by a uniform will which Wieser has called the 'individual economy'. Therefore, the conditions of the individual economy have been made the basis of the following investigations unless explicitly stated otherwise.

The theory of distribution can be established on the basis of the subjective theory of value if we succeed in deriving the importance which an individual attributes to the various factors of production under given conditions from the valuation of the utility yielded by a product. As will have to be shown later, this problem is very closely connected with the question as to the extent to which it is economically possible to expand production which uses the good in question. The problem thus contains a question about man's use of goods which the circumstances demand. Within the context of the determination of the value of a given quantity of consumer goods, however, the problem of value constitutes only a partial problem of theoretical economics. This is so despite the fact that, in the wake of finding the answer to this question, the apparent contradiction between utility and value was overcome and the basis of all value

34

theory was thereby established. The basis upon which the question as to the necessary structure of the economy as a whole, and thus the problem of distribution, can be answered is to be found only within the discussion of the problems posed by the theory of imputation. In contrast to this, adequate attention has frequently not been paid to the problem of imputation. In some of the systems of subjective economic theory it is completely ignored and the explanation of the value of consumer goods immediately moves on to the explanation of prices and further to that of the forms of income. All this occurs because the problem of economic value is erroneously regarded as having been solved completely once the value of consumer goods has been explained. What is thereby overlooked is that a separate explanation of the value of producer goods must be provided because of the entirely different conditions applying to them. The theory of imputation, however, is not merely a special case subject to the same rules as apply to value in general; it is the next and decisive step to be taken in the development of economic theory on the basis of the subjective theory of value. In the paragraphs below, we will show how far economic theory has advanced in this direction to date. Of course, in so far as one believes that a completely satisfactory solution to the problem has not yet been found, we cannot exclude the possibility from the very outset that the determinants of the prices of the factors of production are to be found in the exchange economy alone, and therefore that an imputation of value is not applicable, a view held by several younger authors. Nevertheless, if this view were regarded as valid, the result would be that we would have no satisfactory explanation of economic processes based on the subjective theory of value, and it would also follow that these authors too would lack any basis for many of their investigations.

3 Older formulations of the problem

Suppose that the problem of imputation is formulated in such a way that the question is posed: what part of the level of utility realised by a product is due to the individual producer goods used in its production? It then coincides with a problem which has always occupied economists, namely the question as to the relative productivity of the factors of production. Although it is not quite correct to do so, it actually has been formulated in this way. In a wider sense, therefore, all attempts ever made at answering this question, whose meaning is rather unclear, however, ought to be referred to as 'imputation theories'. There have always been those, as, for example, John Stuart Mill, who openly asserted that this problem was unsolvable since every factor constitutes an indispensable condition for the outcome as a whole. But various attempts have been made towards a solution of the problem. For the most, these attempts were doomed from the beginning because of the materialistic formulation of the concept of productivity they utilized, a formulation resting on ideas taken over from physics, and because of the objective conception of value which went hand in hand with this formulation. J. B. Say's 'theory of productive services' is the best known of these attempts, besides those of the Physiocrats and the Classical and Socialist economists who attributed productivity, 'the power of creating value', to land or only to human labour, respectively. Nevertheless, these theories cannot be regarded as imputation theories in the narrow sense of the word, if only because the doctrines which embodied them do not offer a handle with which to grasp an economic outcome which could be determined independently of the actual expense on producer goods and could be imputed.

Any attempt to ascertain the relative participation of the various factors of production in an economic outcome had to be unsuccessful so long as an adequate explanation had not been found for value, the expression of this outcome. So long as the starting point of the explanation was not taken as the relationship between utility and scarcity of goods, a relationship which determines every economic action, all attempts had to be pushed on to the field of technology. Ricardo and his predecessors and successors were able to describe correctly, for the special case of rent on land, one element of the economic relationship between the value of products and that of one of their factors in the theory of differential rent. By doing so, moreover, they made it possible for the idea of imputing one part of a value, determined independently of the participation of the producer good, to enter into economic theory. Yet the necessary basis for a generalization of this idea was still absent. This should have taken the form of an explanation of the measure in which the economic result was expressed, together with a realization of the independence in principle of the magnitude of the economic from its physical causes. The further development of the theory of rent by H. v. Thünen was the most likely candidate which could have been interpreted as an imputation theory, and its basic principles were actually developed into such a theory by American scholars at a later date (see section 5 below). But it, too, ran aground on its lack of an adequate concept of value. The problem of the participation of individual factors in an economic 'success' could be confronted with any hope of success only after the subjective theory of value had demonstrated how this outcome of economic activity is expressed by value independently of this activity itself. The first to advance this doctrine, H. H. Gossen, remained unknown for a long time, but he was already fully aware of the significance of his work, and indeed attempted to solve this problem along lines which in principle correspond to the later attempts by Menger and Böhm-Bawerk. A systematic development of the theory of imputation has taken place, however, only since the publication of Menger's *Grundsätze der Volkswirthschaftslehre* in 1871.

4 *The development of the doctrine of imputation within the marginal utility school*

The so-called 'principle of substitution', already successfully employed to explain the value of consumer goods, provided the first basis for an attempt to solve the problem of imputation. Menger, like Gossen before him, had already briefly outlined this approach, and Böhm-Bawerk later constructed a complete theory of imputation on this basis. According to this principle, the value of a good employed in a certain use is not always equal to the minimum level of utility realized in this use, but to the minimum level of utility which may be realized in any of the uses which may be made of it. In Menger's explanation of value by the level of utility dependent on the good in question, the reason for this is as follows: When a good whose use originally contributed to a higher level of utility is removed, then the good which is called into substitute for it is that which has hitherto realized the lowest level of utility, and the utility foregone through the loss of the first good will ultimately be asserted at the place which has become free in this way. This explanation was likewise applied to substitutable goods of higher order, and was supplemented for non-substitutable producer goods by the similar consideration that the utility foregone, through their loss and through the prevention of production thereby caused, will in parts be made up for by the utility which the complementary goods realise in new uses. In fact, the utility foregone can therefore be estimated only as the difference between the originally expected level of utility and the one thus realized. But if none of the complementary goods which are necessary for the realization of a given objective have any other use, or can be substituted, then the whole of the utility realized by their combination will be lost if a single one of them is withdrawn. The rules for the imputation of value[1] which follow from this were summarized by Böhm-Bawerk thus:

1 If none of the necessary complementary goods can either be substituted or used in any other way, then the utility to be realised by the product can be imputed in its entirety to any one of these goods in so far as its withdrawal or purchase is under consideration.

2 The value of a producer good which has an alternative use must be estimated to be given by at least the level of utility realisable in this other use; the difference made by its withdrawal to the total utility of the product therefore constitutes the upper limit for the value of the remaining complementary goods.

3 The value of substitutable goods can never be higher than the respective levels of utility realisable in their alternative uses.

The value which in each case is to be imputed to the individual good is determined by the situation in which the valuation takes place, and its limits, which may be very narrow if the goods in question have many alternative uses, are derived in the way outlined above. If the purchase or loss of an 'end-piece' is concerned, while there is no doubt whatever as to the ownership of the remaining complementary goods, then the value which will be imputed to it is all that remains after deducting the minimum value for the other goods. A contrast to this is provided by the situation in which the availability of the necessary complementary goods is not yet assured. In this case, only the lowest level of value resulting from calculation according to the above rules will be imputed to the good, which is to be considered an isolated 'splinter'. In other words, the residue which remains undistributed when all complementary goods have been valued according to the latter method is added on to the value of that good the lack of which threatens to prevent the execution of the production intended. As a rule, the whole of what remains over and above the minimum values of the other goods will therefore be imputed to non-substitutable factors. For goods which have no alternative uses, only that share in value will be imputed to them which remains after the deduction of the maximum values that can be calculated for the complementary goods. The difference in the result of imputation, depending on the situation assumed, leads to the conclusion that values can be attributed to all factors individually, the sum of which either does not exhaust or exceeds the value of the product. This conclusion, however, accords with the general theory of value adhered to by the authors advancing these views who in any case attribute a merely alternating effectiveness to the principle of marginal utility in the determination of the value of the units of a given quantity of goods. It is a necessary consequence of the definition of value by dependent utility on which their analysis is based. This method fails, however, when what is involved is the calculation of the values of a number of producer goods all of which are capable of producing utility only jointly, since in this case the reference to substitutability or to applicability in different uses refers only to cases which stand in need of an explanation to just the same extent as does the case in question. It is to this problem above all that the solution attempted by von Wieser seeks to provide a remedy.

Even before the above-mentioned study by Böhm-Bawerk had been published, Wieser had undertaken a detailed analysis in his *Ursprung und Hauptgesetze des wirtschaftlichen Wertes* [published in 1884 (ed.)] of the conditions which apply especially to the value of producer goods, and in a second book, after a critique of the solutions attempted by Menger and Böhm-Bawerk, he presented a fully elaborated solution to the problem of imputation. This book, which was published in 1889 under the title *Der natürliche Wert*, is still today the fundamental and most detailed treatment of the problem. It is to be regarded as simply the classic presentation of the doctrine of imputation, although it has been surpassed in parts, and complemented on important points, by Wieser's comprehensive treatment of economic theory.

While Menger's and Böhm-Bawerk's attempts essentially consisted in applying to producer goods the idea of dependent utility which had been used successfully in the explanation of the value of consumer goods, Wieser's solution takes account to a larger extent of the specific conditions of production which were brought into the system of the subjective theory of value through his fundamental investigations into the law of costs. At the beginning of his investigations at least, the primary problem he seeks to solve is that of the value of the products themselves. From his solution to this flows his solution of the problem of imputation. Now, the economic principle requires that the same margin of utility is held to in the uses of those consumer goods which can be used for different purposes. In precisely the same way, it also requires that their share in the value of a product is never less, in whatever use, than the largest share they can obtain in any other use which is not, however, actually considered in the planning of production because of an insufficient supply of goods. This means that, in the individual economy, if it is at all possible, production in each branch will be expanded to such an extent that the utility obtained is distributed in its entirety to the different factors of production, given equal valuation of the individual producer goods in the different branches of production. It is only under this condition that, as a rule, the actual decision about the available producer goods is the most advantageous. Furthermore, under this condition it is not possible to put the producer goods to more advantageous uses either by moving some of them to production processes where the utility which can be obtained exceeds the sum of the values of these goods, or by withdrawing them from processes where the opposite relation holds. The only cases exempt from this are those in which a discontinuous utility scale of the product excludes an expansion of production to this point of maximum advantage. In this case, the value of the product is determined by its 'cost-utility', that is, by the sum of values which are to be imputed to its factors of production in their marginal uses (law of costs).

The equality in the value of a producer good in different uses also enables us to represent in equation form the reciprocal relationship existing between the values of products produced by the same factors as well as their relationship to the value of the factors of production. On one side of these equations the same factors of production recur as equal value quantities, so that there exists mutual dependence between them. Substituting concrete values either for products or for producer goods enables us, therefore, to calculate the other elements. Wieser applies this by substituting for the values of the products and thus derives the values of the producer goods. Wieser has supplemented this basic form of imputing values, which he now calls 'common imputation', in his *Theorie der gesellschaftlichen Wirtschaft* [*Social Economics* (ed.)] by a kind of residual imputation for certain goods which he calls 'specific imputation', and which he introduced in partial accommodation to Böhm-Bawerk's exposition. The differentiation between goods which justifies the application of different methods of imputation is based on the great diversity in use of various goods of higher order classified either as 'cost-goods', i.e. producer goods which can be put to many different uses, or as 'specific producer goods', i.e. those which have only a relatively limited number of uses. This classification is, naturally, not an absolute one but is fully applicable only in extreme cases having relative validity only for intermediate goods.

Cost-goods, used in almost all production processes, have a certain equilibrating effect on the utility margin of all the goods produced with their assistance. The marginal utility of products made entirely with cost-goods will therefore vary only within relatively narrow limits, or rather they will display greater differences only in proportion to the number of productive groups necessary for the production of the good. However, the smaller the number of branches of production in which a good can be used, the narrower is the scope for such approximation, and the stronger will be the influence of its specific relative scarcity on the products in question, an influence which will manifest itself in a wider divergence from the general level of marginal utility of the products. The products of such a good will therefore display utility margins which are relatively narrower or wider than the average of the cost-products. The utility margin under discussion in this context is not, however, to be confused with the narrower utility margin mentioned above as being caused by the discontinuity of the utility scales of individual products. Wieser, incidentally, has really left the analysis of this question incomplete; at least, he does not clearly express the difference in the utility margins of the individual products, which necessarily arises also within the group of 'products of general utility margin' because of their differing relative composition. The particular influence of the specific producer goods on the utility margin of products made with them also determines the form of imputation which applies to them. While the cost-goods used are to be assessed at the value which is to be imputed to them in the production of cost-products, the whole of the deviation from the general utility margin, and the unusually large or small value caused by it, is due to the specific producer good. Accordingly, all of the difference between the given value of the cost-goods and the value of the product is to be imputed to the latter. Because of the absence of an equilibrating tendency, such as exists among cost-goods its value depends to a much larger extent on the value of certain

41

products and their fluctuations. Those kinds of income which are determined by the value of these specific producer goods therefore display such particular forms of development that they have been described, under the name of rents, as being subject to separate laws. If several specific factors are used in one production process, then the factor which, because of its greater versatility, is most like a cost-good is to be regarded as a cost-element in comparison with the others; that is, its value, obtained elsewhere, is to be deducted first, and what remains is to be imputed to the specific factor.

Wieser's analysis is based on a conception of the marginality principle which is considered to be erroneous by most of the other adherents to the marginal utility school. It consists of the cumulative assessment, based on marginal utility, of the value of all units of a given quantity of goods.[2] Wieser himself, however, regards it as an essential element of the subjective theory of value without which the principle of marginal utility would be unable to provide a satisfactory explanation of economic phenomena. Hence Wieser regards value as the arithmetic form of utility, and it is this conception alone which justifies his demand for a definite and complete distribution of the utility yielded by the product. It also enables us to attach the same value to several units of one good participating in a production process. On the other hand, only this solution provides a definitive answer to the question: what share in the value of a product is to be imputed to the individual factors of production in a stable individual economy? To determine this is a precondition for the rational organization of production in an economy without exchange.

Apart from the contributions by Böhm-Bawerk and Wieser, referred to above, only J. Schumpeter has actually attempted to solve the problem of imputation in the context of a complete system of economic theory. The main features of his solution correspond to those of Böhm-Bawerk, and seem to differ from them only as is necessitated by the special characteristics of the mathematical method employed by Schumpeter. This is not the place, however, to discuss this method.[3]

5 A second point of departure: the doctrine of marginal productivity

It is true that the dependence of the physical magnitude of a product on the quantitative ratio in which its factors of production have been combined is a purely technical moment, and as such its only significance for the derivation of economic laws can be as a *datum*. Nevertheless, the observation of man's reaction to this phenomenon has given rise to a method for deriving the share in the value of the product to be imputed to each factor of production, which is essentially in accordance with the solutions obtained in direct pursuit of the fundamental concept of the subjective theory of value. Yet the explanation thereby arrived at seems to be more limited in its applicability and the system of doctrines constructed with its aid seems less uniform. Round about 1890, and independently of the efforts of the Austrian school, St. Wood and especially J. B. Clark in America have used this phenomenon to construct a comprehensive system of theories of distribution on the basis of the concept of marginal productivity, rather as H. v. Thünen had done sixty years before in Germany. Numerous American scholars, above all T. N. Carver and also F. A. Fetter, H. R. Seager and F. W. Taylor, participated in the elaboration of this doctrine. In Europe, K. Wicksell, P. H. Wicksteed and E. Barone have analysed it mathematically, and a large number of modern theoreticians have incorporated it into their theoretical systems, in most cases without any further inquiry as to its relationship to the principles of imputation developed by the Austrian school.

Even leaving aside the extraordinary frequency of the cases to which it can be applied, the doctrine of marginal productivity remains of importance, not merely for casuistic reasons but also for reasons of principle, in dealing with the question as to the value of producer goods. If the conditions in which producer goods can be used in the different branches of production were altogether rigid and if no change in them was possible, then it would be only in exceptional cases that complementary goods would be available in sufficient quantity to be combined with all the units of each producer good, so that all of these producer goods could actually be used in production. But all such goods for which a sufficient number of complementary goods were not available would therefore be excluded altogether from the class of economic goods, if there were no other uses for them. It must be assumed, therefore, that there is always a number of cases in which the ratios in which the factors of production can be combined are variable, and that the doctrine of marginal productivity will therefore have to be called upon to provide an explanation of the ratios actually chosen in such circumstances. Nevertheless, after what has been said above, it seems permissible to state that the marginal productivity theory can hardly be regarded as a separate, independent principle for the solution of the problem of imputation. Rather, in the last resort it is based on the assumption that this problem can be solved by the method of direct imputation of value. Consequently, we will not go wrong if we fix our attention first of all on the direct imputation of value in the assessment of the problems posed by the theory or imputation which follows and if we accept, with certain modifications, the derivations established for it as equally valid for the theory of marginal productivity.

6 Various misunderstandings and objections

Few concepts of economic theory have been so exposed to fundamental misunderstandings as the concept of imputation. It is hardly necessary any more to refute once again the proposition that imputation attempts to pass a moral judgment on the earnings of those directly involved in production or of those who participate in production through goods which they own. It should just as little be necessary to emphasize, given the fact that those who originated the theory of imputation explicitly rejected any such proposition from the outset, that the theory of imputation makes no attempt to demonstrate a causal connection between a single factor of production and a certain quantity of the product. Although this interpretation is hardly to be found any more in its crassest form, one which is related to it is nevertheless very widespread and forms the basis of most of the alleged proofs of the impossibility of imputation. This is the idea that imputation of value is based on a kind of technological imputation which establishes a connection between certain quantitative proportions of a product and individual factors of production independently of any value relations. Certainly, as was shown in the preceding section, the representatives of the marginal productivity school attempted to do something like this for a special class of cases, but this misunderstanding seems to be attributable above all to the mode of expression adopted by the leading representatives of the theory of imputation, who failed to point out explicitly that the expressions 'productive contribution' and 'shares depending on participation in' refer exclusively to value shares. For this reason it was possible to advance an interpretation which assumed that the imputation theory of the marginal utility school was seeking a particular economic causality, upon whose basis it would be possible to demarcate in physical terms an economic share in the product. Yet the sole purpose of the theory of imputation of the marginal utility school is a direct determination of the value share to be imputed to the individual factor of production without prior calculation of a physical proportion, though it uses a terminology which seems at times to contradict this. There is no necessary connection between an individual factor of production and its share of the product over and above the value relation. The share of a factor of production in the value of a product therefore changes as soon as there is a change in the factors which determine the value, even if the technical composition in the branch of production in question remains unchanged. The misunderstandings which exist on this point can largely be attributed to the fact that one of the essential presuppositions on which the theory of imputation is based is overlooked. The productive combinations from which the value of the producer goods is to be derived must at the same time be economically admissible. For example, any attempt to calculate the shares which are to be imputed by investigating the returns of an enterprise using different combinations of its factors of production, which has been divorced from the context of the economy as a whole, is necessarily bound to fail, the reason being that these different combinations can never exist under the same economic conditions, and so there is no connection between the valuations (carried out at these different combinations). Obviously any critique which rests on this misunderstanding must reject the theory of imputation as absurd, but in fact it has no bearing upon the theory's validity.

Not all objections, however, can be traced to misunderstandings, above all those advanced by Wicksell, Birk, Taylor and others. These are not so much aimed at suggesting a correction of the results of imputation, but rather to point out that the various solutions attempted do not yield anything which did not already have to be assumed as known in the very formulation of the problem. The significance of these objections will become obvious in the next section.

7 *Critique of existing solutions and an attempted correction of the problem*

Economic value is the general expression for the allocation to particular uses of a good of a certain kind in an economic system. In this capacity, the values of the products are fully exhausted by the values of the producer goods given that the dependent values are equal in each production process. Or, since this is the basis on which the imputation of value is carried out according to the marginal utility school (in Wieser's version), this simply means that the value of the dependent shares coincides with the value which is to be imputed to the factors of production according to the method of direct imputation of value. The marginal productivity theory thus supplements the simpler theory of imputation, which is constructed solely on the basic principle of the theory of value, by taking into account the particular complication stemming from the fact that the ratios in which producer goods can be combined in numerous branches of production are variable. It does so by putting forward the requirement that the value of the quantity of a good produced by the last unit of each factor coincides with the value which is to be imputed to the factor. If the sphere of application of the principle on which the marginal productivity theory is based were the same as that of the direct imputation of value according to the marginal utility school, then it would hardly be possible to ascribe primacy to either of these principles. In fact, however, there is a not insignificant number of cases in which it is not possible to vary the ratios in which the factors of production are combined, though such variability has to be presupposed if the marginal productivity method is to be applied. If a change in the combination of factors for a production process is excluded by the nature of the process, or an adjustment of the ratios, in which the factors are combined, is not carried out at the time in question because of particular reasons (because, for example, the current situation is only temporary), imputation can be carried out only on the basis of the direct method of the marginal utility school.

The perception on which the doctrine of marginal productivity is constructed is the general applicability of the law of diminishing returns first established for agriculture (see article on this in the *Handwörterbuch der Staatswissenschaften*, 4th edition, vol. 1, pp. 11–12). The fact that from a certain point onwards an increase in individual factors of production, while all the others remain unchanged, yields an increase in the quantity of output which is, however, relatively less than the increase in the factor or factors of production in question, has been common property of economic theory for a long time. A fully satisfactory explanation of it now seems to have been provided by T. N. Carver with the aid of the probability principle and the generally valid 'law of variable proportions' which may be derived from it.[4] According to this law, for any given combination of factors of production it is possible to establish that share of the quantity of the product which depends on the co-operation of one unit of every factor in situations in which it is possible to vary the quantity used of the individual factors independently of that of the others. For practical purposes, this share can be regarded quite straightforwardly as the product of any unit of the factor of production in question; hence a proportional distribution of the entire product to the factors which participated in its production can be carried out with the aid of the infinitesimal calculus. But this still leaves the question of imputation quite unsettled. For what determines the combination of the factors of production that is chosen in each individual case? In the usual exposition of this theory within the framework of a market economy it is pointed out that the influence exerted by competition must be such that the same prices are fetched by the shares in the product which are dependent on each unit of the producer good in different branches of production, or, in other words, that the price of the share which is to be imputed must be congruent with costs.

However, to demonstrate the significance of the doctrine of marginal productivity as a theory of imputation, i.e. as a derivation by the individual of the subjective value of producer goods, which can serve as a basis for the explanation of the formation of the prices of these goods, this doctrine must be extracted from the market-economy guise in which it is usually presented. In particular, the social concept of value with which it has been connected by J. B. Clark and some of his students must be discarded. Only then does the marginal productivity doctrine become immediately suitable for the explanation of income distribution without the intermediate step of price formation. As long as the objective phenomena of value are regarded as the result of individual valuations, it is logically necessary to be able to explain the latter first and without reference to exchange. If the basic principle of the doctrine of marginal productivity is applied to the conditions of an 'individual' economy guided by a will, then one will necessarily arrive at the proposition that in every branch of production a combination of factors must be chosen in such a way that the *value* of the product which depends on the last unit of a producer good will be the same in each production process. Now, it will be obvious immediately that mere quantitative proportionality of the final increments, dependent on the same factors in different processes of production, is not sufficient. For the same factors frequently display proportionately different marginal contributions in the production of consumer goods where they are combined in the same way; or they display the same relative magnitude of their marginal contributions only if they are combined in different proportions in the different processes of production. In these cases it is obvious the economic principle is satisfied only if the values of the dependent shares in the product are equal. But this simply means that the combinations of producer goods used in each process of production should be chosen in such a way that it immediately imparts information about the minimum level of utility which the good has to achieve if it is to be used correctly from an economic point of view. This is as true of producer goods as of consumer goods. Hence a direct connection exists between, on the one hand, the reasons why a certain process of production has been embarked upon and expanded to a certain level, and, on the other hand, the determinants of the value of the goods used in this process. The doctrine of imputation in its current form severs this connection because, in the determination of the value of producer goods it sets out from a value of the product which is given independently of this connection, and, therefore, a given organization of production. This is where the reason should be sought for the failure of the theory to arrive at an entirely satisfactory solution of the problem. By assuming that the value of consumer goods can always be derived without difficulty with the aid of the marginal utility principle it has shifted the problem already posed by the value of products, because their quantity is not a fixed datum, to a later step in the explanation. At this later step, however, the problem has been separated from the question of the admissibility of the allocation of the factor since the latter question has already been regarded as solved. Hence it was no longer possible to provide an answer to the problem which relates to its original meaning.

The various representatives of the doctrine of imputation within the marginal utility school varied in the degree to which they were at all conscious of the difficulty contained therein and in the extent to which, accordingly, they tried to take account of it. To ignore the explanation of the value of products as an indispensable logical link between the explanation of the value of goods, which are given in fixed quantities, and the explanation of the relation between the value of producer goods and that of the product, involves a mental jump which is particularly clear in Böhm-Bawerk's treatment of the problem. In his exposition of the law of costs (*Positive Theorie des Kapitals*, 3rd edition, pp. 205–6) [English edition, vol. II, pp. 116–17 (ed.)[5]], as well as in that of the value of complementary goods (ibid., p. 277) [English edition, vol. II, pp. 161–2 (ed.)], the only use of the individual means of production he considers is that in which they are combined in the same way, in fixed 'productive groups'. Consequently, the only problems he sees arising for the value of products are precisely the same as those relating to the value of a given quantity of consumer goods. The quantities produced in the different branches of production are regulated in such a way 'that needs and wants of roughly equal intensity depend on the last unit (of the product) in each of the quantities produced; the marginal utility of each unit will therefore be roughly of the same magnitude' (ibid., p. 295) [English edition, vol. II, p. 173 (ed.)]. He offers no solution for the far more important case in which producer goods can be combined in varying proportions in the different branches of production. Rather, he regards the conclusion derived from his assumption as generally valid and as sufficient for the explanation of the value of all products. In only one case does Böhm-Bawerk take account of a difference in marginal utility in different branches of production: that of the necessary inequality in the satisfaction of individual need and wants due to discontinuities in their scales.

Because of his failure to see the specific problem posed by the use of several goods for one purpose Böhm-Bawerk seeks the problem of imputation also in cases in which a large number of goods, in a strictly economic sense, do not exist. In the well-known case which appears in his exposition as 'first case' (*Positive Theorie*, p. 278) [English edition, vol. II, p. 162, para. 3 (ed.)], several goods are used in the production of a good but none of them are substitutable nor can they be employed anywhere else. Hence only one economic good is concerned, namely the product. This is so because the utility of its elements is determined by their simultaneous existence in the required proportions; that is, because what are involved are elements which can possess utility, and thus value, only jointly. There is no question of an economic imputation of value here, because the individual factors do not exercise any specific influence on the marginal utility of the product. This, of course, does not preclude each one of these factors, essential for the product to have the quality of a good, being treated just like the product, as long as all the other factors are present; that is, since it is an element of the product, the full value of that product is imputed to it. Nevertheless, this does not justify using the same procedure in cases of genuine imputation.

Böhm-Bawerk's conception, however, leads him to erroneous conclusions even in cases of genuine imputation which he deals with as 'second' and 'third' cases. In these the quality of being a good is attributed to the individual elements independently because they can be used elsewhere, or are substitutable, or because all the goods which are used together with them have these properties. It is because Böhm-Bawerk has not lost sight of the connection between the value of the producer goods and the question whether their use in the respective production process is admissible, that he can refuse to accept the basic validity of Wieser's 'distributive concept'. Since his search was wholly concerned with 'dependent utility',that question lay completely outside his vision. But the only answer that can be given to it is that any production process has to be expanded until the sum of the values which can be obtained by the factors of production in different processes is no longer exceeded by the value of the product in question. Böhm-Bawerk, however, regards the state of equilibrium simply as given, and even emphasizes explicitly that the particular use to which a good is put at any time must be regarded as a datum (*Positive Theorie*, Exkurs VII, p. 209) [English edition, vol. III, p. 92 (ed.)]. To arrive at an answer to the question of value, it was necessary for him to introduce a disturbance into the equilibrium state, so that he could then employ his so-called 'idea of loss'. For goods which are not complementary to others, this principle indicates the minimum level of output produced directly by homogeneous goods in an undisturbed state of equilibrium. The loss of one factor of production then results in a series of displacements which changes the efficacy of various factors. The result, though, is that the difference in total output, given both the assumptions made above, cannot be regarded as determining in precisely the same way the efficacy of the factors in question which have been withdrawn. At a later point, Böhm-Bawerk appears to want to represent as innocuous the difference between the sum of the values, which have been recognized to depend on several factors of production which have been withdrawn, and the value of the product. He does so, though unjustifiably, in Exkurs VII of his *Positive Theorie* (p. 200, which, incidentally, contradicts his exposition in the text, pp. 285–6) [English edition, vol. III, p. 88, and Vol. II, p. 166, respectively (ed.)]. The way in which he does this is to maintain that an explanation of the distribution of income must proceed through two stages. The first is the theory of imputation, and the second the theory of price formation with the latter being based on subjective valuations that can be ascertained without the aid of the former. Yet the way in which the complete distribution of the product to the factors of production is determined in his theory of price formation remains unclear, given that it does not take place by way of his method of imputation but that it does do so as a matter of fact.

The solution suggested by Wieser has the advantage over Böhm-Bawerk's solution that it starts from different combinations of producer goods as a matter of principle. Wieser has thus recognized that the value of complementary goods can only be derived by considering those combinations in which the independent character of the individual producer goods, as well as their differing relative scarcity, are expressed by the difference in the value of the products which arises from the difference in the way in which the factors of production are combined. It may almost be said that by introducing the concept of differing utility margins Wieser was the first to apply consistently to producer goods the fundamental idea of the doctrine of marginal utility: that the last need or want which is actually satisfied depends on the available quantity of a good. His formula for imputation has the further advantage over Böhm-Bawerk's that it meets the requirement that the value of a product be completely distributed to the factors of production, with the result that it can serve directly as a basis for a theory of distribution. It also can hardly be denied that the relation between the value of producer goods and that of the product which is expressed in Wieser's equation is correct, all the less so since they merely represent an inversion of the law of costs in a form in which it is made conformable to the subjective theory of value. On the other hand, his equations also seem to fail to achieve what the principle of marginal utility achieves for the value of consumer goods which are given in a certain quantity, namely the derivation of value from the 'data', the scales of needs and wants and the quantity of producer goods available. They do not demonstrate to us the necessity of the uses in which are attained the levels of utility from which the value of the producer goods is derived. As we have shown, Wieser first posed the problem of the value of producer goods, and only after he had resolved it by means of the law of costs did he attempt to find a solution to the problem of imputation. But his solution does not lead back to the pre-economic elements, since his law of costs was constructed on the assumption that the value of the producer goods is determinate. He thus derives the value of producer goods from a value of the products which he can determine only with the aid of the value of the producer goods. That the unsatisfactory aspect of this solution is not more evident can be attributed to the fact that there is at least an implicit indication that the problem, which is basic in this context, is solved by the requirement that the maximum level of utility has already been reached when production is planned. In Böhm-Bawerk's analysis, on the other hand, this indication is explicit. However, so long as this concept is understood in the usual way as absolute obedience to the requirement, based on the ordering of needs and wants, that one need or want must be preferred to another (cf. J. Schumpeter, *Das Wesen und der Hauptinhalt der theoretischen Nationalökonomie*, p. 132), this offers no solution to the problem because direct choice between the satisfaction of two needs or wants is excluded by the complementarity of goods. If, like Wieser, we assume as our basis that value can be calculated numerically – this can hardly be avoided if the problem is to be solved – then even a state of maximum utility cannot be calculated without the distribution to the factors of production of the level of utility realized by the products. It follows that the condition of maximum utility cannot be calculated without prior solution of the problem of imputation.

Any one-sided derivation of the value of producer goods from that of the product necessarily comes to grief on the fact that the value of the product cannot be ascertained without taking account of the resistance to the expansion of production to its physically possible limit, a resistance which differs for each individual factor used in the production of the value of the final goods. This restriction depends on the value which is to be imputed to the factor in question in its alternative use, in so far as it can be employed elsewhere, a proviso which is applicable in the majority of cases. The restriction itself thus depends in turn on the value of other products and its imputation to the factors of production which have produced them. The derivation of the value of either the product from that of its factors, or of the value of production from that of their product, is certainly possible because of the relations which exist between them according to the law of costs. Yet it is meaningless for the theoretical explanation of the phenomenon of value on the basis of the 'economic data', i.e. the quantity of goods and the needs and wants, since neither of these two values can be determined independently of the other. This is so because neither producer goods nor products exhibit independently both the sets of data which are necessary for the determination of value. Rather, the one element, the utility level attained, makes its appearance only in the products, while the second element, the limit to the available supply, is determined absolutely only for producer goods.

This, however, does not eliminate the problem of imputation. It only assumes another form. The problem is not the derivation of the value of producer goods, assuming a given value of the product. Rather, it is the influence which the relative scarcity of a producer good exerts on the admissible level of expansion of each process of production, assuming given alternatives of employment and given complementary goods. The problem of imputation becomes identical with the question of how, **on the** assumption of given quantities of producer goods and given **scales** of needs and wants, the producer goods available are to be allocated among the different branches of production. Any answer to this question, and thus any solution to the problem of imputation, has therefore to take into account the totality of all the complementary goods utilized in an economic system and all the needs and wants which their products serve to satisfy. That it is necessary to do this may make it impossible in practice to apply imputation to any large economic system, but it should still be possible to demonstrate by means of a simplified case that the subjective theory of value is in principle applicable. And in this way it should also be possible to prove that a conceptual solution of the problem of imputation is feasible. The mathematical school, following Walras, has successfully attempted to solve similar problems. Even they, however, have not succeeded in doing justice to the problem of imputation.

At the moment, all that can be said about the final resolution of the problem of imputation is that all elements of the economic system to which the producer goods in question belong have to be taken into account, apart from the obvious fact that their final result must coincide with the relation between the value of the products and producer goods which is expressed in Wieser's equations. The shortcomings which the subjective theory of value has so far revealed in providing an answer to the question on which the problem of imputation is ultimately based, also seem to be the reason why a large number of theoreticians still believe that they cannot manage without the aid of an objective concept of cost. However, reliance upon disutility of labour as the essential cost element does not solve the problem at all, as can easily be shown by considering what happens if disutility of labour is replaced by the relevant recreational opportunities, or simply by leisure, as alternative uses of the 'good' labour while the data remain unchanged. In this case, the problem which one has been trying to avoid arises in connection with its employment with complementary goods.

Notes

1 Eugen von Böhm-Bawerk, 'Grundzüge der Theorie des wirtschaftlichen Güterwerts', in *Jahrbücher für Nationalökonomie und Statistik*, n.s. vol. 13 (1886).

2 On this, see the articles 'Wert' and 'Grenznutzen', in J. Conrad *et al.* (eds), *Handwörterbuch der Staatswissenschaften*, 3rd edn, Jena: Fischer, 1909–1911; also Hans Mayer, 'Untersuchungen zum Grundgesetz der wirtschaftlichen Wertrechnung', *Zeitschrift für Volkswirtschaft und Sozialpolitik*, n.s. vol. I (1921) and vol. 2 (1922).

3 On this, compare the excellent critique by Schönfeld in his article 'Über Josef Schumpeters Lösung des ökonomischen Zurechnungsproblems', in *Zeitschrift für Volkswirtschaft und Sozialpolitik*, n.s. vol. 4 (1924).

4 Cf. T. N. Carver, *Principles of National Economy*, 1921, and the article by his student, J. Davidson, 'On the physical foundations of economics', *Quarterly Journal of Economics*, XXXIII, August 1919.

5 Eugen von Böhm-Bawerk, *Capital and Interest*, 3 volumes, translated by G. D. Huncke and H. F. Sennholz, South Holland, Illinois, 1959 (ed.).

THREE

ON THE PROBLEM OF THE THEORY OF INTEREST*

Ever since the publication of Böhm-Bawerk's great work, the formulation of the problem of interest on capital which he introduced has been accepted almost without exception in so far as its solution is attempted within the sphere of the theory of value. As is well known, Böhm-Bawerk starts his examination of the problem by asking why there is a permanent difference between the value of the capital employed and that of its product.[1] Or in more general terms, why is it that, in every time-consuming productive process, the value of the product exceeds that of the goods from which it is produced? This difference in value, 'the fold in which the interest on capital is hidden',[2] provides the starting point for his explanation of interest and, since the publication of his work, for the majority of theoretical economists working in the field of the theory of interest. Böhm-Bawerk and most theoretical economists who adhere to an 'agio theory' of interest believe that there is only one way in which it is possible to overcome the contradiction between the difference in value which actually always exists, and the rule derived from basic value theory that the value of the means of production must coincide with that of their products, which is by making the *ad hoc* assumption that future needs and wants are regularly valued lower than the same needs and wants in the present. It is for this reason alone that the available means of production are not distributed among the branches of production, which differ in the lengths of their time periods, in such a way as to equate the marginal utilities of the goods produced by them with the same quantity of means of production. A state of equilibrium in which the value of the producer goods does not coincide with that of their products can only exist because of the lower valuation of future needs and wants. It is this difference

---

* First published as 'Zur Problemstellung der Zinstheorie', *Archiv für Sozialwissenschaften und Sozialpolitik*, 58 (1927), pp. 517–32.

in value which makes the payment of interest on capital possible within a static system.[3]

However, the particular solution, which Böhm-Bawerk felt obliged to accept because of the way in which he had posed the problem, did not meet with general agreement. (Indeed, it was precisely the assertion of a regularly lower valuation of future needs and wants which was sharply criticized.) Yet his formulation of the problem was generally accepted as an apparently inevitable consequence of the modern theory of value.[4] The result was, however, that on the one hand the path to more obvious explanations of interest on capital, in particular that of the marginal productivity theory, was barred, and on the other hand the only way out which seemed possible, the one which Böhm-Bawerk himself had chosen, was contradicted by the facts. The question which we wish to pose in this article is whether the way in which Böhm-Bawerk formulated the problem of interest on capital really does make it necessary to assume that a lower valuation is regularly placed upon future needs and wants, in the sense that in its absence the existence of the difference in values mentioned above would be inconceivable. Is it really true that the production of future goods would otherwise have to be expanded to the point at which their value declines to that of the producer goods with which they are made? Or may not there be other reasons why an expansion of production to this extent is impossible and, therefore, why the assumption of a generally lower valuation of future needs and wants is superfluous for the explanation of the difference in values? Put concisely, the question therefore is: does the way in which Böhm-Bawerk formulates the problem of interest on capital make unavoidable the assumption of lower valuation of future needs and wants? There is hardly any doubt that Böhm-Bawerk himself believed that interest could not exist without this particular element which he had introduced. This is the consequence which follows inevitably from the consistent extension of his oversimplified theory of value. But I believe that there is little difficulty in showing that his theory is incorrect.

For such an investigation, however, the Böhm-Bawerkian formulation of the problem requires a partial modification which has already been hinted at above. It is well known that the subjective theory of value asserts the conformity in principle of the value of the producer goods with that of their products only for very specific conditions. These conditions, which relate to the existence of a state of equilibrium, are fulfilled in the case of producer goods only if the production processes which are carried out utilizing given producer goods are expanded to precisely that level (in so far as it is technically possible), at which the value of the products falls to the level of the value of the goods with which they are being produced. However, equality between the values of products and that of producer goods has thereby necessarily already been assumed. Hence the main thrust of the analysis is not towards the ratio of values but towards explaining why, in the cases in question, production is not arranged in such a way that the conditions for equality in values hold. Why then is the production of goods which can be produced in longer or shorter periods of time not expanded everywhere to such an extent that the products of the same producer goods receive the same value? By asking this question we move outside the framework employed by Böhm-Bawerk himself, who regarded the given structure of production in general as a datum not to be subjected to closer investigation, and move closer to that of Wieser, whose explanation of the ratios existing between the values of products and those of producer goods rests largely upon the analysis of the reasons why a certain structure of production is economically necessary.[5]

An answer to the question as to the allocation of given goods, which depends on the fundamental data of the economy, is made more difficult by one well-known phenomenon. This phenomenon, which Böhm-Bawerk called the higher productiveness of roundabout methods of production, denotes the higher productivity which given producer goods are able to achieve in more time-consuming roundabout methods of production.[6] A necessary consequence of this phenomenon is that the decision as to whether given producer goods are to be employed in more or less time-consuming production processes has to be based on a comparison of the utilities of larger and of smaller quantities of the same[7] product at different points in time. Given the premise of constancy in the data, we must assume that the supply of the goods which are to be produced from the given means of production is the same at both points in time under consideration, leaving aside the consequences of the employment of those means of production that are in question; or that it is the disposal over the entire obtainable supply of the producer goods with which we are concerned. On either assumption, it follows from the law of diminishing marginal utility that the utility of a smaller number of units with higher marginal utility is to be compared with the utility of a larger number of units of the same product with lower marginal utility. It is only if the larger quantity of lower-valued units of the product makes up for the smaller quantity of higher valued units of the product in terms of their total values that, on Böhm-Bawerk's own assumptions, a state of equilibrium can conceivably emerge, once the possibility of applying more productive roundabout methods is taken into account.

It follows that the correct Böhm-Bawerkian formulation of the problem should be to ask why the production of future goods is not actually expanded beyond its present level. In fact, why is it not expanded to such an extent that the value of the products of given means of production decreases to the level of the value of those goods produced by them in the process occupying the shortest possible time (even quite possibly to the level of value which they possess when they are used directly as consumer goods)? As has become evident, the result of such an expansion of production ought to be a decrease of the marginal utility of a unit of goods which have been produced by a more time-consuming process of production, to a level below that of the marginal utility of the same unit of the same goods produced in a less time-consuming process. Only in this way can the difference in utility between current and future goods be eliminated. According to Böhm-Bawerk, it would also be a necessary consequence of the endeavour to arrive at complete equality between the marginal utilities obtainable from a given producer good at different points in time, if it were not for the general lower valuation of future needs and wants.

If production is organized in such a way as to provide evenly for the present and the future, such that the marginal utilities of the products in question have to be of the same magnitude at both points in time, this difference in value must necessarily exist. Its disappearance would thus presuppose that means of production have been set aside for time-consuming production processes to such an extent that total provision must have become increasingly better. The marginal utilities of all goods which are produced with the employment of capital would have to decline continuously, and since means of production are thereby set free for other purposes, the marginal utilities of all other goods as well would have to decline continuously.[8]

The satisfaction of current needs and wants should therefore be interrupted whenever a unit of a consumer good serving to satisfy them yields a marginal utility which is greater than that which can be obtained in the future from the same unit of a good produced with the goods which are thus saved.

This is the only possible conclusion, because the value of the greater quantity of a good produced with a certain quantity of a producer good using roundabout methods of production can only be equal to that of the smaller quantity of the same good obtained with the same means of production using less roundabout methods, if the same unit of the good, which is available in a larger quantity at the later point in time, has a lower marginal utility than the unit of the (smaller) quantity which is available sooner. This can be shown particularly clearly by the method of diagrammatic representation employed in mathematical economics.

In our diagrammatic representation, we start from the proposition that we confront two alternatives. From a given quantity of means of production we can obtain either a greater quantity of products at a point more distant in time or a smaller quantity of the same product at a point closer in time. According to the conception of statics which undoubtedly underlies the Böhm-Bawerkian analysis we must assume that the curves representing the desire for the product are the same at both of the points of time in question.

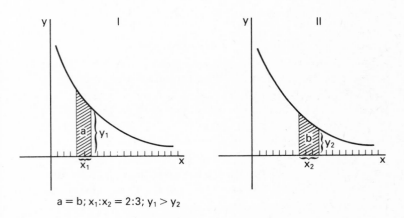

$$a = b; x_1:x_2 = 2:3; y_1 > y_2$$

Figure 1: Conditions for the existence of a state of equilibrium between the employment of a means of production in I, a shorter, less productive process, and II, a longer, more productive roundabout process, according to the older conception of the significance of the comparison of isolated individual utilities. The sections on the abscissa represent equal units of the product, the segments denoted by x_1 and x_2 represent the number of units of the good produced from the same quantity of means of production.

Let, therefore, the two curves in the diagram on page 59 express the diminishing intensity of a need or want as the extent increases to which it is satisfied by a good at the two points in time I and II, the units of that good being measured along the abscissa. Further assume that at the earlier time I, two units of the good, represented by x_1 along the abscissa, can be produced from the given quantity of the means of production, while three units of it can be produced at the later point in time II, represented by the respective segment x_2 along the abscissa, from the same quantity of the means of production.

We have now to ascertain the conditions under which the allocation of the means of production between the two production processes in question leads to a state of equilibrium consistent with the rules of basic value theory, without introducing the assumption of the lower valuation of future needs and wants. In doing so, we have to bear in mind that the utility of a larger quantity of the good to be produced in the more time-consuming process is to be compared with the utility of each quantity of the good produced in the shorter process. Thus a larger section of the abscissa in diagram II must correspond to a given section of the abscissa in diagram I. Now the areas which are enclosed by the segments of the abscissa represent the different quantities of the product, and by the utility curve (value function) represent the total utility of the product obtained from the given quantity of means of production. Hence it follows that they can be of the same magnitude, as is required by the equality between the total utility produced in different processes, only if the ordinate of the utility curve at the point of discontinuation of the satisfaction of the need or want (i.e. the marginal utility) is correspondingly smaller for the good produced in the more time-consuming roundabout method than for the other good.

A further question now arises. Does the fact that such an expansion of production of future goods, leading to a continuous reduction in their marginal utility, does not take place, and that their marginal utility thus regularly exceeds the immediate utility of their means of production, need to be separately explained by assuming that a lower valuation is set on future needs and wants, as Böhm-Bawerk appears to believe? Or are there already other reasons which make impossible such an expansion of production? It may be that people do not so much strive to obtain the highest level of utility for each unit of a good as rather to balance their overall satisfaction of needs and wants over time, and that consequently a state of equilibrium can emerge even without the utility of the present means of production coinciding with that of the future products. If the latter is the case – and from the outset this can hardly be doubted, the bases on which it can be proved being given below – then the higher productivity of roundabout methods will be sufficient of itself to demonstrate the necessity of interest on capital. This alone will not explain its absolute level, since concrete data as to needs and wants and the level of supplies of the individual economic subjects would naturally be required to do so. But it is certain, as soon as we answer the question in the affirmative, that – and this is sufficient for the theory – a definite level of the rate of interest on capital will appear which will depend upon the particular valuation made by the individual, and that interest on capital cannot disappear as long as unexploited roundabout methods make an increase in yield possible.

It must continue to be surprising that such an approach to the problem appears never to have been attempted in the voluminous literature dealing with the problem of interest on capital. Yet it should be pointed out that the fundamental theoretical concepts which provide the framework for an answer to our question have been elaborated only very recently. It has already been mentioned that Böhm-Bawerk in particular regarded the fact that a good is used in a certain way as quite unproblematic, and that inasmuch as he wanted to regard this use, quite inconsistently, as a 'datum',[9] he looked upon it as an absolutely self-evident result of the ordering of needs and wants which provides the starting point of the analysis. In so far as he had any interest at all in the problems which are inherent in the construction of an economic plan, he seemed to be in absolutely no doubt that the isolated comparison of the different levels of utility yielded by the various uses to which a good might be put make an adequate and unambiguous decision possible in all cases. More recent work, especially that of Hans Mayer[10] and L. Schönfeld,[11] has demonstrated that this is not so but that difficult problems arise in this context. The latter in particular has shown that, in principle, it is not comparisons of isolated individual utilities as such which are decisive for the economic plan which is to be adhered to, but that it is always the comparison of alternatively realizable total economic utilities which alone can be the decisive factor. The former can substitute for the latter in a kind of abbreviated procedure only in so far as they generate the same result (though he in fact believes that this is always the case).

There is no need to elaborate on this distinction here. It is enough to show that, under the conditions in which we are interested here, comparisons of individual utilities do not afford a sufficient basis for the determination of the economic decisions which are to be made. The demonstration that this is so is of particular interest not only because the Böhm-Bawerkian version of the foundations of the theory of value has proven to be inadequate within the narrower field of the theory of interest on capital, but even more so because the efforts prevalent among his direct students to formalize extensively and to 'depsychologize' the foundations of economic theory are bound to fail. This failure is of particular interest as well because at least two other main problems of economic theory present the same problems. The difficulties are especially great in the theory of interest on capital because this field is characterized by a combination of two problems, neither of which has been solved satisfactorily. To resolve them becomes particularly intractable if, as is currently so popular, a fixed ranking of the individual ends concerned is regarded as a correct and adequate basis for the derivation of the equilibrium system.

As has been shown already, one of these problems is the comparison of the utility of a smaller quantity of goods, composed of units which have a higher marginal utility, with the utility of a larger quantity of goods, composed of units which have a lower marginal utility. While it is evident that in such a comparison a state of equilibrium must come about at a certain point in time, in this case the conditions for such a state of equilibrium cannot be derived from the mere assumption of a given ranking of the individual uses.[12] The second problem is that of time, which in this context pushes the first into the background since, as will be shown, taking account of it eliminates the significance of the comparison of individual utilities. Formulated by Böhm-Bawerk in an extraordinarily narrow fashion, this problem was not seen in all its implications either by him or by the older representatives of marginal utility theory. It was only Hans Mayer who, in his publications mentioned above, recently showed that it is only possible to construct an economic plan which has any meaning at all if the passage of time is brought into consideration. Hence it is indispensable that the consideration of decisions concerning goods must be provided with a time dimension if the laws of value formation are to be understood.

As happens in other fields as well,[13] the solution which had at first been established for simpler conditions has been applied to new situations, without the existence of the preconditions for their applicability having ever been seen as a problem. That the question of the temporal organization of the satisfaction of needs and wants had already been answered within the framework used to answer the question of their organization at one point in time (strictly speaking, an 'economic period' considered as timeless), appears to have been so self-evident that it was not even posed at all. However, from the psychological point of view, two entirely different possibilities are being questioned. Firstly, by foregoing utility in one position, a higher utility in another position can be achieved simultaneously with or immediately following the former by this sacrifice, the sense of loss thus being compensated by a simultaneous and larger increase in utility, with such a decision yielding, on balance, an increase in total utility of one unit during a short time period. The second occurs when the moment at which the sacrifice is made is distanced in time from the moment at which the higher utility is realizable, with the result that the amalgamation of the two sensations into one unit cannot take place. While experience undoubtedly justifies the assumption that decisions within a short time span are made according to the individual utilities which can be obtained from goods in their different uses, there is no general experience which entitles us to assert that decisions are made in a particular way between two identifiable utilities of a given magnitude which are realizable at two points distanced in time from one other. In particular, we are not entitled to maintain that a future level of utility which is estimated to be higher will be preferred to a level of utility in the present by virtue of this estimate alone.[14]

Comparisons of individual utilities, rather, can be applied only as a type of 'abbreviated procedure' (Schönfeld), in lieu of the ultimately decisive comparisons of total utilities, in cases in which both of the uses considered as alternatives for a good may be carried out equally well without any change in the external conditions of economic activity being required. This *ceter paribus* clause, however, is not satisfied with respect to uses, one of which can be realized only at a point which is more remote in time. In particular, this condition is not satisfied when a state of equilibrium between the two uses can be arrived at only if, as a glance at the diagram on page 59 will show, the same need is satisfied to a higher degree at the more distant point in time than at that which is closer, independently of the use in question. Böhm-Bawerk's formulation of the problem is based on the presupposition that the possibility of producing larger quantities of a good with given means of production employed in more time-consuming processes of production implies that the production of future goods ought to be expanded to such an extent that the level of utility of the larger quantity of goods produced from a unit of means of production falls to the level of utility of the smaller quantity of goods which can be produced from the same means of production in a shorter period of time. This presupposition, however, is based on the erroneous assumption that the comparisons of isolated utilities obtainable from given quantities of means of production at different points in time are actually decisive with respect to the temporal organisation of the provision for needs and wants, as well. As against this, however, an analysis must start from the proposition that it is not comparisons of isolated utilities, in the sense implied here, which are determinant in decisions of this kind, but the striving to achieve a very clearly defined organization or rather gradation of the provision for needs and wants.[15] But nothing can be said in general about the way in which individuals wish to organize their provision for needs and wants at separate points in time. To maintain in general that economic subjects are prepared to suffer sacrifices today for future improvement in their provision is as little permissible as it is to maintain that the present level of provision is generally preferred. In this case, too, the task of theory is simply to provide the framework into which any concrete assumption about the individual ordering of the different degrees of provision at different points in time can be fitted, in the same way as it has hitherto derived laws concerning the formation of value at a given point in time without making concrete assumptions about the ordering of needs and wants which exist at this point in time. The highest level of total economic utility in any economy with a time dimension is afforded by precisely this 'combination of decisions' (Schönfeld) which does not necessarily offer the highest sums of individual utilities but the highest degree of approximation to the temporally distributed satisfaction of needs and wants desired by the economic subject.

For the time being, let these few suggestions suffice to point out the direction in which the answer to the question posed here is to be sought. The primary concern of this essay has been to examine whether the presuppositions of the Böhm-Bawerkian formulation of the problem are correct, and hence if the answer he provides, which appears to be the only way out, is necessary. Even if the explanation given above may not as yet seem adequate, I believe that it provides the basis upon which it can be adequately demonstrated that the factual situation to which the Böhm-Bawerkian formulation of the problem refers is not covered by the elementary rules of the determination of value which he applies. It follows that there is no such rule according to which the value of means of production and of products which are available at different periods of time 'ought' to coincide, and that the existence of such a difference in value does not therefore require any special, *ad hoc* explanation. The reason for this is that the Böhm-Bawerkian formulation of the problem obscures the simple fact that the use of capital does not mean that the satisfaction of a more intensive need or want is sacrificed for the satisfaction of a less intensive one. The question is rather that of obtaining a higher level of future welfare by means of a satisfaction of less intensive sections of a future need or want at the expense of satisfying a smaller section of a present need.

Only one further thing needs to be added to what has been said above. Even though we have concluded that no factual basis exists for an assumption of a general nature as to the relative degree of provision for needs and wants at different points in time, it is still possible that our investigations may need a fictitious assumption of this type as a methodological expedient. As Strigl[16] has shown in detail, and this should be readily comprehensible after what has been written above, the indispensable theoretical tool provided by the static approach can be employed only so long as we start from the assumption that the economic subjects aim at the same level of provision in successive economic periods. Only in this way is it possible to conceive of an economic process to which the picture of static theory applies, since its most important precondition, apart from the constancy of needs and wants, is precisely the constancy of the means of production available in successive economic periods. If we do not wish to confine the static approach wholly to an economy without time, as has indeed happened,[17] but wish to handle the temporal economy as well with the static method, it will be possible to do so only if we utilize this assumption to artificially create the data which make a smooth process possible. It is obviously for this reason that the publications by Hans Mayer cited above, which are the first to deal seriously with the problem of economic decision-making in time though without as yet touching upon the problem of interest, set out from the assumption that one of the essential preconditions of the static approach is the endeavour to obtain the same level of provision in consecutive economic periods.[18]

If we take such an imagined static state of affairs as the starting point of analysis, and attempt to show the individual factors operating on the level of the rate of interest, the picture which emerges is much more plausible than that derived by Böhm-Bawerk. In the latter, the starting point is taken to be a 'normal situation' allegedly resulting from the principles of general value theory, in which the value of the products should always coincide with the value of the producer goods. Specific reasons are then sought as to why this is prevented from occurring and thus a certain level of the rate of interest is attained. But in our approach, we will have to start from a normal situation derived from general value theory and the concept of statics, in which the value of the product differs from that of the producer goods by the full amount of the additional productivity made possible solely by the time which elapses between the points at which they are respectively available. The rate of interest therefore coincides completely with the physical productivity of capital. Only if the rate of interest deviates from this physical productivity do we have to seek an explanation in non-static factors, such as the endeavour to obtain a better provision in the future (saving) or the failure to make a decision necessary to secure an equal level of provision in the future. But once it is realized that a static economy is inconceivable without the existence of the difference in value between present and future goods which is expressed in the rate of interest, the 'dynamic theories of interest' are superseded as well. Such theories owe their existence partly to the fact that the Böhm-Bawerkian formulation of the problem treats the rate of interest in the static system as a kind of abnormality (cf. e.g. Schumpeter, *op. cit.*).

Notes

1 Cf. e.g., *Geschichte und Kritik der Kapitalzinstheorien*, 3rd edition, p. 137 (originally published 1884). [English edition, (*The History and Critique of Interest Theories*, trans. G. D. Huncke and H. F. Sennholz, 1959), vol. I, p. 77 (ed.)].

2 *Positive Theorie des Kapitals*, 3rd edn, Innsbruck, p. 294. [English edition (*Capital and Interest*, 3 volumes, trans. G. D. Huncke and H. F. Sennholz, South Holland, Illinois, 1959), vol. II, p. 172 (ed.)].

3 In no way I am ignoring the fact that Böhm-Bawerk gives three reasons for the difference in value between present and future goods; only the

first two of these reasons refer directly to the lower valuation of future needs and wants, while the well-known higher productivity of roundabout methods constitutes the third reason. Even if we entirely disregard the fact that the *raison d'être* of this 'third reason' within Böhm-Bawerk's system is disputed, it can nevertheless easily be shown that no independent significance can be attached to it, but that the efficacy attributed to it by Böhm-Bawerk presupposes the existence of the other two reasons, that is, the lower valuation of future needs and wants. It is, however, unnecessary to prove this statement here since the assumption of the lower valuation of future needs and wants undoubtedly constitutes the essential element of the Böhm-Bawerkian theory. Anyway, Böhm-Bawerk's own exposition, in the paragraph which begins on p. 460 of the *Positive Theorie* (3rd edition) [English edition, vol. II, pp. 275–6 (ed.)] can be referred to regarding the subordinate character of the 'third reason'. On this point, mention ought also to be made of K. Wicksell's last paper, 'Zur Zinstheorie (Böhm-Bawerks Dritter Grund)', included in the collection *Die Wirtschaftstheorie der Gegenwart*, vol. 3, Vienna, 1927, which came to my attention only when this essay was already in proof.

4 Cf. e.g. Schumpeter (*Theorie der wirtschaftlichen Entwicklung*, Leipzig, 1912, p. 324):

> The demands of a value theory nature which he [Böhm-Bawerk] imposes on any theory of interest are here fully accepted; and our analysis begins with the conviction that it is no longer possible today to put forward any theory of interest which does not meet those demands and is exposed to any of the objections he has formulated.

5 Cf. on this the exposition in my paper, 'Bemerkungen zum Zurechnungsproblem', *Jahrbücher für Nationalökonomie und Statistik*, vol. 124 (3rd series, vol. 69), Jena, 1926, pp. 13ff. [this volume, pp. 33–54 (ed.)], as well as my obituary of Friedrich v. Wieser in the same journal, vol. 125, Jena, 1926, p. 517. Recently, Wieser's formulation of the problem has been adopted, in a particularly consistent and successful manner, by Hans Mayer as the starting point for his various contributions to the fourth edition of the *Handwörterbuch der Staatswissenschaften*, Jena, 1927 (see especially 'Produktion') and in his series of papers 'Untersuchungen zu dem Grundgesetz der wirtschaftlichen Wertrechnung', *Zeitschrift für Volkswirtschaft und Sozialpolitik*, new series, vol. 1 *et seq.*, and by Leo Schönfeld (*Grenznutzen und Wirtschaftsrechnung*, Vienna, 1924). [Review by Hayek in this volume, pp. 183–9 (ed.)]

6 The frequently misunderstood thesis of the higher productivity of roundabout methods of production should be virtually unassailable if it is formulated precisely to mean that more roundabout methods of production are taken into consideration from an economic point of view only if they result in a higher yield for the same initial outlay or the same yield for less expenditure. A more time-consuming productive process which is economically admissible has always to yield a larger product. In this connection, one has to start from the assumption that, in prin-

ciple, there is an arbitrarily large number of ways of producing a good within a given time period of production. But the methods which are given within each period of production yield different results, and within each of these periods only the most productive ones are considered. Every extension of the production period in question increases the number of roundabout processes to be considered, and more productive methods which were previously not considered *may* therefore be drawn into the realm of the possible.

7 I deliberately neglect here the justified objection raised by F. X. Weiss ('Produktionsumwege und Kapitalzins', *Zeitschrift für Volkswirtschaft und Sozialpolitik*, new series, vol. 1, Vienna, 1921) that the higher productivity of the same producer goods employed in more roundabout methods of production generally cannot lead to production of a larger quantity of the same good, but only to the production of a larger value quantity of a different product. To take account of this objection would only complicate the exposition without altering the conclusion.

8 Cf. on this and the following the interesting arguments by R. Strigl in his illuminating contribution which has hitherto not attracted sufficient attention: *Die ökonomischen Kategorien und die Organisation der Wirtschaft*, Jena, 1923, especially pp. 135ff.

9 It is hardly necessary to enter into a more detailed discussion of the internal contradiction implied if, on the one hand, the starting point for the entire explanation of the formation of value is taken to be that the individual decisions over goods are determined in a very definite way by considerations about the optimal organization of the provision for needs and wants (equalization of marginal utilities, etc.) and that therefore a very definite structure of the economy necessarily corresponds to every system of definite values of products; and if, on the other hand, one wants to regard the ways in which the goods are used as data, as Böhm-Bawerk indeed occasionally argues (*Positive Theorie*, 3rd edition, Exkurs VII, p. 209) [English edition, vol. III, p. 92 (ed.)]. Since the demonstration of the necessity of a certain application of a good already explains the necessity for this good to have a certain level of value, and since all the factors influencing its value also influence its application, and vice versa, the admission that the occurrence of applications of the goods has to be regarded as a *datum* which does not require further explanation would imply nothing less than a declaration of bankruptcy of the entire theory of value.

10 See the entries 'Produktion' and 'Bedürfnis' in the *Handwörterbuch der Staatswissenschaften*, Jena, 1927, 4th edition, and also the series of papers 'Untersuchungen zum Grundgesetz der wirtschaftlichen Wertrechnung', *Zeitschrift für Volkswirtschaft und Sozialpolitik*, new series, vol. 1 *et seq.*, whose publication is still proceeding.

11 *Grenznutzen und Wirtschaftsrechnung*, Vienna, 1924. Cf. also the article 'Grenznutzen' by P. N. Rodenstein-Rodan in the *Handwörterbuch der Staatswissenschaften*, 4th edition, and the more recent literature referred to therein [an English translation, 'Marginal utility', was published in the *International Economic Papers*, vol. 10, 1960, pp. 71–106 (ed.)].

12 The problem of interest on capital is one of the three cases in which

the resolution of fundamental economic problems poses this hitherto unanswered question. The other two cases are the theory of prices and the theory of imputation. The author himself intends to deal with all three of them systematically at a later point in time. The present outline merely serves to give a brief sketch of the problem in its most important application, until such time as the author's other commitments enable him to undertake its general elaboration.

13 Cf. my paper cited above on the problem of imputation, p. 3 [this volume. pp. 33–54 (ed.)].

14 To dispose of an objection which might be raised because of my style but would not touch upon the essence of the assertion, let me describe once more in somewhat more concrete terms the situation in question. Suppose that the product of a given quantity of means of production can be used in one of two successive economic periods in which exactly the same needs and wants are to be satisfied. Independently of this, however, the satisfaction of needs and wants which are precisely the same in both periods is provided for in both periods. Furthermore, the product of the means of production, which are still to be allocated, is larger in the later economic period than in the earlier one. Therefore, the utilities of different quantities of the product, which can be produced with the same quantity of means of production, are compared with each other. The marginal utility of the same physical unit of the product, available in the period in which more can be produced with the same quantity of means of production, has to be lower in this period *relative to the remaining level of provision* which is exactly the same as in the other period concerned. It is only with regard to the fact that, given that the level of the remaining provisions is the same in both periods, the marginal utility of a product can be relatively higher in one case and lower in the other than that of the other goods which did remain constant, that we can talk about the marginal utility of the one quantity of goods being higher than that of the other and that the actual decisions in this case do not give preference to the level of utility which is higher in this sense. But it is only a question of terminology if, instead, the converse procedure is adopted which derives the designation of utility as being higher or lower from actual decisions and infers from this that the utility of all other goods changes from period to period despite a constant level of provision. In any case, the way in which Böhm-Bawerk expresses the lower valuation of future needs and wants shows that he himself used the term 'utility' in the former sense, hence an immanent critique of his procedure will likewise have to adhere to this. It is only from this conception of utility that we can derive the Böhm-Bawerkian formulation of the problem, since otherwise a valuation which contradicted actual decisions would not be possible.

15 As soon as the same means of production can achieve totally different results, or different quantities of the same means of production can achieve the same result at the two points of time in question, whether one wants the same utility from equal units of the means of production at both points becomes a totally different question from whether one wants the same level of satisfaction for equal needs and wants.

16 *Op. cit.*, pp. 136ff.

17 Cf. Rudolf Streller, *Statik und Dynamik in der theoretischen Nationalökonomie*, Leipzig, 1926, especially pp. 100ff. and the literature referred to therein.

18 In principle, three empirical situations are conceivable: the endeavour for better, equal, or worse provision in the future. During the first, most general step of the theoretical argument, the second type is assumed purely for methodological reasons. It would be an interesting task to establish inductively on the basis of household accounts which situation is the dominant one. If the influence of these different estimates of present and future levels of provision on the level of the rate of interest is to be ascertained, it would be necessary to have information as well on the increase in physical productivity which can be obtained by extending the degree of roundaboutness of the production process. Only in theory could it be conceived that interest would disappear entirely, given a strong desire for ever higher levels of provision in the future. Any desire for relatively better provision in the present should raise the rate of interest beyond the degree of physical productivity of capital. In view of the large extent of savings, we have to assume that *de facto* the progressive situation in which the striving is for a higher level of provisions in the future is the rule, and that therefore the rate of interest is normally lower than the additional physical productivity of the capitalistic mode of production. On this, cf. the essay by P. N. Rodenstein-Rodan cited above, pp. 1197ff.

FOUR

INTERTEMPORAL PRICE EQUILIBRIUM AND MOVEMENTS IN THE VALUE OF MONEY*[1]

The consequences of economic theory's characteristic abstraction from time

All economic activity is carried out through time. Every individual economic process occupies a certain time, and all linkages between economic processes necessarily involve longer or shorter periods of time. Suppose, however, that the methodologically valuable fiction is employed, at least initially, by which time is abstracted from. The analysis then begins from an economic system in which all individual processes are assumed to take place simultaneously, and hence the prices of all commodities of a given type are formed under the same conditions. The result is that the propositions arrived at in this stage of the analysis can provide no more than a partial explanation of what goes on in the economy as it actually exists. Yet, because so large a part of all economic activity is in fact directed towards the achievement of a certain degree of satisfaction of needs at particular points in time, common usage tends predominantly to describe this part of human behaviour alone as 'economic'.

In the same way, however, prices also fulfil a particularly significant role with respect to the distribution of the individual processes through time, as the guide and regulator of all economic activity in the exchange economy. It is precisely this function which hitherto has received only brief mention in economics. In most cases, the conclusions arrived at in that first stage of the theoretical analysis have been regarded as sufficient for the treatment of all concrete problems, and there has been a failure to supplement them with a basic examination of the significance of the aspect of time for the structure of the price system.

Yet as soon as these assumptions, oversimplified and all too contradictory of reality as they are, are replaced by ones correspon-

---

* First published as 'Das intertemporale Gleichgewichtssystem der Preise und die Bewegungen des "Geldwertes" ', in *Weltwirtschaftliches Archiv* (1928), no. 2, pp. 33–76.

ding more to the facts, it becomes evident that the customary abstraction from time does a degree of violence to the actual state of affairs which casts serious doubt upon the utility of the results thereby achieved. From the moment at which the analysis is no longer concerned exclusively with prices which are (presumed to be) simultaneously set, as in the elementary presentations of pure theory, but goes on to a consideration of the monetary economy, with prices which necessarily are set at successive points in time, a problem arises for whose solution it is vain to seek in the existing corpus of economic theory. Instead of needing to explain merely the necessity for the existence of a particular structure [*Abstufung*] of simultaneously existing prices and its function, what must now be done is to analyse the necessity and significance of relative levels of prices at successive points in time.

The absence of a theoretical basis for assessing different prices of the same goods at different points in time

From the outset there can be no doubt that, even in a stationary economy, in which the same processes are repeated in the same order, the same goods will not necessarily realize the same prices at every point in time. Rather, under certain conditions, their prices will be different at different points in time, and such price changes *must* recur if the economy is to regularly reproduce itself. The reason is that regular self-reproduction of the economy is not at all synonymous with continuity in the flow of the individual processes within it. In fact, under given external conditions, this will never be so. In that mode of analysis which abstracts from time, this difficulty is overcome by supposing – a necessity imposed upon it by its assumption that the economic periods succeeding one another are in all respects the same – that the length of the period is such as to include within itself even those production processes recurring over the very longest periods of time. The first implication of doing so is to lengthen the economic period, to which the elementary theory applies, to such an extent that it embraces even the longest-term of the price fluctuations arising from the discontinuity between the individual economic processes. As a result, such price fluctuations are eliminated from the picture, so that all acts of exchange are conceptually transferred to a single point in time within the economic period. These periods must be of at least a year's duration, given the seasonally determined variations in individual economic processes, and can be assumed to be even longer because of the existence of production processes of such great duration which are performed but once. The outcome is that the simplification permissible only as a first step in the analysis has led in turn to a failure to consider the necessity for the existence of different prices at successive points in time.[2] Now, it does not matter whether we are dealing with acts of exchange undertaken on a number of occasions at different points in time within such long periods, or with those undertaken on a single occasion in a stationary economy. In either case, it is undoubtedly the rule, and not at all merely an assumption, that the conditions by which they are affected will differ from time to time, and hence that the prices realized in them will also differ. Not merely external circumstances such as changes in the time of day and the season of the year, and the particular technical characteristics of many production processes, but also the natural variations in human needs, ensure that even a self-replacing economy cannot present the same picture at every moment in time. On the contrary, the same processes can be repeated within it only periodically. Consequently, as a rule, the transfer through time of goods which are currently available will not be possible at will or without incurring a certain expenditure. It also follows that, in such an economy, the factors which are operating upon the prices of the same sort of goods at different points in time – and hence also these prices themselves – will be different.

In precisely the same way as, in static theory, the difference in the price of a particular good at different locations due to transport costs and the like must be regarded as the precondition for the existence of an equilibrium, the disparity between the prices of the same goods at different points in time in a self-reproducing economy is a necessary precondition for that self-reproduction to take place.[3] Yet more consideration has been given to the case of the inter-spatial price system than to the determinants and the functions of the *intertemporal price system*. It can even be said that existing theory usually concerns itself merely with the utilization of goods given at one place and at one point in time, and, with very few exceptions, completely ignores those features of space and time which do not fit within its framework.

Virtually the sole exception to this is provided by the well-known works of E. von Böhm-Bawerk. But though they are replete with hints of this kind, they have little to offer in the way of positive conclusions for the problems to be dealt with here. The most significant step beyond Böhm-Bawerk is taken by F. A. Fetter, in his exposition of the influence exerted upon the valuation of given goods by the temporal conditionality of their enjoyment. His concept of *time value* [*Zeitwert*] at least touches upon what are the most significant problems in the present context. Nevertheless, in my view, Fetter too does not confront the problem which is decisive in this connection which is the significance of the temporal pattern of prices of a good for the undisturbed functioning of an economy.[4] At most, some brief attention has occasionally been paid to the significance of the difference in the prices prevailing at various points in time, and the consequences of disturbances in their normal structure, in connection with the theory of interest (K. Wicksell, I. Fisher, L. Mises). But so far as I am aware, the full implications of the problem have never been analysed.

The only method which should be used in the economic analysis of a problem such as this is to ask which conditions will give a price structure such that the structure of the economy conforming to it will remain unchanged, and what will be the consequence of any structure of prices deviating from it. As with any other problem involving prices, therefore, the circumstances which determine the exchange ratio between two goods must be ascertained. The only difference is that the goods in question are now located at different points in time, though in technical terms they may be exactly the same good.

Awareness of the necessity for an intertemporal price system to exist is, however, not merely incompatible with the widespread conception that the intertemporal constancy of prices constitutes a precondition for an undisturbed self-reproduction of the economy. It is in fact in the sharpest contradiction to it. In particular, the analysis to be presented below will show that, given a general expansion of production, the maintenance of equilibrium requires a corresponding reduction in prices, and in this case any failure of prices to fall must give rise to temporary disruptions of the equality between supply and demand. Before this point can be considered in greater detail, however, it will be necessary to analyse more precisely the necessity of and the conditions for a temporal equilibrium position, and to establish the criteria for its existence or its absence. It is especially necessary to do so because the view has already been advanced above that it is possible to apply the concept of equilibrium, and the static mode of analysis adopted in doing so, only to an economy which is presumed to be without time.[5] Moreover, it is at least uncommon to treat price changes – or, more correctly, the differences between the prices of technically equivalent goods existing at different points in time – within the framework of an equilibrium system.

Constructing a theoretical basis by treating the problem as one of equilibrium

Yet the concept of equilibrium is just as indispensable a tool for the analysis of temporal differences in prices as it is for any other investigation in economic theory. Strictly speaking, its field of application is identical with that of economic theory, since only with its assistance is it possible to give a summary depiction of the very great number of different tendencies of movement which are operative in every economic system at every point in time. It basically conveys nothing more than the assumption that interrelationships between economic phenomena obey a regularity of their own, shown by the fact that the overall economy strives, under any given constellation of the circumstances influencing it (the 'economic data'), to achieve a quite particular articulation of its component parts. Any attempt to explain economic processes must set out from the proposition that, given the particular constellation of such circumstances that exist, there is only one particular mode of behaviour by an economic subject that corresponds to his interests, and he will continue to change his decisions until he has achieved the most advantageous uses of the resources available to him.

In addition, if there is any change in the external conditions, for the whole of the period within which it falls there is naturally only one way of allocating the goods available to him which offers him the highest satisfaction. If the individual could foresee the change in question, he would make the appropriate decisions at the very outset of the period. If he could not have foreseen it, he will become aware only subsequently that he could have achieved a better result through carrying out a different allocation of his resources, and so he has in comparison suffered a loss. Only in the former case will the outcome of the allocation of resources among individual uses be successful in the sense that it corresponds to the expectations which gave rise to them, and hence there is no occasion to change the decisions that have already been made. Suppose that, at the time a person decides upon a particular distribution of his given resources among various uses, he also has knowledge of all the conditions under which his individual actions will be taken. If this is so, there will be only one quite particular configuration of these decisions which will correspond to an equilibrium position. Hence, if the differences that exist in these conditions at every point in time within a forthcoming period are known, this time period may be as long as can be conceived of, and the differences between the conditions existing at every moment of time within it can be as great as one wishes. But the relations between the particular decisions of the economic subjects, and thus between all the economic processes conducted within the overall time period, must always be basically the same as those which can be derived for an equilibrium system in which time has been assumed away.

Hence, to conclude that an economy can persist in a static condition it is not at all necessary to assume that, at every point of time within the economic period under consideration, wants and production possibilities remain the same. All that needs to be assumed for such a static equilibrium to occur is that the wants and the means of production existing at every point in time are known to the individual economic subjects at the time at which they frame their economic plan for the period as a whole.[6] That this will never be so in reality is obvious, but a large number of the changes in data are known beforehand and, in assessing the effects of such changes, the use of the ideal case of a state of equilibrium enables us to investigate the basic relationships which are dominant in such circumstances.

Even statistically considered, an economic system extended through time must bear in mind the temporal conditionality of the various data. Or, to put it in terms which are more easily understood but also more exposed to misunderstandings, it must take account of those changes in the data through time which are predictable and will exist in any economic system which possesses a time dimension, as for instance, the changes connected with the alternation of the seasons. The purpose of analysing an economic system of this type is to ascertain the relationship which exists between the prices of technically equivalent goods at various moments in the time period under consideration. Such differences in price must emerge because of the difficulties in transferring goods from one point in time to another, in just the same way as such goods will not carry the same price if they are located at different places. In line with the basic concepts of modern price theory, it will nevertheless be necessary to preface an investigation of this type with a short discussion of the subjective evaluation of given goods at different points in time, if an explanation of exchange relationships is to be provided.

Temporally determined variations in the value of the same good

Suppose, then, that for the time being we consider the evaluation as it is undertaken by an isolated individual. We then ask what determines the amount of a good he has, and hence his estimate of its value, at different points of time within a period. Assume that he can predict that the good itself will be obtainable only with varying degrees of difficulty at different points in time, perhaps because of the well-known variance in production-technical conditions (the influence of the seasons upon agriculture!). (The implication of this assumption is that to transfer the good from the time at which it is easily procurable to that at which it can be obtained only with difficulty necessitates a certain expenditure.) The answer is that the valuation of those goods which are available at a time at which they can be obtained only with greater difficulty, or, what is the same in economic terms, at which they are obtainable only in lesser quantity, will be higher than that of those goods which, although technically equivalent, become available in the more favourable seasons. Obviously, the economic subject might seek to achieve the same satisfaction of a particular want at a given point in time, though a greater expenditure would be involved in his doing so. But then his behaviour would be inappropriate, for the same outlay devoted to satisfying another need, with a good whose conditions of supply at this moment were not particularly unfavourable, must yield a more satisfactory outcome.[7] Every attempt, even under such conditions, to make the good in question available at both points in time in such quantity that its marginal utility and therefore its (subjective) value was the same on each occasion, can have only one outcome. Relative to the supply of other goods at the two points in time, the satisfaction of this need will imply either that too great an outlay must be made on it at one of the points, or too small an outlay at the other, or both. The shifts to which this must give rise are evident, and will come to a stop only if one condition is fulfilled: if, in relation to the other goods, the good in question is valued more highly at the second point in time than at the first, and therefore it has a higher value at the second point in time, or all other goods have a lower value, than at the first point (or – as must actually be the case – both are true). It therefore follows that, in these circumstances, equilibrium presumes variation in the valuation of the individual goods at different moments in the period of time to which it relates.

Intertemporal exchange

If we are to move on from the derivation of the graduation that must exist in the subjective values of a good at different points in time to consider the determinants of the graduation of prices through time, our premises must now be extended to include the possibility of exchange between several individuals of goods which are technically equivalent but available at different points in time. In view of the point in the overall analysis at which we have presently arrived, we must first assume that this exchange takes place directly, i.e. without the use of a medium of exchange. The obvious precondition for an exchange to take place is that, on this as on all occasions, those engaged in exchange set relatively different valuations upon the goods to be exchanged.[8] That this precondition can be fulfilled follows from the fact that the temporal ranking of subjective evaluations alluded to above relates wholly to the individual, and so different persons can arrive at two completely opposed sets of valuations. Thus some persons will be prepared to exchange goods available at a given point in time for goods of the same type available at another point in time, and in general they will find that there are others who are willing to undertake this exchange with them. The question now becomes: can this exchange be expected to take place, usually or always, in such a way that equal quantities of the goods available at a given point in time are exchanged for the same quantities of the same good available at another point in time?[9] Or are there conditions under which such a ratio, even if it is established, cannot last, since, while it persists, supply and demand will not be equal, and hence there will be further shifts in supply and demand which continue until another exchange ratio has been established on the market? By simple analogy with any other problem of prices, it is clearly the second question which is to be answered in the affirmative.[10]

Since variations in the relative estimates of the goods to be exchanged that are made by the persons concerned can occur to precisely the same extent as in any other process of price formation, it is certain that the exchange ratio between the good x at moment 1 (in what follows: x_1, where x at present represents a unit of *quantity*) and good x at moment 2 (in what follows: x_2) can just as well assume the form $x_1:2x_2$, or $2x_1:x_2$, or any other form at all, as that of $x_1:x_2$. Equally certain is the fact that the consequences which flow from the existence of a ratio of exchange between the quantities of a good available at different points in time, which is not in conformity with the market position, must be the same as in another context, those following from the setting of a price which is out of line with the market position. If, for example, an exchange ratio $x_1:x_2$ is arbitrarily established on the market, while for an intertemporal exchange of this kind the ratio $2x_1:x_2$ would be required for an equilibrium between supply and demand, there would then be an excess supply of x_1 and thus an excess demand for x_2 at the ruling price. Suppose that, for any reason, an immediate change in the market price could not take place, then, so long as this price prevailed, production for the second point in time would be less advantageous than if the 'correct' price ruled, since in this case x_2 could be obtained more cheaply by exchange for x_1 than by taking steps oneself to produce the good at moment 2. This must lead in turn to a further shift in the relative supply of this good through time: an expansion of output at moment 1 at the expense of output at moment 2, and thereby, on the one hand, to an intensification of the disproportion between supply and demand on the intertemporal exchange market and hence also to an intensification of the pressure on the existing price of x_1. On the other hand, however, the 'incorrect' price will lead individuals to produce goods for moment 1 to an extent which is in contradiction to a rational distribution of supply throughout the whole time period. Even if the 'incorrect' price should be artificially maintained, a number of the persons whose decision to produce a greater quantity of x_1 was wholly due to the possibility of exchanging x_1 for x_2 at the ratio $x_1:x_2$, will find themselves disappointed in their expectation of improving the supply of x_2 they have at moment 2 by such an exchange since at this incorrect price the supply of x_1 exceeds that of x_2. They must therefore become aware that they would have done better to expand the outlay they have made directly upon the production of x_2.

Differences in the supply of some goods between two points in time affect the intertemporal exchange ratios between all goods

This ought to be sufficient to show that, in a state of pure barter, the exchange between goods of the same kind available at different points in time will not as a rule take place at the ratio 1:1, but according to the circumstances can take place at any other ratio, and that what happens in this case follows precisely the same rules as does the formation of the prices of two different goods. Strictly speaking, goods which are technically equivalent but available only at different points in time ought to be considered different goods in an economic sense, just as can be said of goods which are technically the same but located at different places.[11] As soon as this is kept in mind, it no longer appears surprising but is in fact obvious that, even in a static system, goods which differ only in being available at different points in time will realize different prices. The next step in the analysis is the exact derivation of the necessity for a definite graduation in the set of money prices of technically equivalent goods at different points in time from the recognized necessity of the existence of definite exchange relations for intertemporal exchange. But before this step can be taken, the analysis of intertemporal barter must be taken a step further, and it must now be shown to what extent the factors influencing the ratio of exchange between goods of the same type at two points in time also exert an influence upon the ratio of exchange between all the other goods available at these two moments.

To say that, in the exchange of the quantities of a particular good which are available at different moments, a ratio of exchange which deviates from 1:1 must result, however, leaves unconsidered a substantial part of the consequences which arise from differences in the difficulty of acquiring a good at different points in time, linked with the impossibility of transferring it from one point in time to another. The analysis must now be extended to deal with the exchange ratio which will exist between the stock available of all the other goods at the two points. The first effect of a disparity in the possibility of acquiring a good at two separate instants of time must be that the exchange ratio of this good to the other goods will not be the same at each of the two instants. Suppose, for example, that at the first point in time the good x can be exchanged for the good y in the ratio $2x_1:3y_1$, but that at the second instant, at which x can be obtained only with greater difficulty, a ratio of (say) $2x_2:4y_2$ will at first prevail. Nevertheless, the extent to which the price of x in terms of y at the second instant exceeds that in the first instant will not in general be fully proportional to the greater difficulty of acquiring x at that second point. The reason is that proportionally more labour and other productive forces must now be employed in the production of x and less in that of y. On the one hand, therefore, the rise in the value of x will be less, but on the other hand the value of y will rise in comparison with its value at the first point in time, and the greater outlay necessary to obtain x_2 will not be fully reflected in the ratio of exchange between x_2 and y_2. The result is, however, that the value of y_2 will rise above that of y_1, both in its direct uses and as means for the acquisition of x_2, and hence engender efforts to exchange y_1 for y_2.

Consequently, if we once again assume that, as will generally be the case, the transfer of y from the first to the second point in time is not possible without making a certain outlay, then the exchange ratio between y_1 and y_2 cannot be $y_1:y_2$. On the contrary, it must shift in favour of y_2 in such a way that the shift which takes place is not due to the behaviour of any of the factors influencing the production of or the demand for y. To restore the state of equilibrium which has been disturbed by changes concerning one good, changes must also occur in the intertemporal exchange ratios between the other goods which must move in such a way that those quantities of the other goods for which the good in question can be exchanged at a future point in time cannot also be obtained in intertemporal exchange more cheaply than the good itself. The disparity in the exchange ratios between different goods at separate points in time therefore makes an agio advantageous, and hence creates the necessity for another exchange ratio, even for goods for which there is no reason to suppose that factors peculiar to them are operative which would cause the intertemporal exchange ratio to diverge from 1:1.

In summary, it may therefore be concluded that what follows from the difference in conditions that must always exist at different points in time at least so far as it involves the supply of a number of goods, together with what is only a limited possibility of transferring goods from one point in time to another, must be the formation of definite exchange ratios for intertemporal exchange between goods of all kinds available at separate points in time, in the same way as exchange ratios are formed between goods which are simultaneously available. Moreover, neither of these two groups of exchange relationships is explicable in isolation from the other; both can be understood only as component parts of a unitary system, which must incorporate intertemporal exchange ratios. The exchange ratios for goods which are simultaneously available thereby constitute at most a subordinate system of limited independence, in the same way as this can be asserted of prices ruling at one point in space as compared to the price system which prevails for the country as a whole, or of the latter in relation to international prices.[12]

As is often the case in the discussion of economic problems, the main difficulty in grasping the temporal exchange relations described above is that the technical characteristics of the identity of goods which dominate our thinking make it very difficult for us to avoid regarding goods which are the same in technical terms as also being the same in economic terms. That this must be so for goods available at separate moments of time is also a result of the fact that technically identical commodities with differing temporal quality cannot be utilized with equal facility to achieve a given aim, indeed in some circumstances only a part of them can be thus employed. From the viewpoint of the economic mode of analysis, the status of those goods which are technically identical but are not simultaneously available, and hence also the conditions to which their value and price are subject, cannot differ from that of any of those other goods which, while certainly largely of the same origin, are ultimately produced in basically different production processes (in the widest sense of the phrase) which thus renders them directly utilizable only for different ends. Like the goods which are technically identical but located at different points in space, which have repeatedly been instanced in the preceding discussion for the purpose of comparison, such goods can best be described as goods which are closely related in their production. A particularly close relationship thus exists between their value and their price, but their value and price do not always have to be the same.

Intertemporal exchange ratios and successive money prices

Up to this point in the analysis, the basic assumption has been that, in the economic system under consideration, all acts of exchange were undertaken without the use of a medium of exchange. While this assumption was maintained, prices in the narrower sense could not enter into the analysis, only prices in the sense of exchange ratios between any goods at all. It was therefore impossible to discuss intertemporal quantitative relations in terms of the structure of the money prices realized at different points in time, but only under the restriction of direct exchange between two goods available at different points in time. It has already been shown that there must exist a definite ratio at which two goods available at separate instants are exchanged. But is the existence of such a ratio necessary if the exchange does not take place directly, but is split up into two steps: the acquisition of the means of exchange by surrendering one good at the first point in time, and the acquisition of another good by surrendering the means of exchange at a later point? This is the main question which has already been posed at the outset of our analysis. In more precise terms we are interested in whether the temporal gradation of most money prices fulfils a definite and necessary function, and, if it does, what the consequences are of a deviation of the temporal gradation of prices, due to the operation of external factors, from this 'natural level'.

In essence, this question has already been answered in the affirmative by the arguments presented in the preceding section. As soon as it is recognized that the possibility of transferring given goods from one point in time to another links together all exchange relations at and between each of the two points in time into a system in which they all tend towards a state of equilibrium, it clearly follows that the relative magnitudes of the quantities of goods obtainable for a given quantity of means of exchange at different points in time must be characterized by the same regularity of behaviour. There is only one distinction between this case and that described more extensively in the preceding section which is that while the outcome in both cases is the same, in the former it is achieved not by the roundabout method of interpreting an exchange between two other goods, but by the fact that because the medium of exchange generally permits the individual to store it for the future in a way which is costless (or even yields a positive return) and more effective than that provided by most other goods, it is itself stored and at the second point in time expended to acquire the good desired.

These arguments should be sufficient in themselves to show that, in an economic system which is extended through time and is in equilibrium, the relative level of the money price of any good must vary in accordance with the conditions prevailing at every instant of time. The only thing which remains to be done is to demonstrate, with the aid of concrete examples, what must be the consequence for the regular self-reproduction of the economy of any disturbance of this system of prices by influences which are wholly unrelated to the basic impulses of the economy.

Nevertheless, it is probably necessary to explain in somewhat greater detail the relationships involved in this context. For it may not be immediately obvious that e.g. the existence of the same money prices at two different points in time is equivalent in every respect with that of an intertemporal exchange ratio of 1:1, nor, likewise, that all other ratios existing between two prices at separate points in time are compatible with the same intertemporal exchange relation. In particular, it might be objected that the different subjective value of money at separate points in time, even if the prices of the goods are the same, in itself creates the required equilibrium in all individual economies. Hence, it might be argued that if the overall supply of goods is greater at the later point in time while prices remain unchanged, equilibrium will be maintained by the fact that, while the same price is being paid, it is paid precisely in money of lower marginal utility. Yet the equality of money prices at different points in time has exactly the same meaning as the intertemporal exchange ratio 1:1. The issue raised by variation in the marginal utility of money is therefore not in any sense a new one in that it would have already been necessary to deal with it in any explanation of exchange relations conducted in terms of a state of barter. In that state, too, as has already been shown, the magnitude of the marginal utility of most goods must certainly differ as between the various points in time. In addition, this must be the case even when equilibrium has been achieved. It is precisely the efforts to eliminate, to the greatest extent possible, disparities in availability which motivates the intertemporal acts of exchange, and leads to the emergence of definite exchange relations in which the differences in availability necessarily continuing to exist will be expressed. In the same way, too, the difference in the marginal utility of money merely expresses the differences in availability which must exist as between the two points in time, without thereby being able to replace the necessary gradation of the prices which prevail at successive points in time. The following sections of this article, in which assumptions of a rather more concrete character are employed, will show the consequences of attempts to stabilize prices by monetary policy in such circumstances.

The equilibrium price system in circumstances of periodically recurring changes in the conditions of production

Such changes in data as are predictable, which can as such be taken account of in the economic plan, and whose effects can therefore be handled with equilibrium analysis, can be divided essentially into three groups: those which recur with precise periodicity; those which are of uniform tendency in both direction and extent; and finally, those whose unique occurrence can be confidently expected for a definite point in time, as the result of developments which are currently observable or of known human decisions. The effects of such changes in data can most clearly be seen in the first of these three groups. It is in the analysis of the effects of the changes in external conditions which naturally recur in relatively short periods of time that it is most obvious that only by conceptually reducing them to an equilibrium system can they be understood. But this also shows how unjustified and inappropriate are all attempts to restrict the applicability of the equilibrium concept exclusively to systems which extend through periods of time within which all external conditions remain constant. Rather, to enable the use of equilibrium analysis, it is only necessary to assume, as we have done, that no deviation from the expected course of events takes place during the period.

Among the cases in the first group, the price gradations through time with which we are most familiar, and whose necessity is immediately evident to us, are once again linked with the most short-term of such periodic changes, the change in the time of the day. It is scarcely possible to deny that the explanation of the different prices realized by a good or service at different times of the day still falls within the sphere of static theory, yet simultaneously it can equally scarcely be doubted that, from an economic viewpoint, the same services which are produced on one occasion during the day and on another occasion at night must be regarded as different goods. One of the best-known examples of this sort is that fares on the tramways are frequently higher at night than during the day, but the same phenomenon can be observed for the most variegated types of goods, e.g. the prices of theatre tickets at the day and the evening box offices, and the lower night-time prices for electricity which are customarily frequent. To show the basic concordance between this differentiation of prices of technically equivalent goods at various hours of the day with the gradation of the prices of goods which are different in nature but are being sold simultaneously, and the existence of a linkage between them which can be explained only by employing the concept of equilibrium, it is sufficient to subject the example of tramway tickets to closer analysis.

It is clear that, in given conditions, the maintenance of a night service on a tramway is profitable only at relatively higher fares, and that in such a case (assuming, obviously, free price formation) both the provision of the night service at prices which were not appropriately higher, and its suspension, would signify a loss for the entrepreneur. But the only conclusion to be drawn from this example is that, while a night service cannot be conducted at correspondingly increased prices, the entrepreneur could profit by changing the conditions under which he supplies the service. Hence it is only if the night service can be appropriately priced that the necessary changes are not called forth by the market but an equilibrium exists. And the resulting gradation of prices is explicable only within the context of equilibrium, in which the decisions made by every economic subject are such that he achieves the ends he seeks.

Basically the same can be said of those gradations of prices which emerge in the course of the change of the seasons. For them, too, it is easy to show that the difference between the prices of technically equivalent goods at different seasons fulfils a definite function, and, whenever a condition of equilibrium does not exist, it is advantageous for the individual participant in the market to continuously change their decisions, and thus call forth changes in the gradation of prices in the direction of equilibrium. The well-known fact that the prices of agricultural products like corn are different immediately before and after the harvest can be adduced as an example of this. What is perhaps for many purposes a better example is provided by the analogous difference in the price of eggs during and outside the main laying season, because in this case the output of eggs could be increased in every season by undertaking the appropriate expenditure.

The goods instanced above are therefore without exception goods whose supply is subject to greater difficulty at certain times of the year, whether because of climactic or other reasons, greater costs are involved in so organizing their production that they become ready to be consumed at these points, or because they cannot be made available at these times at all, but can only be transferred from an earlier point in time by incurring certain expenditures. It is well-known that these difficulties are also in fact expressed in corresponding differences in the prices of the goods concerned as between different seasons of the year. In this context as well, all that has to be shown is that a quite definite gradation of these prices is a necessary precondition for a continuance of the regular repetition of the economic processes currently taking place to just the same extent as it is with simultaneously existing prices. This is best shown by analysing the consequences which must follow from the establishment of two prices at two points in time between which no such equilibrium relationship exists.

Assume that, at the first of the two points in time to be considered, the good in question can be produced at significantly lesser cost than at the second, but simultaneously that the money price obtainable for it is the same at each of the two points. Given the argument presented above, this assumption clearly implies either that too high a valuation has been placed on the good at the first point, or too low a valuation at the second. As a result, expenditures to ensure a future supply of the good are less attractive, and conversely larger sums will be spent upon getting hold of it in the present. For at the existing prices, it is most advantageous to satisfy the demand for the good at the second point in time by selling it at the first point and using the proceeds to purchase it at the second. But this must mean that, at least for a number of individuals, the expectations which have induced then to make certain dispositions with respect to this good will not be fulfilled. In particular, some of them will not be able to obtain the good at the given prices at the second point in time. By assumption, at that point it is more difficult to produce, and hence in most cases will be supplied to the market in lesser quantities, even at an equilibrium price. In the present case, however, its scarcity at the second point in time, and hence the disproportion between supply and demand then, is still further intensified by the fact that an equally high price existing at the first point in time does not make it appear profitable to incur those expenditures involved in making the good available at the second point, though the purchasers would still be prepared to defray them at that point. Because of the stability of prices, which has been foreseen, the situation at the second point will therefore be such that not even a subsequent rise in the price to the level corresponding to equilibrium would be sufficient to bring supply and demand into equality with each other. Preventing the necessary configuration of prices existing at different points in time thus leads to a still further intensification of the tendencies towards a change in prices, tendencies which must sooner or later be realized if a complete disorganization of the market is not to result.

The analysis of the converse case yields similar results. Assume that a natural product realizes the same price in two separate seasons, but that in the later season it can be produced in greater quantity at the same cost because of more favourable weather conditions. It will then obviously be advantageous to expand the output of the good for the more distant point in time at the cost of that for the point nearer in time. At the latter instant, the goods are obtained more cheaply by purchase than by producing it for oneself; a greater quantity of it is obtained at the point further away in time in return for one's own production than one has expended in the intervening period upon providing it for oneself. Output for the first point in time will therefore be sharply cut back, and that for the second point unduly expanded. A situation must then result in which, in comparison with the supply that would otherwise be available, on the one hand a deficiency of this good must emerge at the first point in time and on the other hand a surplus at the point more remote in time. Once again, some of those demanding the good at the first point in time will be unable to purchase it at the price they expected to prevail and likewise some will not be able to sell it at the second point in time at the price they expected. Supply and demand will not be equal to each other at either point in time because at each point the same price corresponds to the marginal costs of quite different quantities of output and to the marginal offer made by a number of purchasers, the latter of which is inversely related to the former.

Under certain circumstances, the conclusions arrived at previously with respect to the prices of individual goods at different points in time will also hold for the totality of goods in an economy and so also for the so called 'general price level'. To show this as clearly as possible, let us take an extremely idealized example. Assume that an isolated people feeds itself predominantly with a fruit which can be brought to maturity at any time of the year, though only at very different cost, but at the same time cannot be preserved for more than a few days. Then the price not merely of this fruit but also of most other commodities will differ at different times of the year. The implied assumption is that the work necessary to obtain the fruit is undertaken a relatively short time before it ripens. When production conditions are unfavourable, a part of the tools and capitals otherwise employed in other directions will therefore be transferred to the cultivation of this fruit. Consequently, at this time there will be a deterioration in the supply of all those other goods which can only be stored at a certain cost, and this deterioration will not be compensated for by a rise in the supply of foodstuffs to the level it attains in more favourable seasons. The quantity of most goods possessed by the people will therefore differ very greatly as between one time of the year and another. Indeed, at one time they will be relatively well provided with most goods, at another time relatively badly.

Suppose that in these conditions the various goods could be obtained at any time for the same money price. Then everyone would gladly save a part of his money income in the good time, in order thereby to improve the supply of goods he can obtain in the bad time. But it is perfectly clear that if all individuals seek to act in this way, prices in the bad period must be driven up, and they will continue to rise during it until the money unit will not be able to purchase a greater utility for anyone than it could at the good time of the year. As against this, however, and at least with respect to goods which are transferrable from earlier points in time, it would not pay to assume the higher costs connected with doing so, and hence not even the degree of equalization of availability that is economically possible would be achieved. Naturally, in this connection we completely abstract from the existence of credit for the time being, since otherwise the result of saving would be neither a decline in the sums of money expended during the period when saving was occurring nor a rise in expenditures during the period for which the savings had been made. On the contrary, no change in the overall sum of money expended in the economy need occur in this case because of the investment of the money saved by the individual savers. Nevertheless, to bring credit into the picture would only make the analysis unnecessarily complicated without forcing any essential change in its conclusions.

These **conclusions** can be stated thus: a difference between the levels of **all or at least** most prices prevailing at different points in time may **also be n**ecessary, hence under certain conditions *movements of the so-called 'general price level' fulfil a definite function.* It is hardly necessary to devote much space to that naive conception of the Quantity Theory which provides the only basis for denying the necessity of changes of the price level stemming from the goods side. At this point, the significance of such conceivable seasonal fluctuation of the 'price level' for the theory of the value of money need only be briefly mentioned. The absurdity of always wanting to attribute changes in the general price level to some kind of avoidable changes in the 'value of money', due mainly to the imperfection of our monetary system and to be avoided wherever possible, is clearly shown by the possibility of such regularly recurring movements of prices as e.g. a continuous general price rise in the winter months. This merely expresses the greater difficulties to which supply is subject at that time, and hence differences in the value of the majority of goods at different points in time. Leave aside the fact, which will be dealt with elsewhere, that it is impossible to establish a general 'value of money'. It would also be quite nonsensical to speak of a difference in the value of money, because the difference in the value of goods is expressed in terms of the difference in money prices. If use is made of the inexact concept of a general value of money, consistency would also require denial of the fact that, within an equilibrium system extended through time, temporal differences in the value of money may exist, in the same way that Mises disputes the possibility of spatial differences in the value of money.[13]

The equilibrium price system in persistent and also in once-and-for-all changes in the conditions of production

Up to this point in the analysis, the description of the linkages between prices at different points in time can hardly have been subject to contradiction, even if, as far as I am aware, they have hitherto never been set forth explicitly. But what could be more surprising at first sight is the further assertion that basically the same relationships exist in cases in which the shifts in the data are not of a periodic nature but consist in a known, uniform movement in one direction. In what follows, an attempt is made to prove that, in the case of such a movement as well, only one quite particular relative level of prices at successive points in time ensures the maintenance of equilibrium, and that any other pattern of prices leads to shifts in the structure of production which ultimately must call forth a disparity between supply and demand and thereby induce further price changes which as a rule involve losses. This conclusion constitutes the essential point of the present analysis, and provides the most important basis for the thesis as to the relations between 'movements in the value of money' and the natural gradation of prices, with which the following section will be concerned.

First of all, assume once more that the prediction can be made with certainty that, over a longer time period, the cost of production of *one* good will continuously decline. Suppose that, because of the construction of a drainage system decided upon for health reasons, a certain area of a soil particularly appropriate for the output of a particular natural product, but hitherto under swamp, becomes available each year for cultivation. If the price of this natural product did not continuously fall in such a case, it would not be worthwhile to increase output, even before the expected expansion of the production area had been achieved, through more intensive utilization of the area already available at the cost of its later productivity, as would undoubtedly correspond to a state of equilibrium and also be in the general interest. The owners of the fields already under cultivation would then so direct their current production, in the expectation of receiving the same price at a later time, that they could produce the same quantity at the same cost for the entire future as well. But as soon as they have to compete with the product of the better soil which has been newly opened up for cultivation, it is evident that they would have done better to have increased their production at the earlier time at the cost of that at the later. If the assumed constancy in the price obtainable for the good when the supply of it has been expanded is to hold, one of the following conditions must be fulfilled: either all other prices must have risen correspondingly, or at this price supply and demand will not be equal, but the former will exceed the latter. This immediately becomes evident if we consider that, by assumption, the good in question comes on to the market in greater quantity at the later point in time, and hence can only be disposed of by a fall in its price relative to that of all other goods. It follows that either the producer will not be able to dispose of a portion of the product he supplies at the later time, or he can only acquire a smaller quantity of other goods with the same money proceeds. Hence his position in either case will be worse than if he had increased his output at the earlier time instead of producing part of it at the later time. If he undergoes this experience more than once, and if the factor reducing costs can be assumed to continue operative, the producer will finally have to decide in his own interests to expand his current output by more intensive cultivation of the soil; but for so long as he has distributed his production uniformly through time, confident of the validity of his price expectations, he will thereby suffer losses.

As in every other case, a price structure which is not compatible with equilibrium will have two main consequences; on the one hand, a widening of the differences in supply that are minimized in equilibrium; and on the other hand, whenever equilibrium has not been achieved, the prices actually realized will not represent the greatest returns that could be obtained by the producer. The same conclusion can be shown to apply in every other instance of a predictable, regular alteration in the conditions of production of a good in one direction or the other. To avoid prolonging the discussion inappropriately, let us now pass directly to the case in which the changes do not take place in the conditions of production of one good alone. Assume that the predictable improvements in methods of production and the resulting reduction in costs take place uniformly throughout the whole economy. The type of economy involved is familiar in economic theory as a 'regularly progressing economy'. In this case, it is the investment of a relatively constant volume of current savings which leads to continuous rises in output in all branches of the economy. The same analysis can in principle also be applied to the opposite situation. The productivity of an economy may continuously decline because of the enduring operation of particular factors, e.g. the exhaustion of the mines, climatic changes, or declining population and hence diminishing division of labour. The question to be answered in this context is whether – in the same way as with a uniform expansion or contraction of the quantity of a good produced – changes in the overall quantity of output bring about certain changes in all prices and so also in the so called price level. Similarly, must any deviation of prices in successive instants away from this quasi-static gradation of prices give rise over time to the same outcome as can be established in the case of a single good?

The practical significance of this question becomes evident when it is realized that the answer given to it must also be valid in basic respects for the case which undoubtedly occurs frequently in reality, in which every producer can reckon upon being able to sell his product at unchanged prices, or at prices which have not declined by the full extent of the reduction in costs, even after the improvements in production have been made, because the organization or the regulation of the country's monetary system prevents any general fall in prices. This instance will be considered in greater detail in the following section. For the moment, however, the analysis will continue to be based on the assumption that has enabled us to make direct use of the equilibrium concept up to this point, namely that the expansion of output is not merely known to individual entrepreneurs, but can also be predicted in general terms as arising from factors which are generally known to be operative.

If, during such a general expansion in output, the expectation is held with certainty that the prices of products will not fall but will remain stable or even rise, hence that at the point more distant in time the same or even a higher price can be obtained for the product produced at lesser cost, the outcome must be that production for the later period, in which supply is already at a relatively adequate level, will be further expanded at the cost of that for the earlier period, in which supply is relatively less adequate. Even a person who has no intention of saving will, in this case, expect the greatest advantage to arise from his distributing his output in such a way, because by doing so he will raise his total income for the period as a whole. On the basis of the present market situation, he will believe that he can count on being compensated for the temporary constraint on his income, which operates until his increased output comes on to the market, by a greater rise in the earnings he will then derive from it.

It follows that there is no difference in this respect between the outcome of an increase in the output of *one* good and that of a general rise in output. The expectation that prices will not change calls forth an excessive rise in output for the future. This expansion will proceed on the assumption, on the part of the individual, that he will be able to maintain himself in the intervening period in his accustomed fashion and to pay for the goods he needs during this period with the future proceeds of his increased output. In just the same way as in the cases previously discussed, however, the quantities of present goods which producers want to obtain at the given price will not be available, precisely because of the expansion of output for the future. Now, as between the two points in time, conditions of production have changed. But by assumption, the exchange ratios between current goods and future goods that currently prevail reflect the existence of the same money prices at those two points in time. Hence these exchange ratios will now reveal themselves as too favourable for future goods, hence the supply of current goods will remain below the demand for them.[14]

However, the exaggerated stimulus to the expansion of output for more distant points in time at the expense of that for nearer points will make it more difficult for the same levels of prices, which are already in themselves inappropriate, to persist during the whole period, and in time must exert an ever-intensifying pressure on prices. The discrepancy between supply and demand at the prices ruling will be expressed initially in too low a supply and later in too great a supply. Even during the first period, the upshot will be that those who do not succeed in covering their demand during that period at the low prices they expect to prevail will see themselves forced to offer higher prices. Consequently, because a fall in prices in the future is not expected, a temporary rise in current prices must take place, even before the increased output comes on to the market. But then the assumptions upon which the entre-preneurs have decided to expand their output for the later point in time reveal themselves to be incorrect. Not only will they have to discover that they would have realized better prices by shifting their production to a point nearer in time, in addition, they will have to pay a price higher than that which they expected for the goods necessary for the continuance of production at the later point, and for that reason, for at least some of them, part of the profit they expected will be converted into a loss. In other words the situation in which they now find themselves means that they will not be able to sell their products at the later point in time at prices which cover costs.

These consequences, which are brought to a head by the expecta-tion of stable prices as production grows, are therefore the same as those of an inflation, if not in degree then certainly in nature. For prices to remain stable as output increases, the quantity of money must be expanded. But even if the money supply is increased just sufficiently to prevent a fall in prices, it must have basically the same effect on the structure of production as any other expansion in the quantity of money not 'justified' by an increase in output. By preventing the temporal gradation of prices determined by the 'goods situation' from being established, it gives rise to shifts in production which prevent the necessary equalization of the supply of goods as between different points in time. Moreover, at a later stage, when some of these shifts have already been irrevocably completed, it obliges much greater changes in prices which must result in the loss of some portion of the expenditures made.

Basically the same conclusion holds in the case of a continuous decline in output with unchanged or even falling prices. Here the disturbance to supply and the hindrance to the equalization of supply as between different points in time operate in the opposite direction, but will probably have less serious consequences because of this. As a rule, goods which have incorrectly been produced in too great a quantity for present needs can subsequently be shifted into the future relatively easily, while a shift of the output of goods in the opposite direction will usually be impossible or, if it can be done, will involve substantial costs.

To some extent, the case in which the changes in the conditions of production consist in a change in the size of the population calls for particular attention, though it can only briefly be dealt with here. Since it cannot be possible in this case to shift the utilization of the variable productive factors, it follows that an 'incorrect' price structure cannot lead to their being employed at the incorrect point in time. Neither the new labour power nor the exchanger disposing over it is in existence at the earlier point in time. With arguments analogous to those presented above, it can be shown that, if output rises because of an increase in the number of workers, an equilibrium will emerge only with the establishment of a quite particular set of relative prices at the two points in time. Similarly, any deviation of prices from that set must give rise to the type of consequences already described above. But to go into the process in detail would take us too far afield at this point.

Similar types of propositions as to the significance of intertemporal price structures could also be stated for the instance in which a once-and-for-all change in the conditions of production is assumed to take place, for example in the case of the expiry of a patent. In this case, however, the concept of equilibrium hitherto deployed could no longer be validly used to depict actually existing tendencies. The results achieved in an analysis of this type would then have greatest significance merely in serving as a foil against which the particular features of the actual course of events could be more sharply highlighted.

The influence of automatic changes in the quantity of money under a 'tied' monetary system upon the 'natural' level of prices

Any currency policy which seeks to arbitrarily influence the 'value of money' will prevent the establishment of that natural structure of prices through time corresponding to the intertemporal exchange relations originating from barter, and alone able to ensure undisturbed self-reproduction in a monetary economy as well. Furthermore, the same is true of the mechanism of any monetary system at all, either actually existing or merely conceivable. Above all, a tendency towards the stabilization of prices is operative not merely under a currency 'manipulated' with respect to that very aim, but also with any tied currency [*gebundene Währung*] or commodity money [*Sachgeld*]. The effect of such a tendency must be to counteract any tendency to that general change in prices emanating from the 'goods side' as already described and prevent the materialization of a movement in prices in accordance with the temporal equilibrium system. As is well known, a tied currency[15] is described as a monetary system in which the quantity of money is automatically regulated by the possibility of converting a fixed, given quantity of one good into a definite quantity of money and vice versa, whether through direct transformation or exchange. For the sake of simplicity, discussion will be confined to the gold standard as a typical manifestation of such a tied currency. Obviously, however, any conclusions arrived at with respect to it can equally well be applied to any other tied currency.

The essential characteristic of every tied currency and of the gold standard in particular is that every change in prices, so long as it is not merely a matter of two such changes accidentally compensating for each other, leads to changes in the quantity of money and hence to further changes in prices. Suppose that, in the case of the gold standard, we temporarily abstract from changes on the side of gold production and in the industrial demand for gold, and concentrate upon the effect of its operation in the case of a change in the prices of some randomly chosen goods (which are not produced by gold itself or serve in its production), or a fairly general change in prices. It is then evident that the operation of the gold standard will regularly be such as partly to prevent or even to reverse the change in prices arising from other causes. Since some of these effects are of the most minor order and without practical interest, let us confine the discussion to the case of a rather general price change, for instance to that of a fall in prices which originates from extensive improvements in the conditions of production. The increased purchasing power of gold following upon a greater output of commodities will have the familiar consequence of a rise in both the production of gold and also to a still greater extent in the transformation of gold into money, so that prices will be pushed up still further or a further fall in prices wholly or partially prevented. The result is that the difference in prices which necessarily arises from the relationship between the supply of and demand for goods at two separate points in time, and which serves to bring about equality in provision between them, is partly prevented from being established. The responsibility for this outcome is wholly unrelated to the original motivations to engage in economic activity, but stems solely from the particular economic form, the system of indirect exchanges. Yet, as obstacles are set in the way of the establishment of the natural price structure, not merely will the possible equalization of supply as between various points in time as depicted in the preceding sections be prevented from taking place, but in addition the equilibrium between supply and demand will be disrupted.

The tendency of a tied currency to stabilize the 'value of money', even if in a lesser degree than a free currency regulated towards this end, namely its tendency to prevent the establishment of that temporal set of exchange relations expressed in money which must of necessity have been established in a barter economy, must necessarily lead to disturbances of the economic process. *Given what has previously been said, it must be assumed, in sharpest contradiction to the prevailing view, that it is not any deficiency in the stability of the purchasing power of money that constitutes one of the most important sources of disturbances of the economy from the side of money. On the contrary, it is the tendency peculiar to all commodity currencies to stabilize the purchasing power of money even when the general state of supply is changing, a tendency alien to all the fundamental determinants of economic activity.* That is true to an even greater extent of every currency which is regulated with the aim of keeping the price level as stable as possible, since with such a currency changes in the general level of prices stemming from the goods side are wholly prevented. A tied currency, on the other hand, achieves a balance at mid-point, so to speak, between the tendency to a change in prices and their stabilization. Remaining with the example of a fall in prices originating from the goods side, the fall in prices will in this case certainly induce an expansion in the flow of gold into the monetary circulation. But the new equilibrium will emerge before prices have been brought back to their previous level. On the one hand, an increase in the output of gold will bring with it higher costs of production, yet on the other hand, an outflow of gold from its industrial uses will also raise the price of gold in relation to the prices of other commodities.

It would be possible to conceive of a structure of money prices at successive points in time being established which corresponds to the intertemporal equilibrium system, only if the monetary system was one in which any change in the quantity of money was excluded. In practice, as will be discussed later in this article, it is impracticable to regulate the monetary system in this way. But it is worthwhile considering for a moment the situation in which the quantity of money is kept constant, with respect to its significance for the price structure and its relation to the 'natural' price system. In this case, a cancelling-out of the price fluctuations emanating from the side of goods by changes in the quantity of money is not in question. Let us temporarily abstract from certain disturbances which have already been discussed in other connections and are to be dealt with again in connection with the underlying assumptions being made here. For, in a situation of indirect exchange, such disturbances always offer resistance to the achievement of full equilibrium. Now, if the quantity of money is invariable, obviously prices must fall as output rises and rise as output falls, and indeed both occur in such degree that the changes in costs which gave rise to a change in the volume of output are expressed in the change in prices. For example, suppose that production methods have been improved and hence costs reduced. Under otherwise equal conditions, the prices of products must fall precisely to the point at which the increased output now producible with the same quantity of resources can be sold at the same total revenue as the smaller quantity previously produced. If product prices do not fall, there is a stimulus to expand still further, at the cost of current supply, the greater future supply initially made possible by the improvement in production methods, because it promises a greater return than production for the present. If to simplify matters we temporarily also assume that the rise in output takes place in all sectors simultaneously and equally, and that after this general rise in output the relative volume of demand for the various products remains the same, this implies that the price movement permits just that expansion of output with which a state of equilibrium will be regained.

Circumstances become substantially more complicated if the change in the conditions of production and thereby in quantities produced takes place only in individual branches of industry, since shifts in the relative quantities of output and relative prices would then have to take place, but to pursue this would take us too far afield at this point. Yet a brief consideration of the case which frequently does occur demonstrates that the picture gained under the assumption of a generally uniform and simultaneous rise in output, and the conclusions drawn from it, are not completely impractical. What we have in mind is that improvements in productive methods do not occur simultaneously everywhere but they do so successively within a short period of time. Yet the organization of the monetary system does not permit a decline in the general price level and hence all producers can reckon upon being able in the final analysis to sell their expanded output at the same unit prices again after prices have temporarily declined. Clearly, the consequences of this frequently held and well-founded expectation must in general be the same as those of a stability of prices which can be expected to persist with a similarly predictable general rise in production, namely an expansion of output for the period because of the more favourable conditions, which is excessive in comparison to the equilibrium level. Analogous considerations lead to essentially the same conclusions for the converse case of a declining level of output.

Hence the disturbances which can arise because of the use of a medium of exchange in an economic system are in no way to be considered as the consequence solely of a change in the absolute level of money prices. On the contrary, in some circumstances they must be seen as originating in the absence of such a change. Neither the equality between the money prices of individual goods or of all goods or of the 'general price level' at two different points in time, nor the equality of the prices of two different goods at the same point in time, is essential to equilibrium, although it is obviously possible for these equalities to exist in concrete cases. A difference in the 'value of money' at different points of time within the intertemporal equilibrium system is therefore completely compatible with the existence of equilibrium. All that a disturbance of the equilibrium would do is to establish a structure in the value of money at the various points in time which would create an uneconomic configuration in the relative levels of individual prices at those different points, which fulfil a quite definite economic function. *In describing the damaging effects which can arise from money, however, it is not changes in the value of money which should be at issue, but disturbances of the intertemporal price system which are without any economic function.* The theoretical significance of this conclusion can be grasped only if it is realized that the prices established with the assistance of money do not correspond to the equilibrium prices of the hypothetical system which does not possess a medium of exchange, and therefore must yield the same outcome as any other price structure inconsistent with equilibrium. If this proposition is not brought into the analysis, any concrete change in the so-called value of money, or constancy in it, becomes wholly without interest.

It is not at all new to argue that, if disturbing influences from the side of money are to be avoided, the 'value of money' must not remain unaltered as the situation in the market changes but should continuously be adjusted to the changed conditions. Particularly in the bimetallic controversy of the 1870s and 1880s, the thesis was advanced from many sides that, as productivity rose and hence costs of production fell, a corresponding decline in prices would be desirable.[16] In addition, among various authors the view is to be found that changes in the general level of supply ought to find expression in corresponding changes in the value of money. Yet there was no theoretical basis presented for this view, and in my opinion it can be provided only by considerations of the type discussed above. To my knowledge no one has hitherto analysed the function fulfilled by the relative levels of prices at different points in time. In its absence, however, the sole criterion by which the significance of concrete structures of prices could be assessed was also lacking.

Only recently, and with respect to a particular problem, has Haberler[17] investigated the significance of general price movements for the undisturbed progress of the economy. In this context, he has convincingly shown that a fall in the price level due to continuous improvements occurring in all branches of production does not have the same troublesome consequences as a deflation. Theory has hitherto scarcely progressed beyond this distinction between the effects of changes in the price level originating on the one hand from the 'goods side' and on the other from the 'money side'. The view advanced here, that changes in the price level coming from the 'goods side' are not merely not detrimental but are even necessary if disturbances of equilibrium are to be avoided, may still appear to many to have something of the air of paradox. This is especially so because the view that is dominant today, according to which only an invariable price level will ensure an undisturbed course of production, and every general rise in prices must lead to an over-expansion, every general fall to an unjustified restriction of production, appears to be confirmed by general experience and the results of statistical investigations. Nevertheless the results of my analysis do not seem to me to be in any way in contradiction to the facts.

Parallel changes in prices and production

With only few exceptions historically, the best known of which are immediately to be noted, rising output and rising prices and falling output and falling prices run parallel to each other. But this is completely compatible with the recognition that, under otherwise equal conditions, a rise of production can take place only with falling prices, and a decline in production only with rising prices, if equilibrium is not to be disturbed. The restrictive assumption 'under otherwise equal conditions' implies that the changes have taken place in the conditions of production alone, and that simultaneously such changes in the level of demand as would counterbalance the effects of the former have not also fortuitously occurred. Under these conditions, however, the circumstance discussed above, namely that the existing monetary systems prevent the necessary price changes, at least in part, must always imply that any improvement in the conditions of production leads at first to an excessive expansion of output, and any deterioration of those conditions to an excessive restriction of it, in relation to the given demand.

But suppose that a secondary disproportionality between supply and demand has come about because of such an incorrect movement of prices. The direction of the relative movement of prices and quantities must then be precisely the opposite of that arising from a simple change in the conditions of production. This can be shown most clearly by the familiar diagrammatic presentation of the conditions for the establishment of equilibrium by means of the supply and demand curves. In this case, a change in the conditions of production, demand remaining constant, always causes a shift of the equilibrium point along the demand curve, which implies either falling prices and rising output or rising prices and falling output. But the equilibrium point must always shift along the supply curve if production and prices are adjusted to *one another* but do not conform with demand. In this situation in particular, production and prices must simultaneously fall or rise if 'incorrect' prices have called forth an incorrect volume of output. Production, which is temporarily guided by 'incorrect' prices, will therefore always have to traverse a path towards equilibrium along which prices and quantities of output develop in parallel. On the contrary, however, there is no contradiction in saying that production and prices must move in a numerically opposite sense if equilibrium is to be maintained as conditions of production change. The regular parallel movement of both phenomena therefore merely confirms that the economy does not in practice take the shortest route from equilibrium to equilibrium, hence in a type of moving equilibrium, but continually oscillates around it.[18] This is not simply a well-known fact but the circumstances under discussion here show it to be an actual necessity, even for the case in which no unforeseen changes occur.

Under the existing monetary organization, which militates against changes in the general price level, the necessary price changes can enforce themselves only if an erroneous guidance of production has already come about. In particular, it must be assumed that the immanent tendency of the gold currency towards stabilization in fact also administers an excessive stimulus to the expansion of output as costs of production fall, and thus regularly makes a later fall in prices with a simultaneous contraction of output unavoidable. Since, conversely, every deterioration in the conditions of production in the given situation must have analogous consequences as well, it may even be regarded as theoretically probable that the actual movement of the economy will describe continuous fluctuations around equilibrium. But it is an equilibrium which can never be achieved, because of monetary influences which hinder the establishment of the natural price structure. Yet while the parallelism in the empirical movements of prices and production can be explained by these particular circumstances, it naturally provides no proof at all that a rise in prices must regularly lead to a rise in output, and a fall in prices to a fall in output. Rather, it is quite probable that, if the adjustment of prices were to proceed without any disturbance, the connection between prices and output would be completely the reverse, and price movements would then be an expression of the necessary differences in supply as between the different points in time and not of regularly recurring disturbances of equilibrium (i.e. shifts between supply and demand).[19]

It is not our task here to elaborate these reflections into a theory of economic crises, especially since our neglect of the phenomena of credit would mean that any such theory at which we arrived would be completely lacking in reality. It is sufficient at this point to have established that certain disturbances of economic equilibrium are not merely linked to the introduction of credit, but, if probably to a lesser extent, are indissolubly linked with the use of a medium of exchange in itself. Hence attempts to stabilize the purchasing power of money are likely to be least successful of all in eliminating such disturbances. There can be no doubt that they show themselves more markedly in a credit economy and thus can be observed more easily there. From this viewpoint, it may also be justified, in depicting the significance of monetary phenomena for the course of an economy, to set out from the assumption that exchange is mediated by credit alone and not at all by cash. This is the procedure adopted by e.g. R. G. Hawtrey[20] and L. A. Hahn.[21] In any judgment of the efforts to eliminate whenever possible the influences which emanate from the side of money to disturb economic equilibrium, it is nevertheless of decisive significance to recognize that these disturbances are inseparably bound up with the operation of all conceivable monetary systems. Only if the quantity of the means of exchange could be fixed once and for all[22] would it be possible to eliminate merely the most important influences from the money side discussed above, influences which prevent the automatic adjustment of the economy to changes in external conditions.

Obviously this is out of the question, given the ever-present possibility of using a surrogate money in place of real money. The quantity of that surrogate could not be rigidly tied to that of the real money, and its creation would have precisely the same effect as that of any other expansion of the money supply. In addition, it cannot be argued that it would be desirable to fix the quantity of money in this way with the aim of preventing the operation of all active influences from the side of money. Probably it has been fortunate for mankind that the organization of the monetary system has forced it into taking a step forward for which it would not have been prepared to accept the sacrifice involved. Indeed, from what has been said above, this is true of the operation of all tied currencies in a progressive economy and not merely of the effect of credit in the relevant sense, though it is certainly the latter which is generally recognized today. It is not our task to discuss this issue further at this point. But it is certain that this step forward is inseparably connected with those disturbances towards whose elimination efforts are currently being devoted, and that therefore success in such efforts could be achieved only by setting up obstacles to progress. If the foregoing is correct, we must finally give up all thoughts of completely eliminating monetary influences by restricting money to the role of a passive mediator, so that the economy proceeds as if money were not employed in it. We will have to come to terms with the idea that money always exerts a determining influence on the development of the economy, that the principles derived for an economy without money can be applied to an economy with money only with substantial qualifications, and hence that it can never be the goal of monetary policy to ensure that money exerts as little influence as possible upon the path which the economy traverses. On the contrary, the aim must always be to ensure that the unavoidable influences exert their effect in as desirable a fashion as possible.

At this point we must turn away from any further investigation of the inherent tendencies of any monetary economy to recurrent disturbances of equilibrium, and in particular their significance for the explanation of the familiar 'economic fluctuations', *business cycles*. Nevertheless, some practical applications of the conclusions at which we have arrived may be briefly outlined. Above all, it is necessary to consider an exception already noted above to the empirical rule that rising prices imply rising levels of production and falling prices falling levels of production. As is widely known, much surprise has been aroused by the fact that the extraordinary cyclical upswing which the United States economy has experienced in recent years has proceeded for the most part with falling prices, and especially, that it has gone on evenly without bringing with it a crisis, at least for an unusually long time. On the basis of the view advanced above, the presumption would be that the upward movement of production has been able to continue for so long not despite but precisely *because of* the simultaneous fall in prices. For exceptional reasons that need not be discussed here, it has not been possible for those forces to assert themselves which generally prevent a fall in prices as costs of production fall, and hence the price structure and price expectations have not been such as to stimulate that excessive expansion of output for points more distant in time which otherwise regularly leads to sales difficulties. The secret of the duration of the boom in the United States is thus to be sought precisely in the fall in prices, and the boom can be expected to continue only so long as the fall in prices persists. Now, that prevention of a rise in prices during the cyclical upswing also demanded by ruling opinion would be insufficient by itself to prevent the emergence of a disproportionality in the development of the individual sectors of production, a disproportionality which would determine the later reaction. But a fall in prices corresponding to the decline in costs as output rose would be at least as effective in preventing an over-expansion as the rise in interest rates which the dominant doctrine regards as being the only step necessary, and in addition it would do so in a way which was economically more appropriate.[23]

The same considerations also show the baselessness of the concern recently expressed in many quarters about the threatened scarcity of gold, in so far as all that is feared is that the current output of gold will not be sufficient to 'adjust' the quantity of money to the growth of the economy, not that the scarcity of gold could become so acute that the gold in circulation is withdrawn to satisfy industrial demand. But a mere cessation of the tendencies stabilizing the 'value of money', which under the gold standard have hitherto counteracted a fall in prices caused by a rise in the level of production, is all that would be desirable. Yet even a gold currency under which these stabilizing tendencies operate unchecked is unconditionally preferable to a monetary system in which the purchasing power of the monetary unit is maintained as a matter of policy. It has already been shown above that, in a tied currency as opposed to one which is artificially held stable, the necessary changes in prices are only in part prevented from taking place, and hence relatively lesser disturbances to equilibrium are to be expected. The reason is that, with a tied currency, larger quantities of money are obtainable only at greater cost, and money flowing out of the circulation can find a place in industry only at a falling price. Hence, in the new equilibrium which emerges after the level of prices has been changed by a change in the conditions of production, prices will be somewhere between their former level and that which must obtain if the quantity of money were invariable. In this case, therefore, only a partial compensation through passive changes in the value of money takes place.

However, the gold standard (and every other commodity money) has one further advantage. Any attempt to get complete fixity in the quantity of money must come to grief on the fact that it is only possible in part to regulate the quantity of the various surrogate monies. On the other hand, to compensate for changes in their quantity by a change in that of real money meets the problem that it is not possible to ascertain the quantity of them in circulation. Yet no other criteria exists by which the quantity of money could be regulated such that the establishment of prices is not disturbed. The gold standard however, ensures that changes in the quantity of surrogate money are automatically compensated for within the same limits as permissible change in the general level of prices. If the expulsion of gold money from the circulation by surrogate money can never proceed to the point at which the total quantity of means of exchange remains unchanged, at least a partial correction ensues, while no criteria exist for a systematic correction in the case of a manipulated currency. The greatest disadvantage of the gold standard lies in the possibility of decisive alterations taking place in gold's conditions of production due to the discovery of new deposits or better extraction methods, yet it is precisely this drawback which can most easily be overcome. In general, however, the conclusion of our analysis is that the gold standard is still to be regarded as relatively the best, i.e. as the monetary system which creates *relatively* the fewest disturbances for the natural formation of prices.

On the origin of the theory that the quantity of money must be accommodated to the 'demand for money'

There is no basis in economic theory for the view that the quantity of money must be adjusted to changes in the economy if economic equilibrium is to be maintained or – what signifies the same – if monetary disturbances to the economy are to be prevented. Yet it is still generally presented as a self-evident proposition. Even if the concept of the demand for money can only be subjected to an intensive critique at other places in this investigation, it still appears to be appropriate in this context to add a few remarks as to the origin of the concept and the misunderstandings connected with it. It seems to me that the most important reason for the dogmatic acceptance of this view is to be found in an uncritical transfer of a practice perceived as necessary for individual nations to the overall world economy, or to that assumed isolated economy which usually takes its place in theoretical discussions. I believe, however, that it can relatively easily be shown that it is quite impermissible to make this transfer, because the change in the quantity of money which fulfils a necessary function for one nation trading with others is not merely useless but even directly deleterious for the overall world economy.

The theory that the money supply is distributed among the individual nations in proportion to their demand is a familiar one, and can be traced back to North and Hume.[24] It shows that the overall supply of money in existence must automatically so distribute itself among the various nations that there must always be more money in an economy in which a greater volume of transactions is carried on, a greater volume of output is produced, than in an economy which is smaller in these respects. This theory as to the necessary relative supply of money in two countries at the same point in time now gives rise to the idea that in every individual country as well the quantity of money must grow in proportion to the volume of transactions to be effected by it. There is, however, a crucial difference between the two cases. In the first case, the changes in the relative quantities of money in the individual countries are a necessary precondition for the restoration of equilibrium, namely for the change in the relative price levels in the two countries which has become necessary. But there is no change in the absolute quantity of money in the two countries now linked together into one economic system. A change in the total quantity of money would not imply at all that the equilibrium that has been upset within the economy is now restored, but merely that a temporary disturbance of equilibrium in the production of goods has been created for the purpose of bringing about a new equilibrium with the output of gold. The difference between the two phenomena has not been more clearly grasped because it has been usual, in the analysis of movements of money between different places, to content oneself with showing that under certain conditions changes in the relative quantities of money circulating in several countries must ensue. As a result, there has been a failure to realize that it is not by this change alone that the equilibrium between them is restored. So far as the individual in the monetary economy is concerned, the increase in his money income is only a necessary link in the chain of processes which enables him to obtain an increased share in output in return for an increase in his participation in production. The same is true for an economy in that an increase in its monetary income is merely a necessary precondition for it to increase its share in the output of the world taken as a whole. Obviously, however, the unique function thus fulfilled by a change in the quantity of money circulating within a group cannot be discharged by a change in the quantity of money in the world as a whole.

The distinction can best be shown with the aid of two examples. Assume, firstly, that there is a rise in the agricultural output of a country with lower costs of production, and that therefore it is the recipient of an inflow of gold. The reason for the inflow is familiar: money always flows to the place at which its purchasing power is greatest, and hence the quantity of money in the country involved will continue to increase until the relationship between prices there and abroad is once again in equilibrium. This is the explanation usually advanced and yet it relates to only one part of the adjustment process. By virtue of its incompleteness, it gives the completely erroneous impression that, for example, the assumed country that has occasioned the gold movement by raising its productivity will end up with a useless increase in its stock of money in exchange for at least a part of its additional output. The conclusion therefore appears to follow that it has made a sacrifice, so to speak, in the interest of the maintenance of international price equilibrium. But this is as little valid for the assumed country as it is for a person for whom an increase in his money income is the first step to an increase in his real income. A distinction between the case of the individual and that of the country certainly appears to lie in the fact that a rise in the money income of the individual is drawn from the other economic subjects, while a gold movement to one country need not in any way imply a rise in the money income drawn from abroad. But as will immediately be evident, this distinction is merely apparent.

In discussing the example we have set up, we have to begin from the proposition that, in one country, the prices of agricultural products decline because of improvements in production. Because of this, it will be more advantageous for foreign countries to buy such products in this country (to the extent that, taking transport costs, etc. into account, they can in general be exported), and the quantity it exports must rise, without any presumption that the value of its total exports must thereby fall. An import of gold will take place because of the fall in prices only if the overall value of the quantity now exported has risen in relation to that previously exported. If we assume that this is indeed the case, then the increase in demand from abroad, which will lead to a renewed rise in prices or at least to prevention of a further fall, will take the form of an import of gold, other things remaining the same. The reason is that, by assumption, the prices realized in this country for all those commodities the importation of which might be increased, would be lower than those prevailing abroad (since otherwise this country's imports of them would already have risen). Hence the import of gold represents the most advantageous mode of payment. How long will this import of gold continue? For as long as it itself, or the rise in the incomes of the sellers of agricultural goods which it represents, does not bring about such a rise in the prices of other goods that it will become advantageous to import those goods instead of gold. It would take us too far afield to pursue this process in all its details. A little reflection will show that ultimately our country's share in the value of total world output has increased to the same extent as the relative level of the money income of the inhabitants of our country has risen by comparison with that of other countries because of the gold inflow.[25] The change in this share will be due partly to the fact that the people of our country retain for their own use an absolutely greater part of their increased agricultural output and an absolutely and relatively greater share of their unchanged output of other exportable goods, and simultaneously can import more of other goods. After the conclusion of the transition period within which the gold movements have taken place and exerted their influence upon prices, the share of our country in the value of world output will therefore have risen by precisely as much as the value of the total output of the commodity whose output was initially increased, and the precondition for this increase in the share of world output was precisely a corresponding rise in the sum of money incomes in the country.[26]

The flow of gold from one country to another, and the rise in the 'money supply' thereby brought about in the latter, therefore merely constitute necessary intermediate steps in the process by which a movement of goods is called forth, steps which in the monetary economy must precede a change in the market positions of the two countries. The fact that the money income of a group of people linked together in a particular place rises proportionately, and indeed not merely in terms of that part of it composed of sales to foreigners but also that originating in the reciprocal exchange within this group, must result in a relatively greater quantity of money permanently remaining within this group. This phenomenon can certainly be described as an increase in the demand for money, but to do so offers no explanation of it. Nevertheless, it is precisely this description which renders it easy to conclude that these so-called changes in the demand for money are independent causes of the gold movements, and further that an adjustment of the quantity of money to the changed demand for it under all circumstances is a prerequisite for the maintenance of equilibrium.

But it is obvious that the function discharged by changes in the quantity of money available in the world (i.e. movements of gold into and out of its monetary use and the changes in gold output called forth by price movements) simply cannot be similar to that of movements of money from country to country, since the world's share in its own real income can hardly vary. In the preceding sections, it has also been shown that such changes in the quantity of money must give rise to disturbances in quite definite ways. These conclusions need only be added to here by looking at a somewhat different aspect of the same process, which stems from the arguments in the paragraphs above and clearly shows that changes in the total quantity of money can never contribute to the maintenance of equilibrium but on the contrary must always disrupt it.

For this purpose, suppose we vary somewhat the example chosen earlier. Assume now that the cheapening of agricultural output takes place not merely in one country but in the whole world, and the fall in price resulting from the increase in output gives rise to an expansion of gold output and associated with that an expansion in the quantity of money. Certainly, in this case as well a number of persons whose products and services are first demanded because of new gold inflows will initially enjoy a rise in their money incomes, which for them signifies a rise in their real income as well. But this nominal rise in income will not in any sense imply an enduring change in their market position, since similar rises in nominal income will take place successively with all other persons, and hence in the final analysis the share of social output falling to each individual will not have undergone any essential change.[27] Nevertheless, the temporary rise in the profitability of the sectors of production first affected by the gold inflow will have led to their expansion, an expansion which must show itself to have been unjustified as soon as the gold inflow slackens because of the rise in prices which takes place as a result of it. In the moment in which this extra demand slackens off, a part of the extra output stimulated by it will no longer be able to be sold at prices which cover costs but only at a loss. Hence the branches of production concerned will ultimately have to be contracted back to their level at the beginning of the gold inflow.

The final effect of the gold movements will therefore be that the economy, in return for temporarily giving up a larger part of its overall output to the gold producers, will once again achieve an equilibrium between supply and demand only after it has incurred certain losses. Apart from the losses caused by this disruption of equilibrium, every individual must see an additional source of loss in the fact that at least a part of the rise in his money income does not represent for him a means to an increased acquisition of goods but constitutes his ultimate payment. Hence the only recompense he obtains for that part of his output with which he has acquired it is that the stock of money he possesses has been uselessly enlarged. In contrast to the case of a movement of gold within the economy, therefore, changes in the total quantity of money in the economy do not provide a basis for the individual economic subjects to alter the extent to which they satisfy their needs. Rather, in this context the change in the quantity of money is the definitive and conclusive outcome; and so, when the money supply is expanded, the individual is forced to accept as final payment something which he had no desire to take as such.

Appendix: Necessary changes in prices and interest

The view has been advanced above that, with the growth of output as a result of technical improvements and the like, prices must fall if an excessive expansion of production is not to ensue. But it could be objected that it is already the function of the interest rate to maintain equilibrium between production for the future and that for the present, so that any further regulation of that relationship by the movement of prices is unnecessary. At first sight this appears to be an obvious objection, but it overlooks one problem: that in so far as the interest rate is most widely held to be a static phenomenon, what is involved are two completely different functions, which must be performed by the interest rate on the one hand and movements of prices on the other. The interest rate must exist because, for reasons which are not of any further interest here,[28] it is impossible to utilize current means of production to expand the output of goods producible in the distant future to such an extent that their price falls to that of the means of production employed to produce them. The interest rate, so to speak, serves to maintain equilibrium by preventing inappropriate expansion of future production. Yet there must be changes in prices if, because of alterations in production possibilities, disparities have emerged between the price of the means of production and the goods produced by them, disparities which will not necessarily have to persist because of capital scarcity. If the interest rate remains stable, and even if it is subject to variation, shifts in the relative price levels of present and future goods may also be necessary if equilibrium is to be maintained.

For example, suppose that a new technical process is invented that enables a greater quantity of output to be produced than hitherto from the given quantity of means of production in a country's single capital-utilizing branch of production. There may well be a rise in the interest rate, but this by itself will never be able to prevent a temporary overexpansion of the output of the product concerned if the price of that product does not also simultaneously fall. In the most favourable but by no means most likely case, the lowering of production costs may give rise to a lasting expansion of the demand for means of production and thus to a rise in interest rates. But this by itself would not outweigh the particular stimulus to production arising from the fact that a greater quantity of the product still saleable at the same price can temporarily be produced at the same cost. The rate of interest especially will not rise to a higher level, since a permanent difference must now open up between the price of the means of production and that of the outputs they can now produce. Even if the prices of the products do not fall, what was initially a very substantial difference between the two sets of prices must narrow in time to the level determined by the interest rate. But we have assumed precisely that the prices of the products do *not* fall. So the expansion of output proceeds until a point has been reached at which the intensified demand for means of production has driven their prices up to a corresponding level. It is immediately obvious that this expansion can take place only at the cost of a restriction of current consumption, which has been based wholly upon the higher level of money returns expected, but it will cease to operate as soon as this profit has been realized and paid out in purchasing articles of consumption. The price of current goods will then rise again, so that part of the expansion of output already undertaken will have become unprofitable and will therefore have to be retracted. What this implies in turn is merely that this temporary expansion was just as excessive as that which is called forth for instance by inflation.

Within the framework of this analysis, this exposition must suffice to show that the 'natural' movements of the interest rate in the case of a rise in physical productivity will not be enough to prevent an excessive expansion of output for the future, if a corresponding decline in produce prices does not take place simultaneously. The preceding remarks therefore cannot lay claim to constitute a complete treatment of the problem. All that was possible was to point out the direction in which is to be sought the solution of the questions arising in the analysis of the special problems discussed here. To provide adequate answers to them would be possible only within the framework of a complete theoretical system of economic theory. As a supplement to these remarks, it can only further be indicated that the essential difference between the independent character of interest on the one hand and the intertemporal grada-tions of prices on the other arises from the fact that, with respect to the direction in which they must move if equilibrium is to be maintained, they are not at all linked together in any particular way. According to circumstances, it is just as possible for the price of a given future good relative to that of a present good to rise as to fall at the same time as interest rates are rising. For example, as described above, an invention which raises physical productivity can necessitate a rise in the interest rate and a fall in prices; but equally well, enlargement of the stock of capital equipment at an unchanged level of technology can lead to both a fall in the interest rate and a fall in prices. It is well known that, with constant physical productivity (an invariable quantity of output producible by the given goods), a fall in interest must in fact lead to at least a relative decline in the price of the product as compared with that of the means of production. Hence it cannot occasion any further surprise that if physical productivity changes because of new discoveries and the like, quite definite shifts between the prices at successive points in time would become necessary to an ever greater extent, and indeed even with an unchanged interest rate, if equilibrium were to be restored.

Obviously this article has had to abstain from any discussion of the extent to which the two types of temporal differences in value – those expressed in interest and those expressed in the difference in the price of the same good at different points in time – can reciprocally influence or substitute for each other.[29] The fact that each of them fulfils a particular function means that it is basically improbable that a substitution of one for the other could be made without occasioning disturbances of equilibrium. As against that, it can certainly be assumed that each of them can discharge their function properly only if the other also corresponds to the equilibrium position.

Notes

1 This article is intended to form part of a hitherto uncompleted larger work on the goals of monetary policy, which concentrates upon the analysis of the demand often voiced for an artificial stabilization of the 'price level' with the means available to monetary policy. The necessity in this connection of inquiring more closely into some extremely complex problems in pure theory which have hitherto scarcely been dealt with in the literature, and whose only rarely undertaken systematic treatment is as a rule inadequate, makes it seem to me to be desirable to provisionally publish by itself this attempt at a presentation of some hitherto neglected interconnections. In this context, I can only emphasize that it is above all the way in which the problems are raised in this article which seems to me to be important, independent of the solutions to them proposed and still more of what are certainly deficiencies in detail

still present in the argument. Certainly, I need not further point out that the results of such an isolated analysis of what is so important a theoretical problem cannot claim to offer an adequate solution to practical questions of currency policy. To the extent that in this article attempts are made to apply its results to concrete phenomena, these can really be regarded only as a contribution to their understanding, not as an adequate explanation of them.

2 At least one extremely idealized case of an economy functioning in time could be adequately explained only if it were also possible to assume that infinitely short, consecutive economic periods were completely the same. But since this is basically excluded by the essentially discontinuous flow of most economic processes, it cannot be applied at all in relation to the propositions derived from the assumption discussed above.

3 Cf. in this connection especially L. Mises, *Theorie des Geldes und der Umlaufsmittel*, 2nd, newly revised edn, Munich and Leipzig, 1924, pp. 151ff.

4 Unfortunately, to my knowledge Fetter has dealt with the problem of *time value* only in the two editions of his textbook in a way imposed upon him by the exigencies of that form, but has never given a more detailed exposition of it. In general, Fetter's earlier expression *time value* also appears to get closer to the nub of the question than the phrase *time preference* which for other reasons he substituted for it. The most valuable comments are nevertheless to be found precisely in the second book referred to below, in which he restricts in this way the more general expression he originally used, but deals with time more searchingly as one of the aspects to be considered in decisions as to economic allocations. See F. A. Fetter, *The Principles of Economics*, New York, 1904, and later editions; *Economic Principles*, New York 1915, and later editions, vol. I, pp. 20, 29 and especially pp. 101ff. and pp. 235–77. Reference should also be made to the most recent and very interesting essay by Fetter which became known to me only after I had completed this article: 'Interest Theory and Price Movements', *The American Economic Review*, vol. XVII (1927), no. 1, Supplement, pp. 62ff. Hints at similar considerations, whose only purpose was to prepare the ground for his well-known theory of the underestimation of future needs, can also already be found in E. von Böhm-Bawerk, *Positive Theorie des Kapitals*, 3rd. edn, Innsbruck, e.g. pp. 439 and 587ff. [English edition, (*Capital and Interest*, 3 volumes, trans. G. D. Huncke and H. F. Sennholz, South Holland, Illinois, 1959), vol. II, pp. 265 and 347ff., respectively (ed.)].

5 Cf. R. Streller, *Statik und Dynamik in der theoretischen Nationalökonomie*, Leipzig, 1926.

6 In addition, it must be obvious that, if a reciprocal dependence between economic activity at different points in time is to exist, the possibility of employing the same good either at one point or at another for the satisfaction of needs and wants must always exist.

7 Cf. my article 'Zum Problemstellung der Zinstheorie', *Archiv für Sozialwissenschaft und Sozialpolitik*, vol. 58, (1927) pp. 517ff., for one result of the comparison of the utilities which can be attained at two separate

points in time, which only apparently contradicts what is written above. [This volume pp. 55–70 (ed.).]

8 But it is not necessary, as is often assumed, for the values attributed by those participating in exchange to any arbitrarily chosen unit of the good to be exchanged at both of the two points in time in question to be precisely inversely related, therefore e.g. A values some quantity of the good x more highly today than in a year's time, while B values this same quantity of the good available to him today less than the same quantity in prospect for him a year later. Rather, the precondition for an exchange to be possible is merely that the one market participant values any quantity of one good (i.e. in our case, any quantity of the good at one point in time) more highly than any quantity of the other good (i.e. of the same good at the other point in time), while for the other market participant the valuation of this arbitrarily chosen quantity of the good is the opposite, or – what amounts to the same thing – that there is a divergence between the marginal utility of the two goods to the two persons. The outcome of the exchange conducted to its economic limits is then that, for all arbitrarily chosen units of the two goods (or of the one good at two points in time) the divergence between the respective marginal utilities is the same for both individuals, or – as this can probably be expressed most simply – *the marginal differences are equated.*

9 For the relation between this problem and that of interest, see the Appendix to this article.

10 Only during the correction of this work did I receive the article by G. P. Watkins, 'Parity in the exchange of future money and future commodities', *Quarterly Journal of Economics*, vol. 42 (1927–28), pp. 366ff., in which a similar answer is given to the same question raised in another context.

11 Cf. Mises, *op. cit.*, pp. 151ff.

12 In general, the above considerations are completely analogous to those with which it can be shown that in all cases in which a commodity exchange between two countries takes place, a definite relationship, a state of equilibrium, must exist not merely between the existing prices of the goods exchanged between the two countries but also between the prices of all the other commodities in them. This is not manifested in the same relationship having to exist between the prices of all commodities in the two countries but in the fact that any change in the price of any one commodity in one of the countries can basically occasion a change in the price of any other commodity in the other country.

13 Cf. Mises, *op. cit.*, pp. 151ff.

14 In order not to overburden the analysis, the reader is once again referred to the Appendix to this article for treatment of the connections between this phenomenon and that of interest which have been neglected here.

15 The lack of an established, more accurate term makes it necessary to use in this context what is really a juristic rather than an economic concept: *Währung* (literally: currency), though this conflicts with the use made of the term elsewhere in this work. The expression also immediately used directly above, 'commodity money' (*Sachgeld*) (Mises) is too

narrow, since it does not include the various types of credit money which also fall within the category of tied currency. Cf. Mises, *op. cit.*, pp. 33ff. To be completely accurate, one would perhaps have to speak of a money tied in value to a quantity of metal for which it can be exchanged (*stoffwertgebundenem Geld*).

16 Cf. the remarks made by C. M. Walsh in his valuable book *The Funda-mental Problem in Monetary Science*, New York, 1903; on the representatives of the *cost standard*, *ibid.*, especially pp. 235ff.

17 G. Haberler, *Der Sinn der Indexzahlen, Eine Untersuchung über den Begriff des Preisniveau und die Methoden seiner Messung*, Tübingen, 1927, pp. 112ff.

18 Cf. H. L. Moore, 'A moving equilibrium of demand and supply', *Quarterly Journal of Economics*, vol. 39 (1924/5) pp. 357ff.

19 That a connection normally exists between rising prices and rising production on the one hand, and between falling prices and falling production on the other hand, is shown by experience, though it is by no means always necessarily so. But this furnishes a beautiful example of how dangerous it is to derive theoretical propositions from the results of statistical investigations or even to seek to base practical demands upon them. Even the highest correlation coefficient between movements in production and in prices cannot prove that rising production can take place only if prices are rising or that falling prices bring about falling production. Yet it is precisely from such considerations that efforts to stabilize the value of money derive their strongest support, though even the points emphasized in this article show how dubious they are. The false reasoning which led to their adoption was that, if a rise in prices led to a rise in output, and a fall in prices to fall in output, the price level must be maintained stable to eliminate all influences upon production originating from money. But naturally the aim of efforts at stabilization, to achieve certainty as to the future structure of prices, can least of all be achieved by seeking to prevent those price changes which are necessary for the maintenance of equilibrium in production, and such efforts thereby call forth disturbances of equilibrium which must ultimately lead to intensified price movements.

20 R. G. Hawtrey, *Currency and Credit*, London, 1919; 2nd edn, 1923. Also in German translation: *Währung und Kredit*, edited from the 2nd English edition by F. Oppenheimer, translated by L. Oppenheimer, Jena, 1926.

21 L. A. Hahn, *Volkswirtschaftliche Theorie des Bankkredits*, Tübingen, 1920, and later editions.

22 For those advancing this demand, see Walsh, *op. cit.*, p. 5.

23 In this connection, see the Appendix to this article, pp. 111ff.

24 Cf. J. W. Angell, *The Theory of International Prices, History, Criticism and Assessment*, Cambridge, 1926.

25 It must be noted that these remarks convey nothing at all as to the extent of the movement of the prices of individual goods or of all goods, especially also of the agricultural goods whose costs initially fell. They do not do so because the change in national income was wholly due to simultaneous changes in prices and the quantities of goods consumed. All that can be said with certainty is that the overall price of the total product, which changed because of the initial rise in the quantity

produced in one branch of production, has risen by just as much as total income.

26 At this point, where my concern with this complex of problems is subordinate to a more particular inquiry, the question as to whether the rise in the sum of individual incomes bears a fixed numerical relationship to the newly added money can be left open. The question is also uninteresting, because, in consequence of the change in individual prices, no measuring-rod for the increase in real national income is available. Only the change in the share of the individual countries in the value of world product is basically capable of quantification, and this in turn could be derived from the relative change in the total money income of the individual countries. Yet the latter is immune from any measurement.

It may nevertheless be noted that the propositions advanced in the text shows that the view of the mercantilists as to the significance of the relative supply of gold of the various countries as an indication of their wealth are not so basically erroneous as is customarily believed, even if the maxims of economic policy they derived from their imperfect insight into the interrelationships were naturally of no use at all in achieving the goals they desired.

A view which is in many respects related to that presented in the text above is to be found in F. W. Taussig, *Principles of Economics*, 2nd. edn, New York, 1915 and later, vol. I, ch. 35, section 1, pp. 502ff.

27 Cf. Mises, *op. cit.*, pp. 116ff.

28 See also my article, 'Zur Problemstellung der Zinstheorie', *loc. cit.* [This volume pp. 55–70, (ed.).]

29 See also the well-known relevant works by Irving Fisher, especially *Appreciation and Interest* (Publications of the American Economic Association, vol. XI, no. 4), New York, 1896, and *The Rate of Interest*, New York, 1906.

FIVE

THE FATE OF THE GOLD STANDARD*

There has been much talk about the breakdown of the gold standard, particularly in Britain where, to the astonishment of every foreign observer, the abandonment of the gold standard was very widely welcomed as a release from an irksome constraint. However, it can scarcely be doubted that the renewed monetary problems of almost the whole world have nothing to do with the tendencies inherent in the gold standard, but on the contrary stem from the persistent and continuous attempts from many sides over a number of years to prevent the gold standard from functioning whenever it began to reveal tendencies which were not desired by the country in question. Hence it was by no means the economically strong countries such as America and France whose measures rendered the gold standard inoperative, as is frequently assumed, but the countries in a relatively weak position, at the head of which was Britain, who eventually paid for their transgression of the 'rules of the game' by the breakdown of their gold standard.

That the otherwise conservative managements of the central banks deviated in a relatively light-hearted manner from the traditional rules of monetary policy can be attributed to the influence of new ideas on monetary policy, propagated by the academic fraternity, which obtained wide circulation during the post-war years. In order to understand what actually happened, therefore, a brief consideration of the origin and significance of these new ideas is necessary.

The rise of the concept of stabilization

What must be remembered first of all is that, as a result of the general paper money inflation in Europe and the associated drift of

* First published as 'Das Schicksal der Goldwährung' in *Deutsche Volkswirt* (February 1932), in two parts; no. 20, pp. 642–5 and no. 21, pp. 677–81.

118

gold to America after the end of the war, gold was devalued to such an extent that precisely at the time when the return to the gold standard was the most pressing need in most European countries, in America the fact that even gold did not constitute a completely satisfactory basis for a currency in all circumstances was felt more strongly than ever before. Little attention was paid to the fact that even this fall in the value of gold had only occurred because of the abandonment of the gold standard in Europe, and would never have reached the stage that it did had not the few countries which had maintained gold payments used the cessation of competition for gold so as also to inflate, though at a lower rate than those which had departed from gold.

The second important factor which determined the development of ideas on monetary policy was that the above-mentioned facts were partly contributory to the extraordinary influence exercised by two particular representatives of the mechanistic Quantity Theory of Money and of the concept of a systematic stabilization of the price level, Professors Irving Fisher and Gustav Cassel. The fluctuations in the value of money mentioned above necessarily aroused wide interest in Professor Fisher's proposal for stabilizing the value of gold, which he had been advocating for a long time; and the lively propaganda which was being circulated, particularly by the Stable Money Association which he had founded, had succeeded in making the concept of price stabilization as the objective of monetary policy into a virtually unassailable dogma. Professor Cassel, who deserved the greatest credit for the stabilization of European currencies, contributed a further, extraordinarily effective argument in favour of the policy of stabilization, the influence of which upon actual developments it is impossible to overestimate.

This was his prediction that gold production was not adequate for the annual increase of 3 per cent in the world stock of monetary gold which, on his calculations, would be required to maintain stability in the price level.

Fear of the imminent shortage of gold, and the desire to arrive at a systematic policy for stabilizing the value of money, gave rise to two further ideas which dominated the period, and were expressed particularly in the resolutions of the conference on international economic relations in Genoa in 1922; a preference for the *gold exchange standard* as the object of stabilization in individual countries, and the recommendation of '*Cooperation between Central Banks*'. Both desires were to become extremely significant for the development of monetary policy over the next few years. Perhaps it is therefore appropriate at this point to also name the man who acquired special influence as the propagator of the ideas expressed by the Genoa Conference – even if he were not, as one might suspect, its instigator: Mr R. G. Hawtrey of the British Treasury. Together with the two men already mentioned, and the most influential member of the group to whom we shall shortly refer, Mr Hawtrey seems to be one of the stabilization theorists referred to above, to whose influence the willingness of the managements of the central banks to depart more than ever before from the policy rules traditionally followed by such banks can be attributed.

Two further points of antecedent history must be recalled before we can attempt to understand developments during the last six years. At the end of 1923, J. M. Keynes's *'Tract on Monetary Reform'* appeared. Keynes, who had risen very rapidly to international fame by his writings on the Peace Treaty, not only associated himself in this pamphlet with the group who argued for stabilization of the value of money, but also in my opinion set in circulation an erroneous interpretation of contemporary events which gained general acceptance in Britain, and formed one of the bases of the monetary policy which ultimately led to the suspension of convertibility. Keynes maintained that the American Federal Reserve Banks were pursuing a systematic policy of 'sterilising' incoming gold, i.e. preventing the monetary circulation in America from increasing in accordance with the increase in the supply of gold and thereby putting the adjustment mechanism of the gold standard out of operation. Although this assertion was immediately and categorically opposed by the American experts (particularly by Dr B. M. Anderson), and, as we shall see, the Federal Reserve System certainly did not err in the direction of a policy which was too restrictive in the period which has since elapsed, the assertion that America had continuously contravened the recognized rules of the gold standard was not exposed to any criticism in Britain. The conclusion drawn from this was that Britain had become powerless with respect to the gold withdrawals, since America appeared to be a bottomless pit in which the gold of the whole world could be swallowed up without affecting the level of prices there.

The last point which must be briefly mentioned concerns the Federal Reserve Board. In its Annual Report for 1923, which quickly became famous, it rejected the policy of a complete stabilization of the price level. Nevertheless, it joined the stabilization theorists in as much as it expressed its conviction that the intensity of crises and depression could be substantially lessened, not only if every boom were checked at the appropriate time by raising the discount rate, a proposition which could hardly be disputed, but also that every recession in general business activity could be immediately counteracted by a sharp cut in the discount rate. This belief is of great significance for an understanding of its subsequent policy. For as we shall see, the Federal Reserve Board has not merely strictly adhered to this programme, but in addition, it may be noted, the demands of the extreme representatives of the concept of stabilization were continually urged upon it during the Congressional enquiries ('stabilization hearings') which took place throughout the whole of the subsequent period.

The beginning of Britain's difficulties

The actual problems in whose solution these ideas were to play something of a fateful role began with Britain's return to the gold standard in 1925. Whether it was wise to return to the pre-war parity with the aid of a difficult process of deflation is extremely questionable. The events which have since occurred make it seem likely that Britain would have done better to have remembered Ricardo's advice. More than a hundred years previously, he wrote that he would never recommend a government to ease back to par a currency whose value had declined by 30 per cent. By doing so Britain must have got itself into a very difficult position, since there is always a certain length of time before domestic prices adapt to the new level of foreign exchange rates. Furthermore, as a result of stabilization at the conclusion of the process of deflation, prices in Britain were above the international level at the same time when domestic prices in the various continental countries were below the world level as they gradually stabilized at the end of the process of inflation and would remain so for many years to come. If the gold standard were to be permanently adhered to by Britain, the deflation would therefore have had to continue until the British domestic price level had also reached an equilibrium with the rest of the world. The British, however, wanted less than anything to do this, and the new ideas of stabilizing prices and the economy as the aim of monetary policy were welcomed as justifying deviation from the orthodox rules of monetary policy. The situation in which

121

the British economy found itself doubtless exhibited all the symptoms which, according to the doctrines of the stabilization theorists, made a policy of credit expansion appear advisable. Given the existence of falling prices, increasing unemployment and the persistently unfavourable position of the most important industries, even the years before 1929 looked like depression years in Britain.

For those managing monetary policy, this amounted to a serious dilemma. It was in fact solved, in the years which elapsed until the final breakdown of the gold standard, by the Bank of England's restricting itself to the minimum of measures unavoidable for the maintenance of a momentary, highly unstable currency equilibrium, and utilizing every opportunity to avoid the tightening of credit dictated by the international situation. In diametric opposition to the basic concept of the gold standard, the gold which was draining away was constantly being compensated for by bank loans, so that the overall circulation was kept stable at a time when it would have had to diminish if a genuine gold standard had existed.[1] It is only natural that in this situation the Bank of England became the most enthusiastic protagonist of 'co-operation between central banks', which was to have released it completely from these unpleasant necessities. The discussion as to the relative significance of national determination of monetary policy came increasingly to the fore in Britain during these years and reached a peak with the publication of the report of the Macmillan Committee, which also represented a great success for the nationalistic trend in monetary policy led by Keynes.

The dangers of the policy of stabilization

However, the theoretical foundations of all of this are very weak. Without mentioning its other shortcomings, the theory of stabilization of prices had been developed for a closed economy and could not readily be applied to a country which is a member of an international system. Yet Britain in particular was the country least able to look upon her domestic situation as something fundamentally different from her international relations. Her problems could be said to arise in the first place from the deterioration in her international situation, which in turn was the result of a level of prices and wages which was relatively too high even after the deflation. In the period since 1925 Britain's international position deteriorated still further, with the futile policy of stabilization followed by the Bank of England making no small contribution to this. There can hardly be any doubt that during this period, at least in the United States, the rate of progress in production technology and the associated reduction in costs was substantially faster than in Britain. The existence of a common currency system, and especially the presence of the gold standard in both countries, led to the result that even if an equilibrium between the domestic value of currency in Britain and in the United States had initially existed, there must be an enduring tendency for gold to move to America, thereby inevitably creating constant pressure on the British level of prices. These processes are a necessary element in the mechanism by which the distribution of the world's gold is adjusted to the changes in the conditions of production.

It hardly needs mentioning that the payment of war debts constituted a further highly significant factor which necessitated a relative fall in prices and therefore a contraction of credit in Europe as compared with America, even if in Britain's case its significance was essentially smaller since Britain was merely the place through which these payments passed. The attempt, in the face of all these circumstances, to nevertheless avoid the inevitable fall in the national level of prices, would not have been relatively successful for so long if it had not met with sympathetic co-operation and efforts along the same lines in the United States because of the supremacy there of the concept of stabilization. The already mentioned fall in costs which occurred in America should have led, if it had not been compensated for by an enormous expansion of credit, to a corresponding fall in prices. On the one hand, this fall in prices would not have harmed production in any way, since it would merely have resulted from the fall in costs, and on the other hand, it would have forced the ultimately unavoidable reduction in costs in Europe by absorbing Europe's gold. That such a fall in prices corresponding to the reduction in costs can take place without any detriment to production was clearly demonstrated by developments in the United States between 1925 and 1927, when there was a boom despite continuously falling prices. At that time, i.e. until 1927, it seemed an obvious conclusion to draw from the fall in prices in particular, that the United States would succeed in avoiding an inflationary expansion of credit, and thereby the following crisis as well, and thus in perpetuating the favourable economic conditions. It became evident, however, that even before 1927 prices were being prevented from falling to the full extent of the reduction in costs by a systematic expansion of credit, so that in 1927 the threat of a reaction emerged. And the first signs of this reaction gave rise to an enormous acceleration of this expansion of credit for which the policy being followed by Europe and particularly Britain gave America the opportunity, and which led directly to the crisis of 1929.

America and co-operation between central banks

That the United States did not, as is frequently maintained, sterilize incoming gold until 1927, but made it the basis for a quite lavish expansion of credit, is a fact which emerges from all the statistics but particularly from the development of the deposits in the member banks of the Federal Reserve System between 1925 and 1927, which rose from approximately 18 to over 20 thousand million dollars. The unmistakeable signs of a reversal in the boom which made itself felt in 1927 are, nevertheless, the best indication that the United States expanded credit during these years more than was good for it. This expansion would probably have been less if the sustained 'cheap money policy' followed by the Bank of England had not freed the Federal Reserve System from any worries that excessive gold withdrawals would occur. From 1927 onwards, however, the significance of this factor can hardly be in doubt. The fact that the Federal Reserve Banks were rekindling a boom which had passed over into a decline by further huge injections of credit, and could then maintain it for another two years at a previously unheard of level, was possible only because the European Central Banks were willing to follow the path of credit expansion. However the moment they began this policy movements in the opposite direction began, but despite this the draining away of gold came to a standstill after a few months. Yet the Federal Reserve Banks were not forced to abandon their policy of expansion. The conscious co-operation between central banks certainly played a great role at this critical moment. It has even been maintained that, at the conference of the central banks which was held in August 1927 in Washington, it was agreed that in future no central bank would be permitted to withdraw gold from another without its consent,[2] though this hardly seems credible to me.

Yet whatever form this agreement may in fact have taken, there can be no doubt that it was because of such tacit or explicit co-operation during the period 1927 to 1929 that an expansion of credit was made possible which would not have been possible under the automatic gold standard of the pre-war years.

Given this co-operation, the accusation that the United States had caused Britain's problems by hoarding gold is absurd; all it means is that America should have stimulated inflation even more and thereby caused an even greater crisis. It is asking rather a lot of America that it should single-handedly, and at the cost of severe jolts to its productive apparatus, have brought about international equilibrium exclusively by credit expansion on its part, while no attempt was made to implement a corresponding tightening of credit on the part of the other countries. The fact that this claim could be made at all can only be attributed to the dominance of the concept of stabilization, which was based on the idea that an expansion of credit which serves merely to keep the level of prices stable could not have any detrimental effects, even if it was simply a question of the domestic price level within that member of an international system whose productivity was rising most rapidly. It could equally well have been asserted that no detrimental effects could flow from an expansion of credit which was just barely adequate to stabilize the price of that commodity whose cost of production was declining most rapidly. The fact that this point has fatal implications for the concept of stabilization and that the present crisis is attributable above all to persistent inflation until 1929, an inflation which moreover was not even sufficient to keep the level of prices completely stable, is generally recognized in America today. The best proof of this is afforded by the recent report by a committee of the Federal Reserve System, which recommends a substantial tightening up of the existing regulations on reserves for the system's member banks to prevent a return to such inflation.

The accusation that France systematically hoarded gold seems at first sight to be more likely to be correct. France did pursue an extremely cautious foreign policy after the franc stabilized at a level which considerably underdevalued it with respect to its domestic purchasing power, and prevented an expansion of credit proportional to the amount of gold coming in. Nevertheless, France did not prevent her monetary circulation from increasing by the very same amount as that of the gold inflow – and this alone is necessary for the gold standard to function. The only thing which must be said about France's monetary policy in this context is therefore that France had learnt from the experiences of the other European countries. After they had at first permitted a very rapid adjustment

125

of their price level to that of world prices and the associated expansion of credit once their currencies had stabilized, they were all stricken by a more or less severe 'stabilisation crisis'. France's policy, however, actually enabled it to avoid any such crisis. Here, too, it was the attempt to ward off the danger of inflation stimulated by Britain's monetary policy in particular which determined France's monetary policy.

Britain's 'gold shortage'

For the period before 1929, it can scarcely be seriously maintained that the economic development of the world was hindered in any sense by a shortage of gold. On the contrary, we have during this period experienced an expansion of credit to an extent such as hardly existed previously in countries on the gold standard. It is therefore also highly improbable that since that time the world's gold reserves, which were adequate for an expansion of credit of this extent, should suddenly have become inadequate, and that a shortage of gold should be the cause of the present decline in prices. In fact, there was only a single country in which there was a continuous gold shortage at that time, i.e. Britain. Britain's gold shortage could be attributed basically to the same cause which can lead to a shortage of money for any private person, in that she was continually spending more than she earned. If Britain had not been the country from which the rest of the world had been accustomed to draw its views on monetary policy for over a century, it would hardly have come about that the existence of a gold shortage in Britain would readily have been accepted throughout the whole world as sufficient proof of the need for a policy to combat the gold shortage. Britain's dominant influence in the field of monetary policy, which had been a blessing for the rest of the world so long as Britain was in a strong position, must become detrimental to the world as soon as Britain's international position became unfavourable. For the gold standard and, indeed, any international standard, merely constitutes the means by which changes in the relative economic position of a country work out their effects on its share of world income. Consequently, whilst every country which is in a favourable position continually advocates sound principles of monetary policy, opinion will always turn against the gold standard in a country whose international relations are deteriorating. Yet this is merely the means by which tendencies work themselves out, tendencies which cannot in any case be eliminated.

It was not a big step from the desire to be released from the unpleasant necessity of adapting the general standard of living to the lower level of national income by reductions in wages and prices, to a theoretical justification of a monetary policy which rendered inoperative the tendencies of the gold standard in that direction. A special treatise would be required to provide a more detailed exposition and criticism of the errors which are already widespread today with respect to the functioning of the international gold standard and the mechanism of international capital movements, errors which are at the basis of the policy followed by the Bank of England. The most important error is the distinction drawn between temporary movements of gold, which cannot be attributed to deep-rooted causes but merely to momentary circumstances and hence should not be allowed to bring about any changes in the domestic volume of credit, and 'genuine' movements of capital, which should provide the only occasion for effecting changes in the rate of interest. What is left unexplained in this is why movements of gold should under any circumstances represent movements of capital which are not genuine. Nor is it explained why a country which is unable to cover its current obligations from current output and is therefore required to pay partly in cash, i.e. to offset the deficit on current account by capital payments, should nevertheless still be in a position after doing so to make just as much capital available to domestic industry for investment purposes as previously. These theories are neither new nor do their advocates take the trouble to show that the refutation of them provided by the classical economists more than a hundred years ago, a refutation which was finally held to be definitive, is unfounded. Yet this did not prevent them from being joyfully seized upon by those conducting policy (*Praktikern*) and put into practice. Indeed, it can be said that monetary policy was conducted on the basis of gold theories even before they had been clearly formulated. J. M. Keynes's *Treatise on Money*, which represents a grandiose attempt to justify this policy, and the report of the Macmillan Committee which is formulated entirely in the spirit of Keynes and predominantly influenced by him, are much less revolutionary in this respect than may appear if they are compared with the traditional rules of monetary policy. What they essentially did was merely to elevate to the status of principle the violations of the traditional rules of the gold standard which the

Bank of England has been continuously perpetrating during the last six years.

Of course, the Bank of England was not alone in its efforts during this period to deprive the movements of gold of their effect. Britain is merely the most important country in which such attempts were made and the only one in which this policy was not only consistently pursued but in which the attempt was also made to justify it theoretically. In order to explain why these attempts became so general after the war, one factor must be mentioned here which had seduced central banks into undertaking such attempts: the general disappearance of gold from circulation and the concentration of the entire gold supply in the central banks, in a word the general introduction of the system of the gold bullion standard. So long as gold was in circulation, and gold for export therefore did not have to be withdrawn directly from the central banks, a reduction in the circulation of money occurred directly as a result of these gold exports, and the central bank, which might not be directly affected at all by this, thus had no grounds for or temptation towards compensating for this by expanding the volume of credit. The shortage of money in circulation led much more directly to an increase in market interest rates and thereby in the long run to an increase in the official bank rate as well. If, on the other hand, the gold for export is withdrawn exclusively from the central bank, it faces an extremely strong temptation not to let a reduction in the credit base take place but to compensate directly for the gold drain by expanding the volume of credit extended.

In practice, this procedure was usually summarized in two well-known rules which in themselves are entirely correct, but which were interpreted in a way which ran completely counter to the meaning which their classical authors had given them. The two propositions were, firstly, that the purpose of movements of gold is the adjustment of the international trade balance, and secondly, that gold reserves are there to be used if needed. But the first proposition must not be taken to mean that the movements of gold represent the final settlement of international imbalances, but merely that they are one element in the mechanism which leads ultimately to an effective payment in goods. Nor does the second proposition imply that gold reserves are held to avoid the necessity to limit the domestic monetary circulation if gold leaves the country. Both propositions are valid for the case of a gold bullion standard and the case of a mixed monetary circulation in exactly the same way in which movements of gold would work themselves out in the case in which gold alone was in circulation. It was not in vain that the great monetary theorists of the classical period from Ricardo onwards always insisted that a non-metallic circulation of money ought always to be so controlled that the total volume of all money in circulation changes in just the same way as would happen if gold alone were in circulation. The only effect of any attempt to compensate for movements of gold by changes in the volume of credit in the opposite direction can be to render the mechanism of international capital movements inoperative and also ultimately to smash the gold standard, the instrument which should serve to make them possible.

Stabilization policy and the crisis

It is quite obvious that the assertion that the artificial prevention of the fall in prices, induced by the reduction in costs, had a detrimental effect, relates to the period up to 1929 and is not meant to depict the fall in prices which has occurred since then as innocuous. On the contrary, this fall in prices is precisely one of the most severe and harmful consequences of the stabilization policy following during the previous period. Instead of prices being allowed to fall slowly, to the full extent that would have been possible without inflicting damage on production, such volumes of additional credit were pumped into circulation that the level of prices was roughly stabilized even in those countries in which faster technical progress gave rise to a tendency for the level of prices to fall in relation to the rest of the world. Whether such inflation merely serves to keep prices stable, or whether it leads to an increase in prices, makes little difference. Experience has now confirmed what theory was already aware of; that such inflation can also lead to production being misdirected to such an extent that, in the end, a breakdown in the form of a crisis becomes inevitable. This, however, also proves the impossibility of achieving in practice an absolute stabilization of the level of prices in a dynamic economy. The maintenance of stability, at a time when the natural tendency was downwards, finally led to a collapse of prices which doubtless led to their falling far below that level which would have been reached if they had fallen slowly throughout the whole period – in precisely the same way as, under otherwise stationary conditions, the reaction to an inflation which was expressed in an increase in prices can lead to a fall in them to far below their original level.

Although there can be no doubt that the fall in prices since 1929 has been extremely harmful, this nevertheless does not mean that the attempts made since then to combat it by a systematic expansion of credit have not done more harm than good. In any case, it is a fact that the present crisis is marked by the first attempt on a large scale to revive the economy immediately after the sudden reversal of the upswing, by a systematic policy of lowering the interest rate accompanied by all other possible measures for preventing the normal process of liquidation, and that as a result the depression has assumed more devastating forms and lasted longer than ever before. The measures of monetary policy themselves, particularly in the form in which they were pursued by the Federal Reserve Banks most clearly, were in complete accordance with the prescriptions of the stabilization theorists. They were supplemented in America by all kinds of non-monetary policy measures, dictated almost without exception by the desire to 'maintain purchasing power', and, although such measures were originally based on the underconsumption theories of crises, obtained weighty support from the stabilization theorists. From President Hoover's appeal to employers in the autumn of 1929 to avoid dismissing workers up to the recent founding of the Reconstruction Finance Corporation, which is supposed to help firms which have fallen into difficulties to avoid collapse, one measure for preventing or delaying the normal process of liquidation followed another in the United States.

Even if it is hardly possible to offer proof for this assertion, given the space at my disposal here, what must still be said is that it is quite probable that we would have been over the worst long ago, and that the fall in prices would never have assumed such disastrous proportions, if the process of liquidation had been allowed to take its course after the crisis of 1929. Only a rather superficial explanation of the crisis, like that advanced by most stabilization theorists, could have led to the assumption that it was possible to avoid a thorough reorganization of the whole production apparatus. Only if it was believed that the cause of the crisis lay in a process of monetary deflation alone, and if no attention at all was paid to the direction which production had taken in the previous boom, could it be believed that the crisis could be overcome by what is in fact a fight against the symptoms. But if, as can scarcely be doubted, the immediate cause of the crisis lies precisely in this real misdirection of production, and the process of deflation represents only a secondary phenomenon caused by this, an element in the process by which production is necessarily forced to readjust, then the measures which the stabilization theorists advocate for preventing the process of liquidation can only have the effect of significantly prolonging the depression and the fall in prices.

No other reason at all exists to make the gold standard responsible in any way for the present fall in prices. On the contrary, all the factors outlined which do really appear to have played a causal role represent an attempt to put out of commission the normal mechanism of the capitalist economy in general and the gold standard in particular. It is, however, at this point necessary to briefly examine one argument, probably the weakest of its type moreover, which has hitherto not been explicitly mentioned but to which an implicit answer has certainly already been given, namely the allegedly harmful effects flowing from the existing unequal distribution of gold throughout the world. Anyone who has followed the arguments up to this point will have little difficult in realizing that what is at issue here is in fact a result of the circumstances that have already been discussed, an effect of the failure of a number of countries to adhere to the rules of the gold standard, and not an independent cause. The pressure which today emanates from this unequal distribution only represents the inevitable intensification of those tendencies which these countries have for so long resisted.

The breakdown of the gold standard in Britain

The world crisis and the process of deflation to which it gave rise did not make the Bank of England's situation any easier, and probably lessened still further its determination to intensify the domestic difficulties by maintaining interest rates at a high level. After 1929, it vied with the Federal Reserve Banks in lowering the interest rate, which fell from 6½ per cent to 3 per cent within a few months. The situation only took a significant turn for the worse, however, when the Bank of England, after maintaining the rate at 3 per cent for twelve months, reduced it further to 2½ per cent in May 1931 and maintained it at that level until well into July. This, at a time when the collapse of the Austrian Credit-Anstalt had already sent up the first storm signals, and although huge withdrawals of gold were already beginning. From this time on, hardly any serious attempts were made to save the pound, and the Bank of England appeared to have reconciled itself to the fact that convertibility would have to be given up sooner or later. Only this can explain why neither the Bank's own gold reserves, nor the loans which were gradually being raised in France and America, were utilized to restrict the domestic circulation by selling these gold assets. What is more, to free the Bank from effecting the reduction in circulation that would otherwise have been necessary, the legal limit for the fiduciary note issue was raised at the end of July, and during July the volume of notes actually in circulation was increased to an extent greater than could be justified by seasonal considerations. It is obvious that, in these circumstances, the credits available for intervention purposes must eventually have been exhausted without having any effect. This apparent lack of determination to do something to protect the pound would in itself probably have led to considerable withdrawals of credit. But when, in September, the well-known additional shocks to confidence increased withdrawals still further, the lack of any struggle as the end came could not have been expected even on the basis of the policy pursued by the Bank of England in the previous years. That it suspended cash payments when the official discount rate stood at no higher than 4½ per cent is surely the most surprising event in monetary policy of the previous era, and the one which stands in greatest contradiction to the traditional rules of monetary policy.

This abandonment of the gold standard undoubtedly implies a final break with the unique tradition of more than two hundred years, on the basis of which Britain has repeatedly returned to the gold standard at the cost of great sacrifices, even after periods of temporary shock to its currency unit. This time the sacrifices which had been made since 1921 were in vain, because the responsible authorities were unwilling or unable to exact what probably would have been the smaller sacrifices necessary to ensure the long-term position of the pound. The greatest responsibility for this, however, must be borne by those who initially opposed the return to the gold standard. For although their position was justifiable at that time, they did not abandon it even when the gold standard had been restored at its former parity, and fought with the utmost vigour against all the measures necessary if that standard were to be finally consolidated. It is beyond all doubt that they found an increasingly more receptive hearing within the management of the Bank. If one wanted to describe the abandonment of the gold standard in Britain as 'the economic consequences of Mr Keynes', and there are many reasons to do so, I believe that even today J. M. Keynes would still regard such a statement not as criticism but as praise.

The prospects for the gold standard

However urgent a speedy, general restoration of a free, unmanipulated gold standard must therefore seem from these points of view, the prospects of Britain's returning in the near future to the gold standard, and of course this would be the prerequisite for a general restoration of the gold standard, are unfortunately very small. The same representatives of a nationalistic monetary policy who, while the gold standard existed, were successful in preventing the international influences to which it gave expression from becoming effective in Britain and leading to the restoration of equilibrium, are now resisting to the utmost Britain's reassumption of the 'fetter' which she has successfully thrown off. Everyone talks about conditions under which Britain alone would be able to return to the gold standard, and these conditions usually amount to no more than the fact that Britain can do so only if the other countries offered her a guarantee that in future she will be able to maintain the gold standard permanently even if she continues to break its rules. In the meantime, the British cannot see that every international currency, every system of stable foreign exchange rates (and in the long run Britain can do without this less than any other country), would impose upon Britain the same unpleasant necessity for a domestic credit contraction from time to time for reasons which have their origin abroad. The hope is simultaneously voiced, perhaps with greater justification, that in the not-too-distant future America and consequently the rest of the world would stimulate inflation so that the value of gold would be reduced to such an extent that Britain could honourably return to the gold standard without sacrifice, and perhaps even at the former parity. In the meantime, plans are being devised for an 'Empire currency' – but in all probability nothing at all will come of this for a long time yet.

Even a *de facto* stabilization of the pound's rate of exchange can be expected in the near future only if this can be implemented easily and without a contraction of the domestic circulation. In other words, the implication is that in all probability the Bank of England's policy will aim at stability of the domestic level of prices, and will show little or no consideration for changes in the pound's rate of exchange. The difficulties confronting such a policy in a country in which almost all foodstuffs are imported, and hence fluctuate in price as exchange rates vary, are not small. To maintain a stable level of prices when prices of imported articles have increased therefore implies that the prices of domestic products must be decreased, which would undoubtedly give rise to complaints about the Bank's restrictive policy and therefore create the danger of inflationary pressure being exerted upon it. This danger becomes even greater if occasionally, as is still possible, the pound should be depressed on the exchanges as a result of large-scale withdrawals of short-term foreign assets. A reduction in the exchange rate of the pound is the only way in which such capital payments to abroad can actually be made, so long as the Bank adheres to the policy of keeping the level of prices stable.

However, even if the prospects of Britain's speedy return to the gold standard are small, nationalism in monetary policy has, nevertheless, probably reached or even passed its peak as an intellectual movement, as has already been indicated. The surrender of the gold standard has brought little change to the industrial situation, in contrast to the high hopes that were entertained for it, and this has had a sobering effect in many ways. It is more important, however, that the publication of the Macmillan Committee's report and of Keynes's *Treatise*, in which the attempt was made for the first time to provide a theoretical underpinning for that policy, provides leads for the refutation of those theories, in addition to the criticism which is beginning to make itself felt. It is to be hoped that in this context the two works do not represent the beginning of a new era, as many believed, but are simply the final flourishes of an extremely fateful era of monetary policy that has now passed.

The history of the gold standard over the last decade bears great similarity to the most recent history of capitalism. Every effort has been made to obviate its functioning at any point at which there was dissatisfaction with the tendencies which were being revealed by it. As a result, it could finally be assumed, with some semblance of authority, to have become completely ineffective. The leading role in this process was initially played by motives relating purely to social policy, but the recent period has seen the appearance of increasingly overt nationalistic aspects, which have already become almost more dangerous in the area of monetary policy even than in that of trade policy. Dare we hope that they will therefore be even more quickly pursued *ad absurdum*?

Notes

1 This was publicly admitted by the Bank's representatives before the Macmillan Committee, seemingly without anyone being aware that this constituted a flagrant offence against the much-discussed rules of the gold standard. The Deputy Governor of the Bank of England, Sir Ernest Harvey, declared (*Minutes of Evidence taken before the Committee on Finance and Industry*, London, 1931, vol. I, Q. 353): 'You will find if you look at a succession of Bank Returns that the amount of gold we have lost has been almost entirely replaced by an increase in the Bank's securities.'

2 Thus, P. Einzig, *Behind the Scenes of International Finance*, London, 1931, p. 36. However, once one reads the statements of Governor Norman before the Macmillan Committee, in which he not only refers to the efforts by the Bank of England to get the central banks to co-operate as one of the two most important activities during this period, but also identifies their task as the 'elimination of the struggle for gold', Einzig's assertion already becomes less improbable. Cf. *Minutes of Evidence, op. cit.*, vol. I, Q. 3490.

SIX

CAPITAL CONSUMPTION*

The economist finds himself in an unfortunate situation today. Anyone else may feel that he has a right to be optimistic about the somewhat more distant future at least. Even if the economic situation is currently as gloomy as it is right now, the rapid progress of our technical knowledge nevertheless seems to open up a secure prospect of a brighter future. To the economist, on the other hand, the current state of his science does not offer any reason for such confidence. It is not because its progress has perhaps been slower than that of other sciences; rather his concern is due to the lack of influence which his science exerts on practical matters. Other sciences are assured of this influence because their practitioners are trained in their fundamental principles at least. The economist, on the other hand, must look on daily while statesmen and politicians act on the basis of theories which frequently no one has dared to advance seriously in economic science for more than a century. As a result, he must be prey to serious doubts as to whether we shall ever enjoy the benefits of technical progress promised by the other sciences, and whether any prospect of the further progress of wealth will not soon be closed off by the consequences of interventions in economic life whose effects are not understood by those who undertake them.

We almost seem to have reached a critical point, at least in some parts of the world, at which the harmful consequences of economic unreasonableness are no longer compensated for by technical progress, and a permanent decline in the general standard of living has set in. What we are confronting here, however, are economic problems towards whose explanation economics has as yet made little direct contribution, even if it offers us the necessary tools for doing so.

* First published as 'Kapitalaufzehrung' in *Weltwirtschaftliches Archiv* 36 (1932/II), pp. 86–108.

In its current state, economics is the product of a very short and extraordinarily fortunate period in the development of humanity. It was developed during a period of unique growth of wealth – a growth which, incidentally, is to be attributed not least to the general acceptance of the doctrines of those who founded the science. Since the selection of the problems which are treated in more detail has always been determined by the historical situation, it is only natural that interest was wholly focused during that period on the problems of a progressive economy. It is equally natural that the hypothetical stationary economy has been investigated only as a means towards understanding the progressive economy, and that the 'economic theory of decline, the dismal counterpart of the economic theory of growth'[1] has been totally neglected.

This study is an attempt to fill this gap. It owes its existence to the conviction – which has been nourished within me by my observation over many years of a country which has continued to consume its capital – that the future historian of our time will undoubtedly have to write this economics of decline if we do not undertake the unpleasant task. On the basis of many observations, it seems likely to me that the country in which I received the decisive impressions for this study is not at all the only country in the world in which this problem is acute. I also think it likely that the only difference between the situation in Austria and that in some other countries is that Austria is a few years further along a path upon which a considerable part of the world has already entered today.

This essay is not, however, an attempt to describe current events. Before trying to investigate any concrete situation from this point of view, we must first of all be clear about the way in which the process of capital consumption would become apparent, and the symptoms which we must expect it to exhibit. This study is devoted exclusively to such a theoretical analysis, and only the conclusions derived from certain hypothetical assumptions are to be developed within it. Those few illustrations taken from real life, mostly referring to Austria as the country with whose conditions I am most familiar, are meant solely as illustrations, and in no way meant to prove that all the considerations presented in this essay actually apply to Austria. To do so would require consideration of a much greater quantity of factual material than is appropriate within the framework of such a theoretical study.[2]

Capital consumption, as a consequence of voluntary decisions by the owners of capital, is never likely to become widespread to such a degree that, over an extended period of time, it would exceed the formation of new capital taking place at the same time and thereby lead to a reduction of the stock of capital in the economy as a whole. Among the measures which can hit capital owners in general are two types which can lead to so great an amount of capital consumption that the reduction of capital in the economy as a whole can become a serious problem. On the one hand, there are the direct interventions by the state which aim at converting capital into income, such as property levies and estate duties. On the other hand, there are the measures which lead to a situation in which the sum of incomes used for consumption exceeds the net product of the economy over a longer period of time, and so capital is constantly being consumed. At the moment, the former type of measures are by no means insignificant. But the importance of the tendencies of the second type operating in this direction seems to me today to be both so much greater and understood so much less that my emphasis shall be almost wholly upon the latter. Only towards the end of this essay shall I touch briefly upon the effects of the first type of interventions, whose consequences are basically the same. The next few sections will therefore be exclusively concerned with the consequences of an increase in current cost of production over and above the value of the current net output of the economy as a whole. The fact that the mere possibility that such a state may exist is initially likely to appear paradoxical to many economists is, as I hope to show, one indication of how little general understanding there is of the true nature of our current 'capitalistic'[3] process of production.

Our analysis will begin by investigating what will happen in a closed economy, in which an equilibrium between costs and prices has hitherto existed, if this equilibrium is disturbed either by an increase in money cost of production due to non-economic factors or to a decrease in productivity while money cost of production remains the same. The former may occur for various reasons: trade unions may succeed in forcing wages above the existing equilibrium level, or additional taxation and social expenditure may increase the cost of employing workers or of using other factors of production. Or, finally, money wages, which were previously at an equilibrium level, may have become relatively too high as a result of a process of deflation. The case of a general decline in productivity is less important in an age of rapid technical progress as long as we disregard the case of exhaustion of natural forces, or a succession of bad harvests, or the case of capital consumption which is to be investigated below. In principle, however, it is also of significance, since what is true for a closed economy with declining productivity and rigid money incomes is basically also true for a country which is a member of an international system and whose exchange relations with the rest of the world deteriorate because of a decrease in demand for its products, or increased impediments to international trade, or because it lags behind the world rate of technical progress. Finally, a general decline in productivity may also occur in a closed economy due to the destruction of part of its capital equipment due to non-economic causes such as war or natural catastrophes, or because it has been converted into less profitable forms by state intervention (subsidies to certain branches of industry).

Now, suppose that as a result of one of these circumstances, money incomes rise relatively to the value of consumption goods which are currently being marketed under the existing organization of production. What are the implications of this? In dealing with this question, most economists so far seem to have been totally under the influence of two apparently unchallengeable truisms, though these truisms are in fact applicable only to production processes which are conducted entirely without capital. This seems to have been the case to such an extent that they have hardly found it worth their while to devote any deeper thought to the question. I am referring to the idea that it is impossible to consume more than is currently produced, and to the assumption that it follows from this that *all* prices must rise simply in the same ratio if there is an increase in money income relative to real income. If, however, part of the difference between the demand for consumer goods and the net produce of the economy as a whole can be taken from capital – that is at least conceivable and, as I hope to show, is even regularly the case – then not only will the first idea prove to be mistaken but doubts must also arise as to the truth of the second assumption which is derived from it. Yet it is above all upon this second assumption that the widespread conviction is based that it is only if the production of consumption goods becomes more profitable that the incentive to invest must rise in general.[4, 5]

What, then, actually does happen in such a situation? The assumption is that wages or, more correctly, the total costs involved in the employment of workers, have risen above their equilibrium level, so that the cost of one hour of labour is greater than the value of the last hour of labour employed. In dealing with this problem, economists have mostly contented themselves with showing that the number of workers employed will consequently decline until the marginal product of labour again coincides with its cost. Of course, this is perfectly correct as long as labour is co-operating only with land or other factors of production given in fixed quantities. As the opponents of this theory have emphasized again and again, the outcome is different when labour is co-operating with capital, since the higher cost of labour can then be thrown on to capital. While those who argue in this way believe the effects to be thus less harmful, they will in fact be far more harmful precisely because of their far-reaching consequences and the difficulty of predicting them. From the very fact that it is possible to pay wages to labour, which exceed its actual contribution to the product, at the expense of capital, an excessive rise in wages of this sort can lead to a reduction in capital and thus to a permanently lower equilibrium level of wages, over and above the unemployment to which it gives rise directly.

Under capitalistic production, if wages or the sum of total incomes are too high, competition arises between current consumption and the amount available for reinvestment (i.e. for maintenance and renewal of circulating as well as fixed capital). Current consumption will be able to claim a larger share of the product of the current flow of original factors of production than is compatible with the maintenance of the stock of real capital (or the conversion of new savings into real capital). If capital is to be maintained, a constant fraction of the totality of the factors of production must always be reinvested in a capitalistic way (or, to be more correct, all factors of production must be continually invested for the same average period). If new savings are to be transformed into real capital, this fraction must become greater (or the average period of investment becomes longer). This will occur only if the relative prices of consumption goods and of the means of production make it profitable for the productive forces available to be distributed to the production of both groups of goods in such a way that capital is maintained or that it grows by precisely the amount of the new savings. A rise in the prices of the means of production relative to those of consumption goods will lead to a relative increase in the production of the former, and thus to an increment in capital. A relative rise in the prices of consumption goods will lead to an increase in their production and to a decrease in that of capital goods, which implies either a decrease in the rate of growth of the capital stock or an actual reduction in its size.

Now, these conclusions appear evident as long as we bear in mind, firstly, that the choice is solely between increasing the output of capital goods and increasing that of consumption goods, and secondly, given the state of technology and the endowment of natural resources, that a permanent increase *per capita* in the physical output of consumer goods can be achieved only by continuously utilizing a greater part of the productive forces to satisfy consumption not directly but by capitalistic investment. Yet, however plausible such conclusions may appear to be, certain naive ideas seem to make it very difficult to consistently pay attention to them. It is not the economic layman alone who appears to have difficulties in following this train of thought to its conclusion in response to the question: if the entrepreneur receives a higher revenue for the final product, i.e. for consumption goods, why will he not generally be able to invest more? Does not the volume of investment undertaken by every entrepreneur depend upon his sales? Why, then, might an increase in demand for consumer goods fail to induce a general increase in investment activity, since the ultimate purpose of all productivity is the production of consumption goods?

But if we remember that our starting point was a rise in the workers' share in the total revenue of the enterprise above that which they contribute to the product of this enterprise, it is not difficult to see why this must lead to an actual reduction in the stock of capital. Production would continue unchanged only if, as a result of the increase in demand for consumption goods, *all* prices rose in the same proportion, including the prices of all intermediate products. But in this case nobody could expect to obtain any result, be it favourable or unfavourable, from an increase in wages. In reality, these effects are much more complicated than this suggests. For example, the fact that the price of shoes has risen in the same proportion as his costs of production is of little comfort to the owner of a mine which produces the iron ore from which the machines which produce shoes are finally made. In no way does the rise in the price of shoes mean that the producer of iron, who purchases ore, will also have more money available to buy it. He will in fact have less money available for that purpose because he will have to pay more for coal due to increased competition for it by shoe makers. Money spent today on consumption goods does not immediately increase the purchasing power of those who produce for the future;

141

in fact, it actually competes with their demand and their purchasing power is determined not by current but by past prices of consumer goods. This is so because the alternative always exists of investing the available productive resources for a longer or a shorter period of time. All those who tacitly assume that the demand for capital goods changes in proportion to the demand for consumer goods ignore the fact that it is impossible to consume more and yet simultaneously to defer consumption with the aim of increasing the stock of intermediate products.[6] The increase in the demand for consumer goods must lead to a redirection of production in the direction of those goods which can be completed rapidly, because the producers of capital goods cannot expand their demand for means of production in proportion to the increase in demand for consumer goods. This does not only mean that the existing workforce is employed differently, but also that a part of the intermediate products in existence is made to serve consumption in a shorter – and less productive – way than was originally intended, and that a part of the intermediate products used up is no longer replaced. But this constitutes nothing else than the process of capital consumption. In what follows, we shall have to concern ourselves with its particular features.

As I have stated elsewhere,[7] such a process of capital consumption takes place intermittently during the downswing of the trade cycle, and most of the phenomena connected with it are more familiar to us in this context than as permanent features. On the other hand, my tracing back of cyclical fluctuations to changes in the opposite direction in the average period of production or in investment has been objected to on the grounds that, while changes of this type may perhaps be of interest as long-run phenomena, they are at any rate of no significance for the explanation of short-term phenomena such as the trade cycle. In my view, however, scarcely any doubt seems possible that cyclical fluctuations in particular offer an example of particularly strong fluctuations of this kind. If capital goods are not replaced, or to only a limited extent, and the factors of production are used in processes which yield consumption goods more quickly, as coal was in the example mentioned above, then this is nothing else but a transition to less capitalistic methods of production. And if there is less use made of machines whose products can be consumed only after a longer period of time, and if capital goods fall in value relatively to consumption goods, this simply indicates that a lower valuation is placed on labour invested for a more distant future.

The implication of all this is as follows: since the demand for consumption goods has risen above the cost value of the consumption goods currently coming on to the market, this increased level of demand must be met at least in part from funds which were originally earmarked for use in a more distant future. Now, however, it has become unprofitable to use them for this purpose. In other words old, previously expended labour has become cheaper relative to labour which is currently becoming available. Hence it is more advantageous to meet current demand from the supply of previously expended labour than to use new labour to do so. (In the opposite case, where current demand for consumption goods falls because of an increase in the level of savings, previously expended labour will on the contrary become more valuable than new labour. It is therefore profitable to store up labour in the form of capital goods. Perhaps this way of viewing the matter will make it easier to understand the differing effects of a transition to more capitalistic or to less capitalistic methods of production. The former can occur without serious disturbances, while capital consumption is always accompanied by unemployment.)

It is not difficult to see that this process must lead to unemployment if wages are rigid. If they were not rigid, incipient unemployment would lead to an adjustment of the wage rate down to the value of the productive contribution of the marginal worker. Lower wages in conjunction with the decline in the level of consumption thereby caused would make it possible for a new equilibrium position to be attained. However, disequilibrium will continue to persist if there is merely a reduction in the number of those employed while wages remain unchanged, and current cost per unit of output continues to exceed the contribution of the workers to the output. In this case, capital consumption will continue until consumption has been reduced sufficiently and capital ceases to be consumed.[8]

The economy in its entirety must continue to decline so long as more is being consumed than produced, and some part of consumption therefore takes place at the expense of the existing stock of capital. As long as this is occurring, current expenditure on consumption goods will exceed current expenditure on the production of these goods. On the other hand, however, the original factors of production will not be contributing enough to replace the total value of the product consumed. Enough, that is, to replace all those expenses which have already been incurred in the past and which should be continually reinvested for the future.

It would hardly be necessary to devote any more space to the way in which a general consumption of capital takes place if all of us were not inclined to end up by saying – even if we had followed, and agreed with, these general considerations: 'Very well, but after all one has seen, one does not get the impression that a very considerable diminution of capital takes place during a crisis.' Why many people find it so difficult to recognize that capital is in fact consumed in such a situation is that they look at existing capital equipment predominantly or exclusively from a technical point of view and consider only its technical capacity, not its economic significance, i.e. its value. In almost all cases, however, a diminution of capital means in the first instance only a reduction in the value of existing productive equipment, which nevertheless continues to exist in an unchanged form for some time. Its reduction in physical terms only occurs in the course of time and as a *result* of its loss of value. The best equipped factory, the most marvellous machine, which until very recently were able to be employed to great advantage in production, and therefore did represent a large capital value, can lose their value rather suddenly as a result of changes in the structure of prices and thus cease to be capital. It is the fact that this factory or that machine has continued to exist technically in the same excellent condition which makes it so extremely difficult for anyone who reflects on these things more from the perspective of the technician than from that of the economist, to see that capital has been destroyed in this case and that we have become correspondingly poorer.

It is undeniably true that most people, and even most businessmen, can grasp technical things, which are so much more concrete, more easily than abstract economic connections; hence the significance and even more so the causes of such a destruction of capital are almost universally misunderstood. Scarcely any economic phenomenon appears more incomprehensible to the common observer than the fact that the loss of the value of a plant, whose technical efficiency has remained unchanged, is not to be taken to represent a merely superficial phenomenon caused by some insidious property of the capitalist system, but represents a genuine reduction in our wealth.

However, there is no difficulty in realizing that the decrease in the value of a plant due to any of the causes discussed here (even if it only occurs because the plant no longer produces a surplus over and above its operating costs), will shortly lead to both a reduction of its physical capacity, i.e. to a destruction of physical capital, and also to further capital losses. This will take place even if we assume that the operating costs which are still covered by receipts also include the necessary depreciation, and that interest is the only return lost. This also holds true if we neglect the fact that in many cases the permanent nature of the devaluation of the plant is not recognized, and that because of this the allowances set aside for depreciation are insufficient. Of course, this will lead directly to capital consumption. Even if we assume that those who own the capital in question immediately reduce their expenses in accordance with the loss of interest; that they still have sufficient gross returns to amortize their capital; and that consequently they lose only part of their income but none of their capital at all. The fact still remains that even after all these assumptions have been made, it will be unprofitable for the majority of capitalists in a certain branch of production to reinvest their capital there and this will nevertheless lead to capital losses for other owners of capital.

If wages have risen to such an extent that workers can claim for themselves the entire return on capital invested by the capitalist, so that income from interest on invested capital has disappeared, this still does *not* mean that there are no further possibilities for investing capital available for new investment in such a way as to yield interest,[9] as Böhm-Bawerk seems to assume in his classic investigation of this problem.[10] On the contrary, a profitable investment of capital available for new investment will be possible at any level of wages, whether that capital is derived from new savings or from funds earned from depreciation (amortization quotas). Since high wages mean that only relative shorter round-about methods of production can be chosen, the interest which can be earned on these new investments will be even higher than that previously obtainable.

But what are these other profitable uses for capital which had become free for reinvestment and which it is not worth reinvesting in its previous employment? Obviously, they are to be found in industries which benefit immediately from the higher incomes received by consumers, in which it is still profitable to employ labour even at these high wages and where capital turns over quickly, i.e. in industries which produce consumption goods directly. Capital will therefore turn towards all industries which directly serve the consumer. Apart from those industries which directly produce consumer goods, capital will be attracted into all the service industries, e.g. hotels, theatre and cinemas, etc. The essential aspect of this, however, is that *only a small part of the capital invested in industries which have become unprofitable can be withdrawn and invested elsewhere.* Precisely because of the fact that reinvestment of the only barely earned amortization quotas has become unprofitable at one stage of production, capital invested in the preceding stages of production can no longer be amortized. The products of the stage of production in question, which have so far been purchased from funds earned from depreciation in the subsequent stages of production, can no longer be sold at all. This is one of the cases in which it becomes evident that even what is regarded as circulating capital by the individual enterprise is quite frequently not circulating capital at all from the point of view of the economy as a whole, as Dr Machlup has recently shown.[11] If at one stage of production that property which makes capital into circulating capital, namely that it can be withdrawn, is made use of, it follows that the circulating capital of the preceding stages of production can no longer be withdrawn because it is not turned over, and is therefore no longer available. It is precisely in these preceding stages of production that production may have to cease completely as a result of high wages in the subsequent stages, and that therefore capital in these stages may be destroyed in its entirety. What makes it so extremely difficult to see the connection between the two phenomena is that capital losses may be greatest in plants which perhaps are not immediately hit by the rise in the wage rate.

This is one of many cases in which the division of a process of production among a number of different plants or 'industries', though from an economic viewpoint it can be regarded as a unitary process in which a certain consumption good is produced, makes it so difficult to see things which would be immediately obvious if the process were to take place within the walls of one factory. Suppose that all the tools, machines and raw materials necessary for a production process were produced in the same factory which produces the final product. It would scarcely be possible to overlook the fact that a rise in the wage rate which does no more than to absorb the capitalists' income from interest must lead to a direct loss of that part of capital which is used in the production of those capital goods which are no longer replaced because it is no longer profitable for the capitalists to continue to reinvest their capital in the same way. While production will cease immediately in this department, and capital will have been destroyed without any change in the physical state of the capital goods, production will continue in the succeeding departments only so long as the available equipment continues to operate without being replaced. Capital will therefore also begin to wear out physically. Whether capital equipment continues to exist physically unchanged or not is of little significance as long as no change is in prospect which will restore the profitability of the process which has become unprofitable (the latter will be the case if we are dealing with cyclical depressions and not with 'structural' processes of capital consumption). Capital embodied in this equipment is lost, whether or not its technical productive capacity has remained the same.

It also follows from what has been said that one of the effects of capital consumption will be the existence of unutilized productive capacity, a phenomenon which must appear totally puzzling and misleading to the laymen observing it. The fact that it is not profitable to produce more capital goods is not in this case the effect of existing capital equipment remaining idle but its cause.

Another important result of our analysis is that the unemployment which is caused by excessive rises in the wage rate will take on very different dimensions in different industries (in general, it will be greater particularly in industries producing capital goods). Moreover, its extent will not necessarily coincide with that to which wages have risen in the industries in question. But further, it is only after some time has elapsed that it will attain its full extent, as the existing productive capacity gradually wears out, because it is no longer worthwhile to replace it. This is an important point because it is only when unemployment has reached its maximum that the areas in which production will continue to be profitable will become evident, assuming that the cost of maintaining the unemployed (unemployment benefit) is borne by industry in the form of a wage tax or something similar. (This is true even if accumulated reserves are drawn upon to finance the increased payments of unemployment benefit since this represents a reduction of the capital available to industry). Not only will more unemployment be created by these increased burdens on industry or by the reduction in its provision with capital, but part of the investment which has been carried out in the meantime will also be lost, and the same process will again be set in motion. In this way, excessive rises in the wage rate can set off a cumulative process of capital consumption and increasing unemployment. It is difficult to see how it can ever be brought to a standstill.

At this point we must mention a second effect of an excessive rise in wages on the provision of capital to industry. Although it is not a genuine case of capital consumption but merely a case of capital transformation, it nevertheless makes more difficult a return to a state of equilibrium and the resorption of the unemployed. In doing so, therefore, it may indirectly lead to a permanent reduction in productivity in so far as a return to a more flexible wage structure is conceivable at all. What I have in mind is the tendency of high wages to stimulate rationalization; an effect which is quite generally regarded as beneficial (although in my opinion erroneously so). In this context, rationalization naturally means the introduction of labour-saving devices and the carrying out of investment projects which have become profitable only because of the increase in the wage rate and have therefore been forced upon industry only by these high wages, as it were. So far as I know no one has yet asserted that the total sum of capital available for investment could be increased in this way. However, this situation has only to be kept in mind to make it quite evident that the alleged beneficial effects of such forced rationalization do not exist. All that can be correctly asserted is that an excessive rise in the wage rate will lead to a situation in which more will be invested in certain industries at the expense of others than would otherwise have been the case. In the long run, however, this yields no advantage at all, as its only result can be a reduction in productivity. As can easily be seen, if there is an excessive rise in the wage rate it is those industries in which additional capital investment replaces relatively more labour in other industries which will enjoy a relative advantage. In any given situation, the amount of labour which can be replaced by a given amount of capital will vary as between different industries.[12] Whether it is worthwhile to use more labour or more capital will always depend on the relative prices of those quantities of capital or labour which can produce the same additional product. If the price of labour rises relatively to that of the capital which produces the same output, this creates an advantage for those industries in which the same quantity of capital can be substituted for relatively more labour, i.e. capital will be employed in industries in which relatively little labour is needed to co-operate with it. But this means that the same quantity of capital investment will raise marginal productivity of labour less, and will lead to the employment of fewer workers, than would have been the case if the place in which it was utilized has been determined with respect to a lower level of wages. It also means that the same increase in capital which might otherwise have sufficed to raise the equilibrium level up to that to which wages have been prematurely and artificially raised will now be insufficient to make it possible to absorb all the unemployed at this level of wages. It follows that hope that the success of enforced rationalization will ultimately justify wages which have initially been too high is totally without foundation, though frequently entertained.

Another way of putting this is to say that excessively high wages will lead industry to give its capital equipment such a form as if there were actually not more workers available than can be employed after this rise in the wage rate. The level of employment may even be lower after the readjustment than it would have been if industry had been forced to maintain its capital in exactly the same form instead of adjusting it according to the change in wages. Of course, such readjustment, which enables the capitalist to obtain a larger share of the reduced social product, need not imply a loss of capital if it were not for the fact that under existing conditions every increase in unemployment would represent an increased burden upon industry, a new rise in costs. If wages are rigid, the outcome of this will be the same as if the wage rate had been increased. Therefore, what in the first instance represents merely a transformation of capital may ultimately lead as well to capital consumption *via* its effect on unemployment, given the existence of unemployment benefits.

Before I conclude the theoretical analysis of the process of capital consumption, I want simply to mention that basically the same processes which are entailed by an absolute reduction in the capital of the economy as a whole must take place even if the provision with capital per head of the population is reduced because the growth of capital does not keep up with population growth. Any reduction in the *per capita* provision with capital necessitates precisely the same transition to less capitalistic methods of production and thus leads to the loss of capital invested in higher stages of production, the same as happens in circumstances which lead directly to an absolute reduction in capital. To attempt to analyse more closely the more detailed particularities of this process would be to go beyond the limits of this essay. Nevertheless, in the following discussion of the most significant secondary symptoms of the process of capital consumption, we should bear in mind that they apply to the case of a reduction in *per capita* provision with capital in just the same way as to that of an absolute reduction in capital.

The peculiar situation of an apparent surplus of invested capital, which is expressed by a lower valuation of existing production plants and by only partial utilization of existing productive capacity, together with a simultaneous lack of capital available for investment, which is expressed by high interest rates and generally low liquidity, finds its necessary counterpart in the situation of those financial institutions whose function it is to gather the capital which is available for investment and to invest it at their own risk. Even if the banks, in the narrower meaning of the word, do not normally provide capital for investment purposes, as is the case in England, they must still get into difficulties since it is in the nature of their business to invest for longer periods money which they have borrowed on short term. There will be a substantial growth in 'frozen credit', in such a situation largely equivalent to lost money, and the temptation which always exists to throw good money after bad will contribute to increasing their losses. Naturally, the situation of the banks must become particularly grave if they provide industry not merely with operating capital but also with investment capital, as is largely the rule in central Europe. Furthermore, the risk of continuing capital losses in the economy as a whole is still further increased under the central European system because the only way of investing which savers have learned is via the mediation of the banks. A large part of the funds which become available for investment each year therefore gets into the hands of investors whose decisions are strongly influenced, possibly in an undesirable fashion, by their concern to preserve funds previously put into investments which cannot be reversed.

The space I can devote to some of the other symptoms which may regularly be expected to occur in a country which consumes its capital must be even more brief. Most of them result from the processes already discussed above. The existence of large unutilized plants whose value has partially been written off will afford protection to existing enterprises of the industries in question against any new competition. The formation of monopolistic organizations such as cartels will therefore become both easy and profitable. Continuous reinvestment in plants whose value has had to be almost completely written off is another phenomenon which frequently occurs in connection with a process of capital consumption, and has often been observed in Austria especially. In most cases, the result is simply that these new reinvestments as well will soon have to be written off, and replaced by yet more new ones in order to keep up with competition. This is only another aspect of that process of rationalization which takes place under continually increasing costs and which I have already mentioned.

The effects of a process of capital consumption on the external trade of a country are too complex to be dealt with in detail here. It need only be mentioned that in such a situation a number of forces will operate towards the emergence of a balance of trade deficit. This will happen partly because sizeable transfers abroad of capital in the form of purchases of foreign securities will regularly take place as a result of capital consumption; and partly because a proportion of the imports made by the country which is consuming capital will not actually be paid for but will be covered by losses incurred by foreigners on their investments in this country.

Another interesting phenomenon is that in almost all countries which can be suspected of consuming their capital, complaints about the great difference between retail prices and wholesale prices or cost of production are general. The fact that branches of industry which supply consumption goods are relatively more profitable, and that industries which produce foodstuffs like breweries, the tobacco industry, entertainments etc. are prosperous is a phenomenon which should be expected to occur during a process of capital consumption. Yet the mere existence of such a situation does not, of course, in itself prove that such a process is at work. The same situation could arise if the rate of saving merely showed a sharp decline without capital actually being consumed. But the emergence of this phenomenon raises a strong presumption that tendencies towards capital consumption are actually operative if it takes place at a time when population growth is slowing down, as is often the case today, and even more when unemployment simultaneously continues to rise.

Yet even if it is scarcely possible to ever make a totally accurate diagnosis, except for extreme cases, there is one symptom which provides a fairly useful clue to the development of the capital of the economy as a whole: the evaluation of existing industrial capital on the stock exchange. We have previously seen that a loss in the value of existing plants is equivalent to a destruction of capital of a corresponding magnitude; moreover, a sufficient proportion of the consumer goods industries is nowadays already organized in the form of joint stock companies. Suppose, then, we wish to give expression to a development in these industries which, for example, compensates for developments in the capital goods industries. The best indicator available of the actual development of the capital of the economy as a whole then appears to be offered by the development of the values of the shares of all the industries of a country (and the relative development in the individual industries) taken over a period of several years.

Comprehensive statistics of this kind, however, which also cover firms which have gone bankrupt and all the smaller enterprises, are rarely available. For Austria, Dr O. Morgenstern of the Austrian *Institut für Konjunkturforschung* has carried out such a statistical investigation and has come up with truly frightening information.[13] According to his investigations, by 31 October 1931 the market value of all Austrian joint stock companies quoted on the Vienna stock exchange had fallen to roughly 18.5 per cent of the market value of the same group of companies in 1913, including the gold value of new foundations of firms and increases of capital since then. That this development is only partially caused by inflation, and that its beginnings are to be located to a large extent in the period after inflation had come to an end, emerges from the fact that the total value of all Austrian joint stock companies quoted on the Vienna stock exchange as of 31 October 1931 is even lower than that of the new foundations and increases of capital which have taken place since inflation came to an end. The absolute amount of the current total value of the share capital of the Austrian joint stock companies on 31 October 1931 was 784,255,607 *schilling*. The significance of this sum will become most evident if it is compared with that part of what is at least dominantly consumption expenditure which is particularly inflexible because it is financed by the state. The former amounts to just on a third of the federal expenditure of the Republic of Austria scheduled in the budget for 1931; and this latter figure does not even include expenditure by the *Länder* and communes! Consequently, if all Austrian enterprises were still in Austrian hands, and if Austria were able to sell all these enterprises abroad at the market prices ruling in the autumn of 1931, the proceeds would not even cover half the annual expenditure of the Republic!

As I announced at the beginning of this essay, I have up to this point dealt in some detail only with one case of capital consumption:

that which is the result of excessively high costs of production, especially of wages which are too high. I have done so because it is this cause which in the last few years has perhaps been the most important and certainly the least understood. However, in emphasizing this one cause, it must not be forgotten that any direct use of capital for consumption purposes obviously gives rise to the same effects. There can be no doubt that this applies to all taxes paid out of the substance of capital, be they capital levies, estate duties or taxation of the reserves accumulated by businesses to finance new equipment, in so far as the receipts from these taxes are used to pay for current expenditure and are not invested profitably. What is remarkable, however, is that even economists are all too prone to envisage capital merely as being the source of income for some wealthy person when they talk of something having to be paid out of capital, and that they tend to ignore the fact that it also represents part of the national productive equipment which will thereby be destroyed. Even though the productive facilities which correspond to these sums of capital do not disappear from the face of the earth, the diversion of these sums for the purpose of consumption still cannot fail to bring about a corresponding reduction in the stock of capital equipment in the final analysis. What is true of the use of capital for consumption purposes also applies, of course, to any redirection of capital towards less profitable purposes such as e.g. subsidizing particular branches of industry, or public works, or something similar. There can be little doubt that in the last few years agricultural and housing policies in particular have been working strongly in this direction in central Europe. As an example of the numerical significance of these factors, it need only be mentioned that in the last few years the municipality of Vienna alone has invested in its housing projects, which are financed by taxation, an amount which is significantly higher than that total market value of the share capital of all Austrian joint stock companies given above.

The fact that everywhere the public has only too willingly encouraged such capital-destroying measures can certainly be attributed largely to the fact that there has been no recognition at all of the possibility that the national capital can be consumed. The public have believed that, after the capitalist has made the capital available and thus done his duty, he passed completely out of the picture, since the existing real capital certainly could not run away. No further effort needs to be expended to show that this view is erroneous. Nevertheless, there are many who recognize that the capital of the economy as a whole can be consumed and yet still advocate measures which have this effect. Frequently they do so because they believe that a nation can afford to consume some of its capital temporarily in order to prevent a decline in its standard of living, in the same way as an individual can temporarily live off his capital in an emergency; it is in part precisely because he can do so that he values his private capital. But he can avoid curtailing his consumption in this way only if he has the well-founded hope that he will be able to earn as much from his reduced stock of capital in the future as he has done in the past from his capital and all other sources. A nation can have little such hope. The effects of capital consumption may for a time be compensated for by technical progress but the greater danger is that it is the very first step on the path towards capital consumption which will in itself lead to a vicious circle out of which it will be extremely difficult to break.

The reason is that the longer a process of capital consumption has lasted, the more difficult it is to stop it. The extent of the decline in the general standard of living necessary to do so grows with every day the process goes on, and a point may ultimately be reached at which it has become impossible to prevent the population from starving unless capital continues to be consumed. In addition, however, there are also strong psychological forces which will operate to intensify a process of capital consumption once it has begun. The first of these forces originates in the discovery that the general standard of living of the population may continue to be raised for some time despite increasing unemployment and despite vehement complaints from the business world. Secondly, the increasing danger of losing one's invested savings will deter an ever-increasing number of savers from continuing to save. In this way, a process of capital consumption may lead in the end to capital actually being destroyed, although its effects were initially offset by the simultaneous formation of new capital. Any attempt to stimulate capital formation must fail so long as there is a very high probability of losing one's savings. Nevertheless, the reduced level of savings should not be overestimated as a cause of capital scarcity. It is likely that by far the greatest part of the supply of 'free' capital which continually becomes available for investment arises not from new savings but from the funds earned by depreciating capital which has previously been invested. That capital scarcity in particular has persisted in central Europe throughout the last decade can probably be attributed to a much greater extent to an insufficient depreciation of old capital than to a reduction in the supply of new savings.

A third and by no means the last dangerous effect of a prolonged process of capital consumption is the specific psychological reaction by the entrepreneurial class. There can be little doubt that the tendency which has become so widespread in central Europe in the last few years to pay fixed and high salaries to officials of corporations, salaries which are independent of profits, is a result of the fact that there has been a long period of time in which no profits have been earned. In this way, though, the entrepreneurial class becomes an accomplice in the process of capital consumption and loses the essential stimulus which should cause it to oppose the process. And it is for this reason that those people whose main task it should be to maintain the capital of their enterprises are pushed into taking up the hostile attitude towards the owners of capital which is so characteristic of the broad public. Nothing could be more revealing of this anti-capitalistic attitude among even the entrepreneurial class than the well-known remark attributed to the president of one of the Austrian joint stock companies who is alleged to have said, during a discussion about the distribution of dividends, that he could not see why he should throw any of the good money of his company to these complete strangers, the shareholders.

This brings me to the last and most general question. It is composed of two related issues. Firstly, can capital consumption be avoided in the long run in a democratic society in which the majority of the population is anti-capitalistic? Secondly, will capital consumption not inevitably make its appearance, at least in a situation in which it can be avoided only by lowering the standard of living? The gravity which the problem of capital supply has now assumed is perhaps most clearly indicated by the fact that serious socialist thinkers, in considerable contrast to classic socialist doctrine, are beginning to present as one of the essential deficiencies of the capitalist system the danger that it cannot guarantee an adequate supply of capital for the economy, and they see one of the advantages of socialism as lying in its ability to effect the desirable level of capital formation.[14] In contrast, socialist politicians and politically inclined economists still regard the danger of capital consumption as a chimera.

The political problem is particularly difficult because the groups which are the primary beneficiaries of capital consumption represent the numerical majority in each society. They are the great masses of wage earners and those on fixed salaries, as well as a large part of those industries which directly serve consumption, and, finally, the retail trade and handicrafts. In contrast, the groups which are directly affected by capital consumption and are therefore prepared to offer political resistance to it are those whose intentions are traditionally deemed suspect by all progressive people, namely heavy industry and high finance. Since nowadays the great masses of the population have been brought up to conceive of 'Capital' in personified form and not as the objective productive equipment of the economy, it is thus difficult to make them understand why it should be in their interest to maintain capital intact.

The filling-out of the theoretical framework provided in the first part of this essay with concrete data has necessarily had to remain highly sketchy. To undertake reasonably thorough investigation of concrete processes and especially of the actual meaning of the trends of economic development during the last decade as described here would involve not much less than an economic history of this period, or at least a history of economic policy during it. Such an attempt could only be made on the basis of highly detailed, specialized investigations, conducted from the viewpoint of the general connections discussed here; but investigations of this type are still almost completely lacking. Recent publications, particularly the highly interesting investigations by the *Institut für Konjunkturforschung* into German capital formation[15] and E. Welter's book on capital scarcity in Germany,[16] have provided us with more detailed and more reliable material on the actual development of the supply of capital within the last few years than we have ever had at our disposal before. However praiseworthy these investigations and however valuable their findings are, I still believe that, if we really wish to understand this development, what above all we still lack is theoretical insight into the essential relationships. And this essay has only been concerned to contribute towards the analysis of this theoretical problem.

Notes

1 In this vein, W. Röpke, *Die Theorie der Kapitalbildung*, lecture delivered to the *Nationalökonomische Gesellschaft*, Vienna, 22 February 1929 (*Recht und Staat in Geschichte und Gegenwart*, 63), Tübingen, 1929, p. 39.

2 There is yet another purpose to be served by the theoretical analysis of the process of capital consumption. As I have hinted towards the end

of my *Preise und Produktion* (*Beiträge zur Konjunkturforschung*, 3, Vienna, 1931, pp. 87, 120), the process of a prolonged shrinkage of the capitalistic structure of production is essentially the same as that which takes place during periodic depressions. However, while in the above-mentioned book I have analysed in somewhat greater detail the events which take place during a boom and a crisis, I hardly touched upon the events occurring during the later stages of a depression. I hope that the present study will complete the picture presented in that book by providing a somewhat more detailed representation of the mechanism of depressions. Above all, I hope to say a little more here about the significance of one factor neglected in my earlier work, the rigidity of wages and prices that currently exists.

3 Whenever the term 'capitalistic' is used in this essay, it will always be done in the theoretical sense of a production process which uses capital, and not in the political sense of a certain social order.

4 This train of thought, which is at the basis of all underconsumption theories, has recently found its expression particularly clearly in J. M. Keynes's preference for an extraordinary surplus of current receipts of entrepreneurs over their current costs of production, including their normal profits. According to Keynes, this surplus is the cause of all booms. I believe, however, that as a temporary phenomenon it must lead to a crisis, and, as an enduring phenomenon, to continuing capital consumption.

5 It almost seems that the strong emphasis which the modern subjective theory of value has placed on the derivated nature of the demand for the means of production – obviously, correctly so in general terms – has had a misleading effect here, and that it has led to a neglect of the 'limits' to production constituted by the state of the supply of capital, as recognized and emphasized by the classics ever since Adam Smith.

6 I believe that John Stuart Mill's famous and frequently criticised 'fourth proposition concerning capital', that 'demand for commodities is not demand for labour', was directed against this misunderstanding, though an adequate justification for that proposition has hardly ever been provided. (Cf. *Principles of Political Economy*, with some of their applications to social philosophy, ed. and with an introduction by W. Ashley, London, 1909, I, ch. V, 9, p. 79).

7 Cf. Hayek, *op. cit.*, esp. pp. 90ff.

8 When *money* wages are fixed and the effective quantity of money remains unchanged, a decrease in the level of consumption will ultimately be imposed by the increase in the prices of consumption goods which must follow upon the reduction in the level of production. If, however, *real* wages are fixed (index-linked wages), capital consumption will not only continue unchecked but even gather pace progressively, because the productivity of labour and thus the equilibrium level of wages will fall as capital is consumed.

9 John Stuart Mill's 'capital disposable for investment'. (*On Some Unsettled Questions of Political Economy*, London, 1844, pp. 113ff.) Or, in more common terminology, 'free' capital consisting of earned amortization quotas (or proceeds from circulating capital which has been turned

over), new savings and perhaps additional credits (cf. F. A. Hayek, *Geldtheorie und Konjunkturtheorie* (*Beiträge zur Konjunkturforschung*, 1) Vienna and Leipzig, 1929, pp. 123–4). This is also the only sense in which that unfortunate term '*Kapitaldisposition*' which has recently found so many advocates can meaningfully be used. (Cf. F. Machlup, *Börsenkredit, Industriekredit und Kapitalbildung* (*Beiträge zur Konjunkturforschung*, 2), Vienna, 1931, pp. 9ff., and G. Halm, 'Warten und "Kapital-disposition" ', *Jahrbücher für Nationalökonomie und Statistik*, vol. 135, Jena, 1931, pp. 831ff). But first, we do not need a new term for this concept; and secondly, as Machlup emphasizes, G. Cassel has used it in a wider sense which forced Machlup to draw a distinction between free and restricted *Kapitaldisposition*. Free *Kapitaldisposition* corresponds precisely to 'free' capital or 'capital disposable for investment', while 'restricted *Kapitaldisposition*' is only an ugly and misleading term for the continually changing value of all the capital goods which exist at any one point in time. But why is a new term needed for this?

10 E. von Böhm-Bawerk, *Macht oder ökonomisches Gesetz?*, reprinted in *Gesammelte Schriften von Eugen von Böhm-Bawerk*, edited by F. X. Weiss, Vienna and Leipzig, 1924, esp. pp. 278ff. It certainly need not be pointed out that, despite this objection to one particular point, this work of Böhm-Bawerk and the elaboration of the ideas it puts forward by L. v. Mises in his *Gemeinwirtschaft* (*Untersuchungen über den Sozialismus*, second and revised edition, Jena, 1932, pp. 424–5), constitutes the most important basis for the reflections contained in the present essay.

11 Machlup, *op. cit.*, pp. 132ff.

12 Of course, for infinitely small additional quantities of capital and labour in equilibrium, the ratio must be the same for all industries. But for all the quantities which actually come into consideration this rate of substitution depends on the relative steepness of the demand curves for additional quantities of capital and labour respectively in the industries concerned.

13 Cf. O. Morgenstern, 'Kapital- und Kurswertänderungen der an der Wiener Börse notierten österreichischen Aktiengesellschaften 1913 bis 1930', in *Zeitschrift für Nationalökonomie*, vol. III, (1931–2), pp. 251ff.

14 Cf. C. Landauer, *Planwirtschaft und Verkehrswirtschaft*, Munich and Leipzig, 1931, especially pp. 79ff.

15 G. Keiser and B. Benning, *Kapitalbildung und Investition in der Deutschen Volkswirtschaft 1924 bis 1928* (*Viertel Jahreshefte zur Konjunkturforschung*, *Sonderheft*, 33), Berlin, 1931.

16 E. Welter, *Die Ursachen des Kapitalmangels in Deutschland*, Tübingen, 1931.

SEVEN

ON 'NEUTRAL MONEY'*

In the various discussions recently devoted to the concept of 'neutral money', there has been some ambiguity in the way in which this concept has been understood and applied. Hence it seems appropriate to again briefly outline the nature of the problem which I sought to pose for discussion under this phrase.[1] Moreover, the way in which I understand the phrase still seems to me to accord not merely with what previous authors have understood by it but also with that for which it is more appropriately reserved. It is all the more unnecessary for me to devote much space to the matter since J. G. Koopmans,[2] in his excellent treatise, has developed the concept wholly in the sense in which I wish it to be understood. Even he, however, has failed to lay sufficient stress upon the distinction which I wish to emphasize in this context. As an example of what I consider to be an inappropriate usage of the concept, I would point above all to the essay by W. Egle,[3] though it has many valuable individual insights.

The concept of neutral money was designed to serve as an instrument for theoretical analysis, and should not in any way be set up as a norm for monetary policy, at least in the first instance. The aim was to isolate the influences which money actively exerts upon the economic process, and to establish the conditions under which it is conceivable that the economic process in a monetary economy, and especially relative prices, are not influenced by any but 'real' determinants – where 'real' relates to the equilibrium theory developed under the assumption of barter. More precisely, what is involved is the clarification of the significance of the assumptions customarily employed in the theory of economic equilibrium: that, while money is indeed present to facilitate indirect exchange, it can be neglected as a factor influencing the relative levels of prices.

* First published as 'Über "neutrales Geld" ' in *Zeitschrift für Nationalökonomie*, 4 (1933), pp. 659–61.

That this is the normal procedure is shown both by the distinction usually drawn by the Lausanne school between money as mere '*numéraire*' as distinct from 'money' (*monnaie*) and the Menger-Mises assumption of the 'inner objective exchange value' of money.

Obviously, a clarification of this problem must possess great significance for questions of monetary policy. Nevertheless, from the very outset the possibility must be envisaged that the realization of this ideal may compete with other important aims of monetary policy, and consequently that the only practical solution attainable is a compromise. But that will be taken up again below.

The answer to the theoretical problem of neutral money sets out from the recognition that the basic identity of supply and demand, which in a state of barter must exist on every market, is disrupted by the interposition of money. It is therefore necessary to grasp the one-sided effects of money, as I have previously called these phenomena in unconscious imitation of Wieser,[4] phenomena which make their appearance when, as a result of the division of barter into two independent acts, the one or other of these acts takes place without its complement. In this sense, demand without a corresponding supply, or supply without a corresponding demand, become evident above all when money is expended from 'hoards' (cash balances are diminished), money received is not immediately expended, newly created money comes on to the market, or money is destroyed. The problem to which this gives rise therefore leads directly to the adoption of an assumption that the flow of money is constant, with the exceptions to which I have made only passing reference in *Prices and Production*. It was only J. G. Koopmans who subjected the concept to a systematic analysis, in his book referred to above.

If the tendencies towards equilibrium depicted in general economic theory are to remain operative in a monetary economy, all those conditions which it is the task of neutral money to indicate must be realized. Now, it is not merely entirely possible but even probable that this cannot be achieved in practice; moreover, even if it were possible, other considerations could make it appear to be undesirable. Suppose that, in addition to the assumption of the existence of a general medium of exchange, we introduce the further, realistic assumption that many long-term contracts are concluded in terms of this medium of exchange in the expectation that prices will be more or less stable. Also, assume that many or all of the existing prices exhibit a certain rigidity and are especially difficult to lower. The result is that there are very substantial 'frictional resistances' to the realization of a 'neutral' money supply, resistances which are of the utmost significance for the framing of a practical norm for monetary policy. In this situation, it is at least possible that monetary policy will have to seek for a compromise between two aims, each of which can be achieved only at the cost of the other: between the complete realization of the tendencies towards an equilibrium, and the avoidance of excessive frictional resistances. Yet we must then be clear that, in this situation, the elimination of the disturbances actively emanating from the side of money has ceased to be the sole aim of monetary policy, or even the only one of its aims which can be fully achieved. In addition, it can only give rise to confusion to refer to this practical aim with the same phrase as is employed for the theoretically conceivable situation in which one of the two competing goals is fully achieved.

Hence the relationship between the theoretical concept of neutrality of the money supply and the ideal of monetary policy is that the degree to which the latter approximates to the former provides one, probably the most important though not the sole, criterion for assessing the maxims of monetary policy. It is perfectly conceivable that monetary influences would always give rise to a 'falsification' of relative prices and a misdirection of production unless certain conditions were fulfilled, e.g. (1) the flow of money remained constant, *and* (2) all prices were perfectly flexible, *and* (3) in the conclusion of long-term contracts in terms of money, the future movement of prices was approximately correctly predicted. But the implication is, then, that, if (2) and (3) are not given, the ideal cannot be attained by any kind of monetary policy at all.

Basically, the theoretical concept of neutral money, which relates to the influence of money upon the price relationships (simultaneous and intertemporal) determined by real factors, cannot bear any relation at all to the concept of some 'price level' (even if this concept is introduced merely implicitly in the form of a 'demand for money' related to a definite price level).[5] Nevertheless, the adoption of the stabilization of some particular price level as the criterion for that policy which represents a compromise between the competing aims is not thereby excluded. Rather, it seems to me that the stabilization of some average of the prices of the original factors of production would probably provide the most practicable norm for a conscious regulation of the quantity of money.[6] For the reasons already given, however, I would regard it as a regrettable confusion of two different problems if this problem of monetary policy were to be dealt with within the context of that of neutral money.

Notes

1 This must not be taken to imply that I claim to have invented the concept or the term 'neutral money'. Rather, see my *Preise und Produktion*, Vienna, 1931, p. 30fn., as well as the work by J. G. Koopmans cited below, p. 228fn.

2 J. G. Koopmans, 'Zum Problem des "neutralen" Geldes', in *Beiträge zur Geldtheorie*, Vienna, 1933.

3 W. Egle, 'Das neutrale Geld', *Untersuchungen zur theoretischen Nationalökonomie*, Heft 10, Jena, 1933.

4 Cf. *Geldtheorie und Konjunkturtheorie*, Vienna, 1929, p. 56. Wieser has already remarked upon the particular effects of a 'one-sided supply of money' in 'Der Geldwert und seine Veränderungen', *Zeitschrift für Volkswirtschaft, Sozialpolitik und Verwaltung*, vol. XIII, p. 54 (1904), *Gesammelte Abhandlungen*, Tübingen, 1929, p. 178.

5 It appears to me that, if an investigation of this problem is to be free from any objection, the price level (or a value of money in the usual sense) must not play any role within it. The concept of changes in the value of money would then have to be replaced by that of deviations from the problematic intertemporal prices equilibrium. Although I can no longer adhere to all that I wrote on that occasion, I still believe that an approach to a solution of the problems arising in this context is to be found in my article on 'Das intertemporale Gleichgewichtssystem der Preise und die Bewegungen des Geldwertes' (*Weltwirtschaftliches Archiv*, July 1928, vol. 28 [this volume pp. 71–117 (ed.)]).

6 Cf. in this connection G. Haberler, 'Die Kaufkraft des Geldes und die Stabilität der Wirtschaft', *Schmollers Jahrbuch*, vol. 55, 1932.

EIGHT

TECHNICAL PROGRESS AND EXCESS CAPACITY*

Many readers may perhaps feel that someone who, at this point in time, is in the fortunate position of being able to observe current events from the place which at present can without exaggeration be called the centre of economic and political events, ought to have more important and interesting matters to discuss than so apparently specialized a question as 'technical progress and excess capacity'. The fact that I had this lecture announced under this title shows that I do not share this opinion. Not only do I believe that the academic economist does well to leave the coverage of current affairs to other, probably more skilful hands, but I also believe above all that a more important field is opening up to him. Indeed, I see it as precisely his first duty to examine the fundamental ideas of our time which dominate the actions of statesmen and politicians and, therefore, probably exert a stronger influence on the development of the world than the most sensational current events. I hope to demonstrate to you that current ideas about the set of problems indicated only imperfectly by the title in many respects exert a very strong influence not only on the economic policy of statesmen but at least equally on the desires and hopes of the masses.

The title of the lecture, however, may really convey too narrow an idea of its main subject. I have used the phrase 'excess capacity' more as the most obvious example than as the only one of those cases in which technical progress may appear to give rise to a squandering and a waste of economic energy rather than an improvement of our situation. The question I would like to pose is: Does the competitive economy make adequate use of the opportunities for increasing general wealth made available by technical devel-

---

* Lecture delivered at the Austrian *Institut für Konjunkturforschung*, 3 April 1936. First published as 'Technischer Fortschritt und Überkapazität' in *Österreichische Zeitschrift für Bankwesen*, I (1936) pp. 9–23.

opment? Or is it true, as is frequently maintained, that our social order prevents us from making full use of the existing opportunities and that in a rationally conducted economy our income could be a multiple of what it actually is? This question is, of course, so wide that I cannot hope to exhaust it even approximately in one lecture. I shall not examine the more extreme assertions made by various prophets and sects as, for instance, those advanced by the technocrats who have almost passed into oblivion once again. The extreme representatives of false opinions usually present little danger. A *Lebensanschauung* and equally an economic ideology exercise their influence much more through those elements which penetrate unnoticed into the intellectual atmosphere of the time and which thereby rapidly turn from unproven assertions into undoubted dogma. I would therefore like to limit myself here to an examination of a number of typical strands of thought which appear in hundreds of different cases and in very diverse concrete guises and which, taken individually, lead to conclusions which appear plausible. Nevertheless, as I shall attempt to demonstrate, these conclusions rest on inferences whose erroneous nature can be shown most clearly by concentrating upon the most general and most abstract cases. I would not wish to deny that in this I am also guided by the desire, surely pardonable for an academic economist, to demonstrate by means of a concrete example the value of the abstract reflections with which theoretical economists so predominantly occupy themselves to the regret or irritation of their contemporaries.

Since the discussion of these problems will frequently take the form of questioning whether we could do better if we planned industrial development scientifically rather than leaving the utilization of technical progress to unregulated competition between the various enterprises, I must first make one comment in this connection. Very often an affirmative answer to this question is tacitly justified with the assumption that an economic dictator would simply be much wiser and possess a greater degree of foresight than the entrepreneur in whose hands the decision lies today. Particularly when the state is invoked as the central planning authority virtual omniscience is often ascribed to it in contrast to the limited entrepreneur. But the state, or whoever else plays the role of the economic dictator, is also made up of human beings, and, if there really were such omniscient human beings then there would be every reason to assume that they would also figure among the most successful entrepreneurs. It must seem more than doubtful whether a mechanism for selection exists which ensures that it is precisely the most capable who are put at the top of an economic administrative apparatus. Of course, I do not wish to deny that a central planning authority would have at its disposal sources of information which are denied to the individual entrepreneur. However, the advantage arising from this seems to me to be completely balanced by the difficulty that, in the case of central planning, it is necessary to put the decision on questions to which only actual success can provide an answer, in a more or less arbitrary way into the hands of a few persons. The general assumption, that a central planning authority will possess a greater degree of foresight, seems to me to be based essentially upon its having the power to force the consumers to buy what it offers to them. We shall yet see to what extent this is to be regarded as an advantage. Apart from this issue, however, it seems obvious to me that there is no reason whatsoever to assume that a central planning authority would have greater knowledge or fore-sight than the individual entrepreneur.

That is all I wanted to say before examining the actual problems. The fact that, in any economic system, we are always working for a future which can only imperfectly be foreseen may appear to be self-evident, yet it is of such significance for our problems – and it is so frequently regarded as a property of the competitive economy – that it would have been wrong of me to have failed to give particular emphasis to its general character in what follows. It will immediately become evident in detail how this feature more than anything else lies at the root of all the waste and loss which technical progress apparently entails.

The first and most obvious case is that of technical invention: advances in our technical knowledge which by their nature are spontaneous and not foreseeable in detail. Clearly, there is no doubt that every time such an immediately useful invention has been made, a large proportion of the plants previously built and of the expenses previously incurred appear inappropriate in the light of this new level of knowledge. From the point of view of a higher level of knowledge, and perhaps also from the view of some indivi-duals who were aware of the existence of this invention before it became generally known, this may appear wasteful. Yet, so long as we do not know any method of determining in advance who at any time possesses the most appropriate knowledge – i.e. as long as we have no reason to assume that the opinion of X on the prospects of a new method of production will always be more accurate than

165

that of Y – we shall have to restrict ourselves to asking what will be the socially most desirable and advantageous reaction towards the new situation once the new invention has become known and been tested.

In popular discussions of this question we frequently find two differing, opposing indictments of the way in which the competitive economy reacts to such an invention. On the one hand, it is maintained that in such a system technical progress is not utilized to the extent desirable. It is difficult to see why an invention which makes production cheaper should not be introduced in a truly competitive economy. I believe that all those who make this accusation will admit after a little reflection that in the cases in which this does not happen it is the existence of a monopoly or a monopoly-like situation rather than competition which provides the motive and the opportunity for this. To be sure, the owner of a plant which would lose its value through the introduction of a new invention may often be interested in preventing its introduction. But others are equally interested in making a profit through the application of cheaper methods of production. The former, therefore, can succeed in preventing the application of a profitable invention only where others are denied access to it. But the most important restriction of competition which enables this to happen, the most drastic monopoly position of this kind which modern legislation creates, is the patent which under certain conditions makes it possible and profitable for the individual to purchase an invention not in order to utilize it but to take it out of service. It seems, however, that this does not result from competition but from the particular monopoly position which patent rights afford. I cannot enter into further discussion of its significance here.[1]

But are there not cases where it is desirable that a new invention should not be introduced immediately; cases in which the application is profitable for the individual but socially wasteful? This brings me to the second type of reproach and one which sounds much more convincing, which is made against the way in which the competitive economy reacts to technical progress. Is it not quite obviously a squandering of economic energy if competition forces the entrepreneur to scrap machines which are still capable of producing, and to substitute new ones for them? Would not the capital, which is used to produce something that could also have been produced without it, have been much better employed in bringing other, additional goods on to the market?

This argument, which I believe to be totally erroneous, has exerted an enormous influence on modern economic policy, though perhaps not in this its most simple and all too transparent form. On the one hand, the capital losses are pointed to which should be set off against profit, but which are not if the loss is incurred by someone other than the person who makes the profit. In other cases, it is pointed out that, so long as many needs and wants remain unsatisfied, it is more important to produce new goods rather than to produce with more modern methods those which are already being manufactured. In this case more than any other it seems an obvious conclusion to draw that competition tends to create useless and wasteful excess capacity instead of satisfying the most urgent needs and wants.

The most significant example of this kind, which has played a dominant role in the economic policy discussions of all countries in the last few years, is the competition between the motor car and the railway. I do not want to mention at this point the particular difficulties involved in arriving at a correct calculation and imputation of the costs of road construction which clearly must be imputed to motor traffic in order to ensure its economic efficiency, in the same way as the corresponding costs have to be imputed to the railways. Leaving this technical problem aside all the arguments put forward in this controversy surface whenever costly plants are superseded and lose their value as a result of technical progress. The loss of national wealth, the dissipation of capital, the contradiction between individual profit and social utility have all been advanced as arguments in order to demonstrate that the waste apparently connected with technical progress ought to be prevented.

What is the situation in reality? When is it desirable for a new invention to be introduced? Would a wise economic dictator act on principles which differ from those operative in the competitive economy? At this point I must ask you to follow me briefly in a somewhat abstract investigation. First of all, I want to demonstrate in general terms under which conditions it is advantageous for the individual entrepreneur in the competitive economy to introduce a new, better method of production. Then I want to investigate the implication of these considerations from a social point of view. There will then be no difficulty in ascertaining whether the economic dictator could reasonably act in a different way and effect a better utilization of the forces of production.

Not every invention which reduces the costs of production makes it profitable to replace all old machines immediately by new ones and to scrap the old ones. If the reduction in cost is relatively small, then, as a rule, the new method will at first be used to produce only that small extra quantity which can be sold at the lower price corresponding to the new cost of production. Given the new competition, the owners of the old machines will doubtless have to accept a lower price, and hence they will probably not be able to fully amortize the capital invested in these machines. However, as long as the reduction in cost made possible by the new invention is not very considerable, they will not regard it as lying in their interest to replace the old machines by new ones, nor can they be undercut to such an extent by the competition of others using the new machines that they have to cease production. It will only become expedient and unavoidable for them to scrap their machines and to replace them by new ones, even if they are still fully productive for a long time to come, when the reduction in cost has arrived at a certain point.

Where, then, is this critical point? The conclusion we come to in dealing with our whole problem depends on the answer to this question. A somewhat more detailed examination of technical details now becomes unavoidable. Unfortunately, the practical as well as the scientific terminology is so confused in this field that I shall have to begin by defining one or two necessary concepts. In what follows, I shall use the terms 'capital cost' and 'operating cost' of an enterprise in a special, technical sense which facilitates a relatively simple discussion of the problem but which does not fully coincide with any one of the many cost concepts otherwise employed. By capital cost I understand the interest yield and amortization of the invested capital of an enterprise, i.e. of the value of its fixed capital such as buildings, machines, etc. calculated on the basis of their current cost of acquisition. In order to avoid irrelevant complexities I assume that the existing plants can be used only as originally intended, and that their scrap value is zero. The exposition is greatly simplified by this assumption, and there will be no difficulty in generalizing the results subsequently by introducing assumptions of this kind.

By operating cost, on the other hand, I understand all those current expenses necessary to maintain a given plant in operation. Naturally, I am aware that it is in general not possible to draw a sharp distinction between operating cost and capital cost in this sense, but that it depends on the time period under consideration.

For example, if we consider only a short period of time, costs which can be regarded as capital cost will become operating costs if the plant is kept continually in operation over a longer time span. Most repair and maintenance costs belong to this not unambiguously classifiable group. This distinction, however, is sufficient for our purposes and we need not pursue these difficulties any further.

The general answer to my earlier question, then, is that it will be expedient and possible to keep all the old plants in operation in so far (and as long as) total costs (i.e. capital cost plus operating cost) of the new, improved method of production exceed the operating cost of the old plant. As long as that is so it will still be advantageous for the owners of the old plants to carry on producing with them and to depreciate part of the old invested capital rather than to close down and to lose it all. Only when the total cost of production has been reduced below the operating cost of the old process by the new invention will the old plants have to be shut down, and production in its entirety will be transferred to the new plants.

What is the significance of this from the point of view of the economy as a whole? Does it not still remain true that the new capital, which could have been better employed, is used to produce the same output which the existing plants could also have produced? No, here is the fallacy: for the new capital is not employed to produce the same output as the old capital at all. As we have seen, so long as the saving does not exceed the quantity produced by the old machines, the new ones would not be introduced in the first place. For their introduction to become profitable the total cost of the new process must be less than the operating cost of the old one, i.e. more must be saved than the irrevocably tied-up capital cost of the old plant.[2] In other words, the new method will only be introduced when the capital costs to which it gives rise are lower than the saving in operating cost which it yields as compared with the old process. It follows that the new capital is not used to replace the old, bygone capital, but in order to save other factors of production. It sets free other factors of production, workers and machines, which can now be used in other ways. The choice actually to be made in this case consists in whether it is more efficient to employ more capital or rather more labour and raw materials to achieve the same result in the production process in question. The decision will obviously depend on which will cost less, i.e. whether the quantity of capital in question or whether the other factors produce more in some other use. It is on this basis that the intelligent economic dictator, at least, ought to decide. But exactly the same outcome is achieved by the competitive economy. For the price which the individual entrepreneur must pay for capital or for the other factors obviously depends on the utility which they would yield in some other use. By deciding for the cheaper factors of production he does precisely what the intelligent planner should do, in that he produces the given quantity with the fewest factors of production and leaves as many as possible free for other purposes.

My main point, repeated here, is that the erroneous impression that capital is used in such cases to produce output which could equally well have been produced by the old capital, rests on the false assumption that it only replaces old capital and that everything else remains unchanged. In reality, what is involved is that in those cases in which the individual entrepreneur is forced by competition to close down his old plants and either to replace them himself by new ones or give way to other entrepreneurs, the discontinuance of production in the old plants constitutes a saving also from an economic viewpoint.

With this, we have finally arrived at a case in which technical progress creates excess capacity. For in a purely technical sense, at least, the productive capacity embodied in the old plants obviously continues to exist. From an economic point of view, however, the situation is different. For example, should demand increase for the product concerned, then the old plants will not be used (or, at the most, only temporarily), but it will be more economical to build more plants of the new type. Although the productive capacity still exists technically, it has disappeared from an economic point of view, and this is also expressed in the fact that the plants have lost their value. Yet on occasion, it may be expedient not to dismantle them but to keep them, in order to satisfy temporary (seasonal or similar) peak demand which, because of its irregularity, does not justify the construction of a new plant.

Does it follow from this that the loss of value in the old plants, which of course hits the owner hard and which he has every interest in preventing, is meaningless from the point of view of the economy as a whole and that it is not to be regarded as a loss at all? Are all the familiar arguments about the necessity of protecting and maintaining existing capital values simply false? To my mind, there can be no doubt that this really is the case. As in other similar cases which frequently occur, the fact that the maintenance of capital value is generally a condition for an economic utilization of existing means seems to have led to the conclusion that the 'maintenance of capital' is regarded as an end in itself. It seems, too, that the maintenance of capital is being aimed at even where it comes into conflict with the real purpose of all economic activity, namely the highest possible degree of satisfaction of needs and wants. However, it is obvious that what confers utility upon a capital good from the point of view of the economy as a whole – in the same way as its owner's claim for remuneration – is solely the fact that it is an indispensable condition for efficient production. However, if capital is artificially maintained in the role *of a necessary precondition* by suppressing other possibilities of realizing the same level of utility, this contradicts the meaning which the maintenance of capital has from the point of view of the economy as a whole. However much the individual capitalist serves the interest of the economy as a whole when he applies his intelligence and his foresight, he becomes a parasite when he appeals to the state for protection against technical progress which threatens the value of his invested capital. This is no less true, and the danger will be much greater, when the state itself is the owner of the threatened capital values, and when it believes that it has to protect them against devaluation in the alleged interest of the maintenance of national wealth, by suppressing new technical methods. In so far as this argument is used to support so-called passenger and heavy goods traffic regulations we can say with certainty that the alleged national economic interest in the maintenance of capital values does not exist, and that a policy which in cases like this aims at the maintenance of individual capital values impoverishes a nation instead of making it wealthier. Of course, it would be a different thing if, for example, Austria could prevent one of the products of its soil which it sells abroad, as, for example, magnesite, from being driven out of use by a new invention. In this case, Austria would have the same interest as the individual capitalist in preventing the introduction of this invention, and, from a global point of view, she would be acting just as anti-socially as the capitalist in the same case. But the ideal that, as a country, we could preserve our wealth by somehow obstructing the introduction of innovations and by forcing our fellow citizens to make better use of the existing plants, is obviously absurd.

There are a large number of closely related cases in which, according to widespread opinion, greater economic efficiency could similarly be achieved if consumers could only be forced to make better use of the existing plants, especially when they indeed stubbornly insist on demanding a large number of goods which are only slightly different from each other. Since, in a certain sense, this also involves cases in which technical development, namely product differentiation, leads to the existence of unutilized productive capacity; and since, moreover, it is precisely these cases which have given rise to interesting scientific controversies in recent times, a brief discussion of this issue may be in order.

What is at issue here are the consequences of so-called imperfect competition as it exists, for example, between similar branded goods, e.g. different toothpastes. In contrast to the ideal case of perfect competition, where nobody can ask more for the same good than anybody else since he would instantly lose all his customers, it is characteristic of restricted competition that the individual producer can keep his price either slightly higher than or a little below that of other producers of similar products without instantly losing or gaining all sales. No doubt it will be instantly evident to you that such imperfect competition is a more frequent phenomenon than the ideal perfect competition with which the theoretician so likes to concern himself. One of the main reasons for the actual imperfection of competition is, of course, that the most advantageous size of plant in many branches of production is so large that there is room for only one or a very few such plants in a given economic region.

For any given plant, the most advantageous quantity of output is obviously that at which average cost per unit of output would begin to rise with further expansion. For so long as average cost is still falling it is clearly cheaper to produce more with the given plant than to share the same quantity of output between several of equal size plants, and, roughly speaking, as soon as average cost per unit of output begins to rise, the cost of production will be lower in a new plant. Hence it will be more advantageous to produce the additional quantity in a new plant. There would then be little in demonstrating that, under conditions of perfect competition, every enterprise will expand its production to the point at which average cost begins to rise.

But the case of imperfect competition is different. It may happen that there is room in a certain branch of production for only one entrepreneur because the willingness of the public to buy is declining still faster than his average cost even before the latter has reached its lowest point. In this situation, so long as the good in question is clearly defined and is sharply differentiated from all other goods, competition cannot arise. The interest of every enterprise would lie in producing more itself at lower cost per unit rather than in admitting a competitor whose costs would be higher as long as his level of output is small. But the situation is different where the products concerned are not really the same but only very similar, perhaps only distinguished by bearing different trade marks, and which have been introduced to different groups of the public. No producer will easily be able to drive the others out completely since certain people will stay with familiar brands for a long time even if they can get very similar products more cheaply.

Yet, it would be in the interest of the public, so the argument runs, to restrict production to one of the similar products, concentrating it in one enterprise in cases in which the demand for a group of very similar products is not large enough to enable more than one enterprise to produce under optimal conditions, that is, at minimum cost. This enterprise could be fully utilized, while product differentiation and the stubbornness of the consumers result in the existence of many factories which are all insufficiently utilized and thus produce at higher prices. Forced standardization and compulsion on the consumers to make use of just one of the different products would certainly be advantageous for all, since everyone would be supplied more cheaply.

This kind of argument has made quite an impression recently and has led to all kinds of suggestions for rationalization and especially to the regulation of the retail trade. Is it correct? It seems to me that there are two very serious objections to it. Firstly, if it really could be foreseen that the consumers would be better off if they had less choice but could get cheaper products instead, who prevents the entrepreneurs benefiting from this and inducing the consumers to buy only their products by lowering their prices? More important, however, is the second consideration: Who is to decide whether the public's preference for certain articles or trade marks is really all that unreasonable? Do we really have the right to say that the consumer is behaving irrationally if he is not yet enticed by a slightly lower price to give up a familiar brand and to buy an allegedly equivalent product instead? The standardization fanatics move on to extraordinarily dangerous ground here. I, for one, cannot generate any enthusiasm for the idea that somebody else should decide for me what I should like or enjoy and what I should not.

Of course these objections do not in themselves provide a complete refutation of these arguments, and I cannot attempt to do so in passing in a lecture. I have mentioned them not so much because of their practical importance but because, for the sake of completeness, it was necessary to touch on those arguments in which the connection between excess capacity and wastefulness has been discussed so comprehensively in recent times. I have also emphasized them because, in this context, the theoretical discussion of costs has at least produced a definition of the concept of excess capacity which is less naive than the purely technical one which still plays an important role. Unfortunately, however, this theoretical development has had no influence at all on empirical investigations, as we shall see in a moment.

The case discussed so far should have demonstrated sufficiently that the existence of under-utilized capacity need not always imply waste. However, I have not yet exhausted all the connections in which the spectre of excess capacity plays an important role in modern economic policy, and I have still to attempt a brief examination of a few related problems. While up to this point I have sought to explain the existence of excess capacity I must now turn to the influence exerted by the existence of under-utilized plants. In particular, I want to deal with the relationship between the existence of such plants and the feasible quantity of output, and the demand for capital, and, finally, with its influence on the possibility of further modernization of factories.

The idea exists that it is desirable under any circumstances to utilize existing plants fully before constructing new ones, and that it cannot at all be profitable to create new plants if the former has not been achieved. This idea is ingrained to such an extent that even now it may not be unnecessary to show, by means of a few examples, that it may often be expedient to create excess capacity on purpose (and this not only for well-known reasons of cartel policy, which often are conducive to such action, but even when real competition prevails). However, a somewhat more thorough examination of these cases, though they may appear all too simple and self-evident, will also clarify certain relationships which will prove to be essential at a later point. In particular, such an examination will clarify what is to be regarded as excess capacity from an economic, as opposed to a technical, point of view.

It is, of course, most evident in connection with daily and seasonal fluctuations that not every temporary under-utilization of existing plants in itself represents wasteful excess capacity. No reasonable person will maintain that it is always uneconomical when existing production facilities are not used twenty-four hours a day, although certain engineers who are fanatical about rationalization should, if they wish to be consistent, regard it as wasteful if I did not use my bed for twenty-four hours a day after I bought it. According to their conception of economic efficiency, I believe, the number of beds available should not exceed a third of the population figure. More instructive, however, are certain cases of seasonal fluctuations. Undoubtedly, it would be possible to produce at the same rate throughout the whole year in many branches of production where demand for the product exists only during certain seasons. It would then be possible to accumulate supplies which could satisfy a demand which may well be concentrated within a few weeks. In this way the size of the fixed capital equipment required could be reduced to a minimum, and these plants could instead be utilized continuously. But that does not prove that this is always the economically most efficient procedure. In many cases in which such an arrangement would be quite possible technically, it turns out in fact to be more expedient (that is, it would not only be more profitable from an individual point of view but also more rational from the point of view of the economy as a whole) to construct plants of such a size that the output for seasonal demand can be produced during a period of the same length or one which is only a little longer, while the plant remains unutilized for the rest of the year. This will always be an appropriate procedure when, for example, the raw materials or the productive forces used are so valuable that the loss in interest for the products which are kept in stock exceeds the expenses for interest (and amortization) for the larger amount of fixed capital equipment. This case is particularly instructive because it demonstrates how the existence of capital scarcity, by making it necessary to economize on circulating capital, can entail inability to fully utilize fixed capital. What we are dealing with here is a particularly simple case of the apparent paradox which plays such an important role in modern explanations of depressions, namely that capital scarcity can lead to a situation in which existing capital equipment cannot be fully utilized and hence it appears as if there is too much capital. I shall return to this relationship between under-utilized productive capacity and demand for capital in a moment.

Firstly, however, I must try to answer the general question whether, and to what extent, the existence of under-utilized productive capacity in the technical sense proves that it would be possible to extend production accordingly. This is, of course, the case for every single industry to a certain extent. The difference between the technical and the economic point of view, however, is to be found precisely in the fact that what is technically possible for the individual industry need not necessarily be possible for all industries at the same time. One or two allegedly economic, and certainly well-meant empirical investigations, recently published in the United States concerning this issue, have sinned greatly in this respect. They were aimed at the obviously exaggerated assertions of the technocrats and other engineers who maintained that a multiple of what is actually produced could be produced with the productive equipment available. Since these investigations arrived at relatively modest estimates of the possible increase in production they met with a lively reception among reasonable people, on the one hand, but were vigorously attacked by the technocrats and people of that type, on the other hand. Closer examination, however, reveals that the results even of these investigations still represent gross exaggerations. The method used in their derivation was to ask representatives of the individual industries by how much they could increase their production if they used the plants available and if they had no difficulties in selling their products (nothing was said about prices in this context). The results obtained in this way for the individual industries were then aggregated and the final result was regarded as the increase in total output possible for the economy as a whole. The more careful and thorough of these two investigations arrived thus at a figure of about 20 per cent by which output of the American industries could have been increased above the level of the boom period between 1925 and 1929. The most frequent answers in the questionnaires sent out in the course of the second investigation to eminent entrepreneurs and engineers put the possible increase in production at between 60 and 100 per cent.

But what meaning can be attached to these estimates of the volume of production that could have been achieved with the available plants in all individual industries if the sale of these quantities was possible? Do they in any way show that the available equipment is utilized inefficiently, or that all industries simultaneously could really produce so much more? Given the way the questions were put, it is obvious that all technically available plants have been counted as potential productive capacity without considering whether it would not have been more efficient, had production really been increased, to construct new factories for this purpose rather than using the old ones. This means that not only technically obsolete equipment has been counted as potential productive capacity, but equally also all equipment which has become unprofitable due to otherwise changing circumstances (as, for example, a location which has become unfavourable) or due to original miscalculation. As we know, in all these cases the reason why available plants cannot be utilized fully is that the price which can be obtained does not even cover the operating cost of the equipment already available. In a genuine competitive economy this can only mean that there is a more urgent demand elsewhere for the other factors of production which would have been used together with the available equipment. The branch of production in question could only be expanded, therefore, if simultaneously the production of another good, which is more urgently demanded, were reduced. This is not the place to examine the fact that in today's economy the scarcity of the other means of production required is often not a natural scarcity but frequently artificially caused, namely by an arbitrary fixing of minimum prices, above all for labour services. In practice, of course, this simply means that no more labour can be employed than that quantity the last unit of which produces just as much as corresponds to the arbitrarily fixed wage.

The same considerations also show the untenability of the assertion frequently heard that there exist no opportunities for profitable investment as long as there are extensive under-utilized plants available, and that after a crisis the available plants will first have to be fully employed before investment activity can revive. We have seen that, on the one hand, it is precisely scarcity of capital which can cause the existence of under-utilized capacity, and that only the availability of more capital will enable it to be fully utilized. On the other hand, we have seen that obsolete or otherwise unprofitable plants are frequently counted as under-utilized capacity. From a technical point of view these should be reactivated only temporarily, but their existence does not at all preclude the construction of new, more efficient plants.

What, finally, should we think of the frequently heard argument that the existence of superabundant equipment exerts a downward pressure on price to such an extent that it is impossible to carry out modernizations which would be economically desirable? This question plays an important role, above all in the current economic policy discussion in England. The demand has been raised in the textile, the ship building and the mining industries alike – already with success in a number of cases – that the state should first help to destroy part of the superfluous plants so that higher prices will then make it possible to modernize the industry in question. It is not very easy to understand wherein lies the advantage of modernization which is profitable only at prices which are higher than those currently prevailing, that is, when after its introduction the same goods would be produced at a higher cost than is the case today. At this point, I am still assuming that in concrete cases the technicians are justified in their preference for modern equipment to the extent that it would actually be more economical to build more modern plants if none at all existed. But, as we have seen, this has no bearing on the problem of whether it is economical to replace the existing plants by new ones. The aesthetic pleasure which the engineer takes in technically optimal equipment, and the whole concept of the technical superiority of a method of production, which does not say anything about its economic efficiency, represents a great danger to which more enterprises may (already) have succumbed than to technical backwardness. It would be highly desirable if the technicians would learn this, and if, instead of regarding as a pernicious restriction the limits imposed upon them by the profitability calculations of a competitive economy, they would learn to regard these limits as a necessary economic check on the economic efficiency of their actions.

You will probably find that my answers to the questions posed above are based on an utopian *laissez-faire* ideal which may be theoretically better but practically and politically not realizable. In a certain sense you may be right. In individual cases and in the modern economy as it is, it may often be impossible or inexpedient to act as it would be correct to do under ideal conditions. Here, too, it is simply the curse of every evil deed that, ever-creating, it must bring forth evil. I shall readily admit that I would probably not always be able to adhere faithfully to the principles delineated here if I were asked for advice on a concrete question of economic policy. However, I believe that it is the task of the academic economist to represent the claims of reason without regard to whether it will have any effect in the near future. Certainly current public opinion may often make the adoption of a reasonable policy impossible; but it is not unalterable, and I am afraid that our predecessors, the economists of the last generation, must bear some of the blame for the current situation. If we are not allowed to hope for more, then there always remains the one hope that we can at least in part make up for the great wrongs committed by some of our predecessors, by the influence which academic teachers exert on the thought of the succeeding generation.

Notes

1 Incidentally the connections are not as simple in this area as is generally assumed, and the cases in which it may actually be profitable to purchase a patent in order to take it out of service are rather exceptional. Let us assume that the introduction of a patent is to any extent profitable. Then, as a rule, the same considerations which caused its application to appear attractive to somebody will be valid for the entrepreneur who purchased it. From this point of view, the destruction of the value of the already existing plants is compared with the value of the patent; the latter must be higher than the value of the plants which are to be written off if the patent really does make production possible at a total cost which is lower than the operating cost of the existing plants. The exceptional case occurs where a new process cannot be employed in general but yields an advantage only when applied together with certain, not generally available, factors of production. For example, an invention may be of advantage only for businesses to which particularly cheap labour is available while it may be inapplicable in districts where wages are high. In this case it would be advantageous for an entrepreneur who operates in a district with high wages, and whose information, etc. does not enable him to move to the more profitable district himself, to purchase the invention only in order to prevent its introduction in the other district. However, he will have the opportunity of doing so at a price which is still of advantage to him only if the inventor does not know that his patent has a higher value for the other entrepreneurs. Otherwise competition will drive the price of the patent up to a level which is higher than the loss in value against which the first entrepreneur wanted to protect himself through its purchase. The profitability of taking a patent out of service presupposes, therefore, not merely inequality in the conditions of production but also an imperfection of the market due to which the patent can be bought below its real value. Even in this case it would actually be more rational for the first entrepreneur to sell the patent which he had obtained to his competitors at a higher price than to take it out of service. Other psychological considerations, nevertheless, make it unlikely that he will act in this way.
2 In so far as this capital is not irrevocably locked up, that is if the existing plant has a positive scrap value, this will, of course, be taken into account

in the calculations of the entrepreneur, and the results of the calculations will be modified accordingly.

TWO REVIEWS

MARGINAL UTILITY AND ECONOMIC CALCULATION: A REVIEW*

New life seems to be stirring in the field of general economic theory which has been very much neglected during the last decade. However fruitful this kind of research had proved in the first four decades after Menger and his disciples had helped it to regain an honourable position in the German academic world, the rapid development during this period had nevertheless been succeeded by a setback which gave the impression that the possibilities contained in that method had already been exhausted and important results were no longer to be expected from it. In its summary of subjective economic theory into a magnificent and complete system, the great work by F. Wieser in the introductory volume of the *Grundriss der Sozialökonomie* almost uncovered more new problems than it provided positive solutions. It was also to remain the last noteworthy achievement in this field for a long time. Its effect on the younger generation of researchers seems for the time being to have been more that of discouragement than stimulation. It remained the last of, as we may already be allowed to say today, the classical period of the 'Austrian school', and in the subsequent decade hardly anything of importance has been published which took up the investigation at the point at which Wieser had left it. Only very recently, however, have some works been published which point to a revival of interest in the fundamental problems of economic theory and appear to announce new progress in this field. Among these, the work by Schönfeld which is the subject of this review appears to us to be especially worthy of attention for several reasons. While a large number of theoretical works were published even during the period characterized above as more or less fruitless, Schönfeld's book stands out from them not merely by the singleness

* Review of *Grenznutzen und Wirtschaftsrechnung* by Leo Schönfeld (Vienna, 1924). First published in *Archiv für Sozialwissenschaften*, 54/2, (1925), pp. 547–52.

of purpose with which the author seeks to push beyond what has hitherto been achieved, drawing into use all existing attempts in the field. It also and above all stands out by its unusual maturity and clarity of exposition and by the method of procedure adopted by the author, a method which is extremely conscientious and, in its completeness, 'exact' in the best meaning of the word. If the subsequent parts of Schönfeld's treatise[1] maintain the promise revealed by the present small volume, merely an introduction to that treatise, then it should represent a substantial step forward in the development of economic theory. For the time being, however, the fact that the work under review is only an introduction imposes upon the reviewer a certain amount of restraint since the significance of some of the present arguments will be open to final judgment only within the context of the subsequent volumes. At this point, therefore, we will have to limit ourselves to a characterization of the principal positions enunciated in the book and to remarks on some individual points. However, a general appreciation will have to be reserved until the complete work becomes available.

We have referred to Wieser in particular in the opening lines of this review because Schönfeld deliberately follows in his footsteps and emphasizes explicitly that there is no theory to which his own position is closer than to that of Wieser. It is the latter's merit to have pursued further than any of the other marginal utility theorists the connection between the reason why an economic decision has been made, why goods are used in a certain way, and the valuation of the good in question. Even at the expense of a greater unity of his system of doctrines he searched for the connection in places at which others were satisfied with the application of the first result of this approach, the principle of dependent utility, as an explanation of value. Through all difficulties Wieser thus remains faithful to the basic principle of the subjective theory of value: that grasping the basis of economic activity at the same time yields its explanation and its measure. In doing so, however, the results at which he arrives are in contradiction to the simpler systems which are derived from mere generalizations of that initial result, and frequently have earned him disapproval.

Schönfeld takes as the basic principle of his treatise what in Wieser is discernible only as an unexpressed basic tendency. He seeks to fill the gap which exists everywhere between economic data

---

[1] Subsequent volumes were never published (ed.).

and the state in which economic decisions have been carried out and from which most value theorists derive their explanations, except in the simplest connections. Here, too, he follows in the footsteps of Wieser who in his great work distinguishes sharply between general economic theory and the theory of value founded upon it (1st edition, p. 189, 2nd edition, p. 65). Schönfeld, however, wants to go far beyond what Wieser derives from this approach in that he wants to emphasize more strongly the economic service rendered by marginal utility, in contrast to the definition of this concept based on 'dependent utility'. Schönfeld sees Wieser as inconsistent because he derives the definition of marginal utility from a state of the economy in which all decisions have been made while making it perform that 'controlling function' in the decision-making process which plays such an important role in his arguments. Schönfeld now wants to seek a way out of this dilemma by revising the concept of marginal utility as well, through taking into account the role which it plays in the economic decision-making process. To this end he embarks upon the detailed investigation of all those considerations which arise with respect to the allocation of a supply of goods made in accordance with the needs and wants (the 'economic calculation'). It is this which forms the main subject of the treatise.

In the part of the treatise at present under review, this formulation of the problem is only hinted at. It serves in the first place to create the theoretical apparatus with whose aid the basic problem will later be tackled. The most important requisite of this apparatus is the distinction between the theoretically developed economic calculation and the abbreviated procedure applied in practice. The former is the logically complete procedure for the determination of the decisions demanded by given data, in which all possibilities are considered. The latter procedure consists of simplifications which enter in place of these complete considerations, but whose meaning can only be explicated by reference to the unabbreviated procedure which they replace. Schönfeld seems to see the field of application of marginal utility as lying only in the abbreviated procedure, which for the time being is discussed merely in contrast to the system of developed economic calculation. In the meantime, his concern is to elaborate systematically the dependence of the uses of the goods upon their utility and thus to uncover all connections which have to be taken into account even by the logically incomplete procedure. In this context, the most novel and, at first sight, strangest aspect of the entire treatise is the consistency with which Schönfeld begins from a total economic utility conceived of as immediately evident; 'to maximize this is the aim of the individual economic unit'. Schönfeld believes that he can derive the isolated individual utility of a good merely by reference to the total economic utility, and thus explicitly rejects the idea of a purely and simply given system of needs and wants of the economic subject, independent of economic decisions and thus constituting a 'datum' of the theory. At first, this must give rise to doubts because one is accustomed to seeing researchers (in so far as, like Schumpeter, they do not expressly equate the maximum of satisfaction with perfect compliance with the ranking of individual needs and wants) initially begin from a system of needs and wants. Only at a later stage do they have recourse to the assumption, which initially did not figure explicitly as one of the basic assumptions of their system, that maximum total satisfaction is to be achieved independently of compliance with the ranking of needs and wants, a procedure they adopt mainly when the problems which arise do not appear to be capable of solution on the basis of their initial assumption. Such cases arise above all in the theory of complementary goods, though they are also at the basis of the more deep-rooted difficulties of the problems of price and of interest on capital.

If one nevertheless follows Schönfeld further, one becomes inclined to put aside these doubts, at least for the time being, since the possibility is not excluded that he will be able to overcome all these difficulties precisely because at the outset he introduces total economic utility deliberately and justifiably as the determinant aspect of all economic activity. Nor does it appear unlikely that he may thereby be able to show that some of the problems which arise from the usual approach are in fact pseudo-problems. Yet the extent to which Schönfeld treats as self-evident the circumstance that the total economic utility, and not merely the ranking of the isolated individual utilities, is immediately knowable, is such that his remarks in this matter are hardly sufficient to deal adequately with this question. Let us emphasize, only in order to characterize the significance of the change advocated by Schönfeld in comparison with the usual mode of thought, that utility as a datum of economizing activity, given at the outset, thereby disappears. In the place of a given number of needs and wants of a certain intensity, which are given at the outset of the analysis and whose satisfaction by means of a given supply of goods then becomes merely a question of the logic of a system of needs and wants, the total economic utility makes its appearance only after the allocation of all goods to particular uses has been carried out; the maximum of this total economic utility characterizes that combination of decisions which is the economically most desirable one. The economically correct decisions, therefore, cannot be found by means of logical derivation from a 'system of needs and wants' but only through continuous trial and error. In our view, the difficulties connected with this approach appear to lie elsewhere. We shall come back to this a little later.

If one agrees with Schönfeld on this fundamental point then one will be able to follow with approval his further derivations and to enjoy in the course of his representation the many very fortunate formulations of various principles which actually are self-evident but which nevertheless have frequently not been afforded sufficient attention. His real theoretical talent becomes apparent above all in that, even in the most abstract arguments, he never loses contact with reality and that therefore, when confronted with difficulties, he is always able to find a way out which does not do violence to the facts. Supported by wide practical economic experience combined with extraordinary theoretical knowledge, he succeeds in building on his premises in a really convincing way which hardly permits objections to be made to details. Given his basic conception, the next step he takes towards an explanation of economic activity is the derivation of formulae for isolated individual utilities and for comparisons between them, taking into account changes in total economic utility which arise from changes in the use of goods. For Schönfeld too, it is therefore possible to determine that set of decisions about all goods which secures the highest total economic utility only by means of continuous comparisons of isolated individual utilities. It is also here that that temporarily unresolved doubt about his method arises: will it ever be possible to find the condition of highest total utility in his sense by means of continuous comparisons of isolated individual utilities? His approach begins from total economic utility and the circumstance connected with this, that the utility of each good depends on the use made of all the other goods. But this entails the possibility that one can move from a given allocation of all goods to existing uses (or, to use Schönfeld's expression, from a certain combination of decisions) to a combination of decisions which secures a higher total economic utility only by way of changes in the uses of several goods, where each change by itself brings about a reduction in total economic utility. Consequently, that combination of decisions which secures the highest total economic utility cannot be ascertained by means of mere comparisons of isolated individual utilities by which that use of a good is found which contributes most to total utility. However, if one wanted to make a direct comparison of the total economic utilities of all possible combinations of decisions so as to find that which secures the highest total economic utility, then in doing so an explanation of the individual decisions related to utility would be altogether abandoned, and the fact that particular uses of goods take place simply accepted as a 'datum'. This is certainly not Schönfeld's intention, though Böhm-Bawerk at times does actually do so (*Positive Theorie*, Exkurs VII, 3rd edition, p. 209) [English edition (*Capital and Interest*, 3 volumes, trans. G. D. Hunck and H. F. Sennholz, South Holland, Illinois, 1959), vol. III, p. 92 (ed.)].

Among the extraordinarily important self-evident truths which Schönfeld seems to have been the first to have emphasized adequately, and leaving aside the 'operation with entire systems' which has now become possible because of the replacement of the concept of 'individual uses of goods' with that of 'combination of decisions', there is above all the basic nature of the remuneration to which every economic allocation gives rise. The remuneration is expressed in the fact that to every renunciation of one use of a good there has to correspond a use elsewhere (the 'principle of economic *quid pro quo*'). Absent from this principle is the so-called 'idea of loss', which plays such an important role in the writings of Böhm-Bawerk especially. There are other important contributions which can only be mentioned here, such as, e.g., Schönnfeld's more correct formulation of Gossen's law of diminishing needs and wants and the interesting auxiliary concepts of ranking of subsets of quantities and of utilities. A contribution that can also be mentioned only in passing is the 'principle of economic relevance'. Although its meaning is not altogether clearly explained in the part of the treatise under review, it is supposed to enable the number of comparisons of utilities which will actually have to be carried out in the course of economic calculation to be confined to a relatively few, and it seems destined to play an important role in the forthcoming parts of the treatise, especially in Schönfeld's theory of marginal utility.

This book is not easy reading. The superficial reader will quickly be deterred by the courage with which Schönfeld attacks precisely the most difficult problems of economic theory, and by the thoroughness with which he carries out the task in hand, a thoroughness which at times almost seems to degenerate into excessive complexity. However, the exposition offers no difficulties which are not inherent in the subject matter, and it is exacting only in its perfect objectivity, which it also demands from the reader. As a result, one can hardly predict that this book will readily have a noticeable impact. It would, however, be a sad testimony to the current understanding of theoretical economics if a work like this were not to receive the attention it deserves only because it delves so deeply into the subject matter. At any rate, we hope soon to be able to extend the review to the further parts of this work.

THE EXCHANGE VALUE OF MONEY: A REVIEW*

The author of this work believes that, by a systematic analysis of
the factors which determine the value of money, i.e. the general
exchange value of money, he can isolate 'from the structure of
price and income relationships representing the capitalist market
economy the essential nature of money, and express the content of
the purely economic theory of money in an exact fashion' (p. v).
The theoretical justification for and the conceptual delimitation of
the 'general value of money' as a tool of economic theory scarcely
appears problematic to him. Yet, as an investigation into the factors
determining the price level – given that this concept can have any
theoretical significance attributed to it – the work has definite
merits, and like every careful inquiry it has much of value to offer
even to those who set little significance upon its main object of
research.

The analysis sets out from the well-known 'equation of exchange'
in the form given to it by I. Fisher. Neisser very correctly emphasizes
that the equation itself is very far from offering even a theory of the
value of money. All it does is to clearly outline the problems which
an explanation of the value of money faces, by schematically rend-
ering prominent the basic factors involved. Essentially, therefore,
the work proceeds within the conventional framework – certainly
one of its merits rather than a disadvantage, given the addition to
originality rampant in our science. The astuteness and thoroughness
with which terminology which is often ambiguous is clarified, and
the solid basis provided by the now quite generally accepted marginal productivity theory of distribution, undoubtedly makes the
work into a valuable contribution to the more recent literature on
money.

Even if one cannot always agree with the author, his introductory

* Review of *Der Tauschwert des Geldes* by Hans Neisser (Jena, 1928). First
published in *Weltwirtschaftliches Archiv*, 29/1, (1929), pp. 103–6.

remarks as to the possibility in principle that the specific height of the price level can be established – even if partly overtaken by works which have appeared since Neisser completed his study – are already very well worth reading. On the whole, the following remarks as well, on the relationship between the quantity theory and the so-called income theory, are completely apposite. In this context, the generally critical attitude towards the latter scarcely seems justified, certainly so far as regards many of the forms in which it is presented, e.g. that of Wieser. For the point from which Wieser sets out is precisely the relatively independent variability of the real and nominal incomes confronting one another, a feature which Neisser also emphasizes. But the service which the author performs by his explicit emphasis upon the fact that money represents 'pure demand', not dependent upon a simultaneous supply of goods as in the barter economy, and that thereby money 'acquires a life of its own' (*Eigenleben*), must not be underestimated.

Neisser then deals in a very detailed and thorough fashion with the concept of, or more correctly, the various concepts of the velocity of circulation, and offers a clear exposition in particular of the relationship between this and the level of individuals' cash balances. But at the very beginning of this section, we come across the imprecise statement that changes in the velocity of circulation and in average cash balances are always inversely proportional. In fact, the two magnitudes must certainly always change in opposing directions, but in no way do those changes also have to be inversely proportional. (This is also true if one considers, as Neisser appropriately does, the level of cash balances in relation to income, not their absolute level.) Yet this imprecision does not create any problems for the succeeding analysis. It can truly be said of this analysis as a whole that, in his analysis of the factors determining the 'velocity of circulation', the author traces out virtually all the theoretically relevant processes which come into question in this context. Doubtless, precisely this part of the work has particular merits which make it superior to most of the works dealing with the same theme. If, however, these merits are not given a fuller appreciation here, this is probably to be ascribed to a bias on the part of the reviewer which leads him to regard the whole concept of velocity of circulation with a mistrust which Neisser's analysis also cannot overcome. This mistrust arises from the question as to the attitude which should be adopted to the general question of whether average values, as the velocity of circulation is on the author's own definition, have any place in theoretical economics, and whether they can contribute anything at all to the explanation of any phenomena, except to that of changes in other, equally irrelevant average values such as the so-called 'general' value of money.

After a short section on notes and coin, which presents 'without detailed examination the conclusions previously arrived at in monetary theory' (p. 40), there follows an exhaustive analysis of credit money which appears to me to be the most valuable part of the whole book. In it, a whole series of questions, but especially that of the origin of and limitations upon bank credit, is handled with commendable clarity and thereby extricated from much of the misunderstanding associated with such topics. What Neisser writes in the subsection on the quantity of book money, the origin of cheque money, and especially on the inseparability in principle of the cheque deposits that have originated from the deposit of cash and from the granting of credit (pp. 52–6) should be sufficient to finally lay some of the errors which are still very widespread today in discussions of these matters. In addition, it is linked with a critical discussion of A. Hahn's well-known views which is among the best that have hitherto been presented on the much-discussed theories of this author. Finally, the excellent remarks in the same subsection on the effect of even relatively minor changes in the interest rate upon the profitability of individual industries, and thereby on the price level in particular, must especially be drawn to the reader's attention.

The next subsections, which are concerned with the money market and the note-issuing banks, are also highly stimulating. The way in which, in dealing with the money market, the author makes the significance of the demand for cash into the pivotal point not merely of the theory of the money market but of the entire theory of credit shows itself to be very fruitful, especially in his considera-tion of the function of the note-issuing banks as well. So far as regards the arguments he presents in this connection, we can refer here only to his comments as to the appropriateness of cover provi-sions for deposits with the note-issuing banks. These give rise to the suggestion that a certain minimum of the balances due for repayment each day at the note-issuing bank be left uncovered, but for amounts in excess of that minimum the same cover provisions should be demanded as for the bank notes. Again, there are his comments on the conflict between the 'verificatory theory' and the 'dominance theory' of discount policy, with Neisser correctly characterizing the former theory as conclusively erroneous.

If we are to be able to devote some attention to the more important thoughts Neisser presents at the end of his book, we must here completely pass over the following chapter on 'the determination of the national quantity of goods and money'. While in this chapter the essentials of the theory of international trade are analysed in a way which though not original is critical, the last chapter deals with the reciprocal influence exerted upon each other by money and the quantity of goods. The first question to which the author addresses himself is to what extent an expansion in the quantity of money can bring about a rise in production. After what is probably an unnecessarily extended discussion, he comes to the same conclusion as the prevailing view: an expansion of money can have such an effect to only a very minor extent. The remarks which follow on the alleged adjustment of the quantity of money and credit to the 'demand for money', therefore to the extent of commodity transactions, are valuable. They necessarily lead on to the question as to the appropriateness of the trade bill as a basis for note issue, hence to the problem of the so-called 'classical creation of money'. Neisser shows clearly that this theory rests on a complete misconception of the function of the interest rate, and that 'only the interest rate policy of the note-issuing bank, not any automatism in the creation of bank credit' can 'give rise to a parallelism in the movement [of the quantity of goods and the volume of credit]' (p. 148). To be sure, Neisser, like others, bases his belief that such a parallelism is desirable purely upon the uncritically accepted dogma of the necessity of stability in the price level. Some propositions which could be employed in a criticism of this dogma are advanced in Neisser's discussion of the definition of the concept of inflation, but he makes no use of them for this purpose.

To the systematic analysis are added three appendices on war loans and rises in prices, the theory of transfers, and double currency standards and parallel currencies. These go somewhat beyond the framework of the book, and certainly would have been more effectively and appropriately published as a separate book. Nevertheless the application of the results of the preceding investigation to more or less contemporary problems indicates what solid foundations the theoretical analysis lays down for the solution of current problems.

Although the book contains nothing that is essentially new, its critical summary and sifting of those arguments which dominate more serious discussion on monetary problems today does take us a step forward. It is precisely its conservative character which also enables it to indicate the extent to which the most important problems have now been cleared up, and where further work must begin if it is to enlarge our positive knowledge of their implications. Yet, the respectable level attained by the German literature on money in the short space of six to eight years is indicated by the fact that precisely such a book as this is only a summary of what is already familiar from that literature. In contrast to the preceding decades, the German work on money therefore no longer needs to be afraid of comparison with that in England and America.

NAME INDEX

AUTHOR

TITLE

DATE DUE	BORROWER'S NAME

AUTHOR

TITLE

DATE DUE	BORROWER'S NAME